AF545139

BLACK CRACK

IN IRAN

ASLON ARFA

INTRODUCTION BY STEFFEN GASSEL

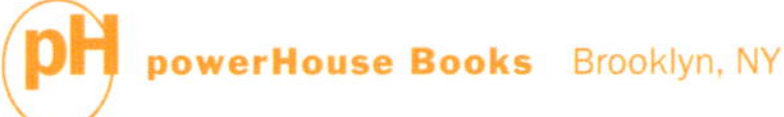
powerHouse Books Brooklyn, NY

 | Published in the United States by powerHouse Books, a division of powerHouse Cultural Entertainment, Inc. 37 Main Street, Brooklyn, NY 11201-1021 telephone: 212.604.9074, fax: 212.366.5247 email: blackcrack@powerhousebooks.com | website: www.powerhousebooks.com

—

First edition, 2010
Library of Congress Control Number: 2010937593
Hardcover ISBN 978-1-57687-554-4
Printing and binding by RR Donnelly, China
Book design by Carol Lin

—

A complete catalog of powerHouse Books
and Limited Editions is available upon request;
please call, write, or visit our website.

—

10 9 8 7 6 5 4 3 2 1

—

Printed and bound in China

AUTHOR'S NOTE

Capturing images of the private lives of Iranians is a difficult task and sometimes seems almost impossible. Certain Iranians do not like to be photographed at all because of their traditions, religious beliefs, and culture; others do not like it because of their fear of the country's strict laws and regulations. You simply cannot take photos of certain daily routines of a typical Iranian family in their own home. Women, for example, do not need to cover their hair inside their homes; however society dictates that they must put on scarves when posing in photos. This is either because they themselves are religious and feel uncomfortable not covering up, or because they believe they must obey the laws. Therefore, the photo you take does not demonstrate their *true* lives.

Capturing real images of Iranian addicts is incalculably more difficult. Neither female nor male addicts like to be photographed. Their resistance comes from a combination of shame, because they are worried about their reputation among people who know them, and fear, because the penalties for possession and distribution of drugs are severe and can even result in death. To make *Black Crack in Iran*, I hung in places in Tehran that were full of criminals, dealers, and addicts. In the parks where I would go to find them, you could see used needles everywhere on the ground. It took a long time for me to get the people to trust me, to let me go inside their houses and take pictures of them while they were living their normal lives and doing their normal chores—including, of course, smoking crack and shooting up.

Sometimes I was completely unsuccessful. For instance, one woman allowed me to photograph her, but her landlord wouldn't let me in the house. In some cases the husband wasn't addicted, and he did not let me take the pictures. Due to these and similar limitations I could not do many of the things I would have liked to, but I believe these pictures are as accurate a portrait of crack addicts in Iran as is possible. It is my intention that by exposing their plight in a raw, intense, and honest way, the attention will bring aid and hope to an otherwise hopeless group.

Aslon Arfa

"Black crack" is completely different from the crack known to Western countries. In the West crack is commonly derived from cocaine; Iranian crack is derived from heroin and is much stronger than heroin in its tar or powder forms. Dr. Mohammad Reza Hadadi, a medical doctor for the Iranian National Center for Addiction Studies explains, "Crack is a common name for all types of crystallized narcotics used as base. All the different cracks make a cracking sound when heated and that is where they get their name. Outside Iran this drug is mainly derived from cocaine, but in Iran it is crystallized heroin." Concerning the process of making crack he adds, "First heroin is added to water and is boiled. Then it is distilled. The substance is passed through a pipe inside which it gradually loses its heat. Upon reaching the end part of the pipe it turns into something crystallized. Of course, most definitely during the process, some other substances such as sodium bicarbonate are added to help it crystallize. Some pills or chemicals may also be added. The purity of the crack depends on the type of heroin used—the purer the heroin, the purer the crack. Its color also depends on the type of heroin boiled in the first place. Heroin can be of creamy color, whitish cream, or even lighter. The darker the heroin, the more impurities it has."

Recently there have been many programs about Iranian crack on Iranian TV, trying to show people how dangerous it can be. Sometimes these programs exaggerate and make claims with no scientific proof. For instance, it has been stated that upon using crack the addicts will suffer from wounds infested with worms, or that crack consumers will have loose body tissue and their body parts will fall off like a leper's. Although these claims are obviously false, this sensationalism shows how concerned the authorities are about the black crack epidemic.

There are clear social consequences associated with the rampant use of the drug. Dr. Mohammad Sadegh Shirazi is the manager of the Aiene Mehr NGO, an organization in Tehran dedicated to drug treatment and rehabilitation. He has said, "Since the medical tolerance for crack is really speedy, the occurrence of risky behavior increases. This in turn may lead to more people suffering from AIDS or hepatitis. For example, a female sex-worker with a crack addiction will be more prone to these illnesses. Because of the quickly forming tolerance to the drug she would need to rapidly increase consumption, and for that she would go for more customers to earn more money. She may have more unprotected sex, because she needs to save the money she would have otherwise spent on condoms for the drug, and also because her sex partners would enjoy it more and return to her." He also says, "On the other hand, crack addicts might be smoking two to three grams round the clock, but would still be experiencing the withdrawal syndrome and therefore, may try more effective ways of consuming it, such as injection. This form of the drug would be more expensive and since they need more money, they would commit more crimes to earn it; therefore, the crime rate would also increase."

All in all, what this amounts to is that it only takes one and a half to two years for a person addicted to black crack to fall into a trap that would take 10 to 15 years for a regular heroin addict to fall into.

INTRODUCTION

Steffen Gassel

A few faded numbers on flaking plaster are all that is left of Fereshteh's last chance for a better life. "I will marry you," the man had said, "but only if you give up the crack and leave your family." He had been a friend of her brother's, whose body—emaciated by heroin—they had lowered into a small, sandy pit in the vast graveyard in Tehran only minutes before.

The man had been a junkie himself. During the short commemoration ceremony he had told Fereshteh of the self-help group that had helped him get away from the drug. "If you join us, you can do it too," he said. "Say yes." But she had shrugged him off—then, and again in the weeks that followed. Three more times he had sought her out in the small, stuffy room in the south of the city that Fereshteh, her mother, and younger brother call home. At the end of his last visit he had scribbled his telephone number on the wall of the cavernous cell. She has never called.

"What do I need a husband for, when I have such a good mom?" Fereshteh asks before putting the red-hot tip of a safety pin to a crumb of crack, sucking in the smoke through a straw. Then, as though to confirm her words, Akram, sitting opposite, reaches across the flame of the gas burner to place a cigarette in her daughter's mouth. Tobacco makes the bitter taste of the heroin more bearable. After five or six drags the daughter leaves the rest of the crack for her mother to smoke. "She is such a good girl," Akram says. "What would we do without her?"

Thirty years after Khomeini's revolution, the Islamic Republic of Iran holds a sad record: no country in the world has more drug users per capita. Official government figures put the number of addicts at 1.1 million, in addition to 700,000 occasional users. But the real figures are probably much worse. According to an estimate by the United Nations Office on Drugs and Crime (UNODC) more than 3.2 million Iranians are addicted to drugs, most of them to opium—but several hundreds of thousands to heroin. And the number is rising fast, particularly among teenagers and young adults. Most at risk are young women like Fereshteh, who is 19 years old.

When did she start with drugs? "At 12 or maybe at 14." She doesn't remember so well anymore. Opium has always been there, for menstrual pains and the flu. It was Reza, an older brother, who had first brought the drug into the house. Back then they had only just arrived in Tehran, penniless, after Fereshteh's father had deserted the family and they had fled the scornful glances of relatives and neighbors in their hometown close to the Iraqi border. One after the other the drug took the lives of four brothers. Then, a few years ago, Fereshteh's older sister died in a traffic accident on a motorbike-taxi. She was 15 and on the way back home from her work as a prostitute. After that, there was no one left but Fereshteh to look after her mother and younger brother.

So, now she follows in her sister's footsteps. Dressed in a black chador, her face made-up in garish colors, Fereshteh takes a motorbike-taxi most evenings. From Shush Square in the poor southern suburbs of Tehran she drives to work in the north of the city. On a good night, one of her regular, affluent customers will call her mobile and ask her to come to his home. But most nights, she has to go with the Afghan builders who pool the little money they get on payday. In groups of three or four they take her to one of the unfinished high-rise blocks in the richer, more anonymous parts of town and share her body among themselves. She earns between 30 and 130 dollars a night this way. The more she gets, the more drugs she is able to buy in the morning on her way home. Only rarely is it enough for more than a day or two.

"We are a nation on drugs," Mohammed Sadegh Shirazi says. The doctor stands under the pale neon light in his practice in the Eastern suburb of Chak Sefid. For more than ten years he has been treating the addicts from the poorer parts of Tehran. In the 1980s and 90s he had to watch while more and more Iranians fell for opium, smuggled into the country by the ton from neighboring Afghanistan. He knew some of the thousands of users who died of an overdose in 2000 and 2001 when the Taliban's ban on poppy cultivation exploded prices and drove many to switch to poor-grade heroin. He was one of the first to raise the alarm when "crack" appeared on the market three or four years later. Within months it became a gateway drug because many users thought it less dangerous than heroin. Sadly, the opposite is the case: Iranian crack is an extra-pure variant, ten times stronger than normal heroin. "These days, I rarely have a patient who only uses opium," Shirazi says. "If it happens, I congratulate him and thank God for it."

Why Iran? Why has this of all countries become haunted by such a massive drug problem? Despite years of first-hand experience, Shirazi, the doctor, has still not found an answer. "Some people say that there are so many addicts here because alcohol is banned and there are no pubs anymore like in the time of the Shah. But I don't believe in this theory. Most of the people on drugs would never dream of entering a bar," he says. "I guess it is more to do with high unemployment and economic problems," and with the low prices. A gram of crack-heroin costs less than USD 5.00 in Tehran, a gram of opium about USD 10.00.

Still, it would be wrong to think that addiction is a problem only among the poor. Iranian crack first surfaced as a designer drug at parties of the rich from the chic high-rise apartments in North Tehran. From there it made its way into the parks and low mud-brick houses of the simple people at the other end of town. Only, it is here that the misery of addiction is most visible.

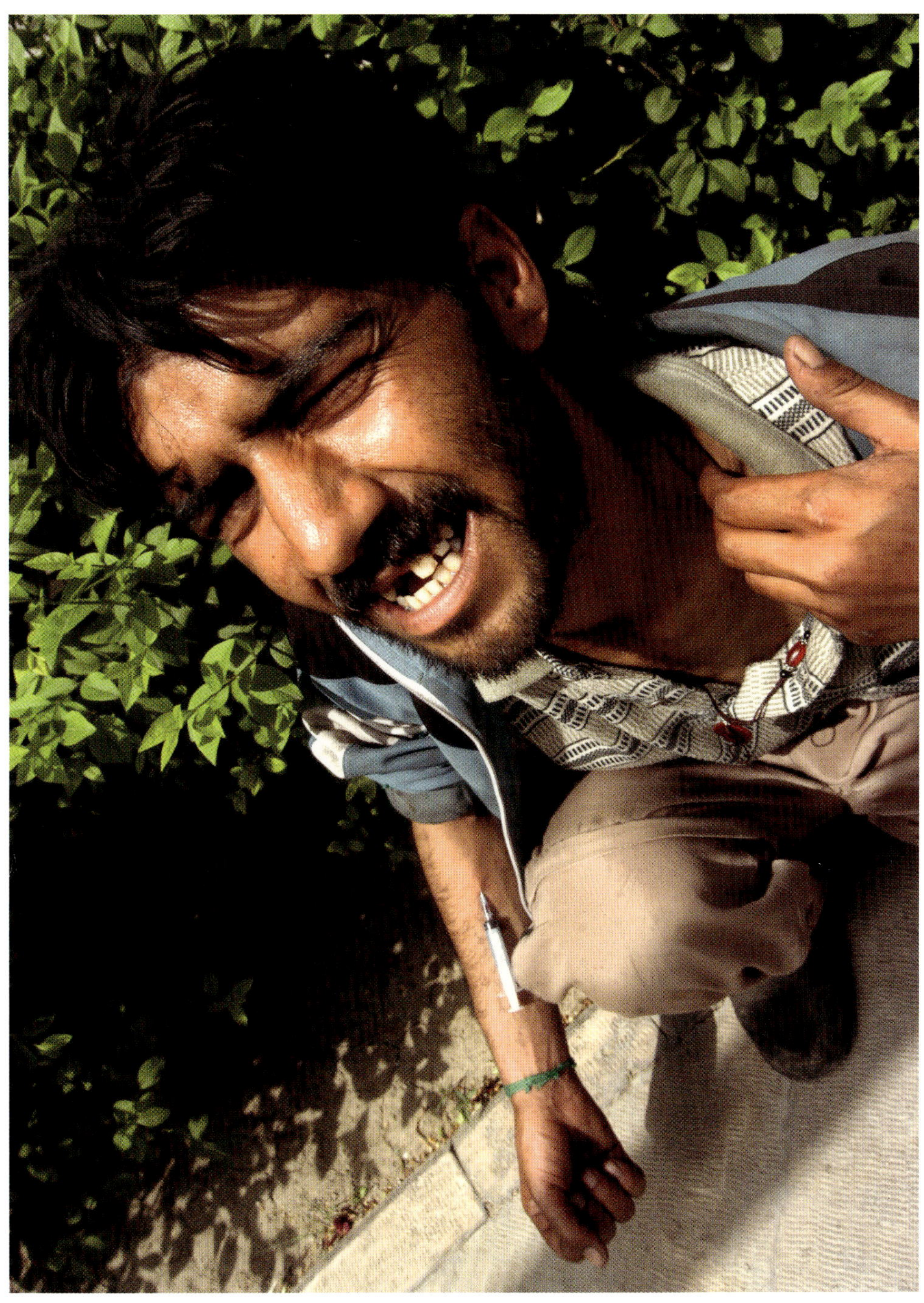

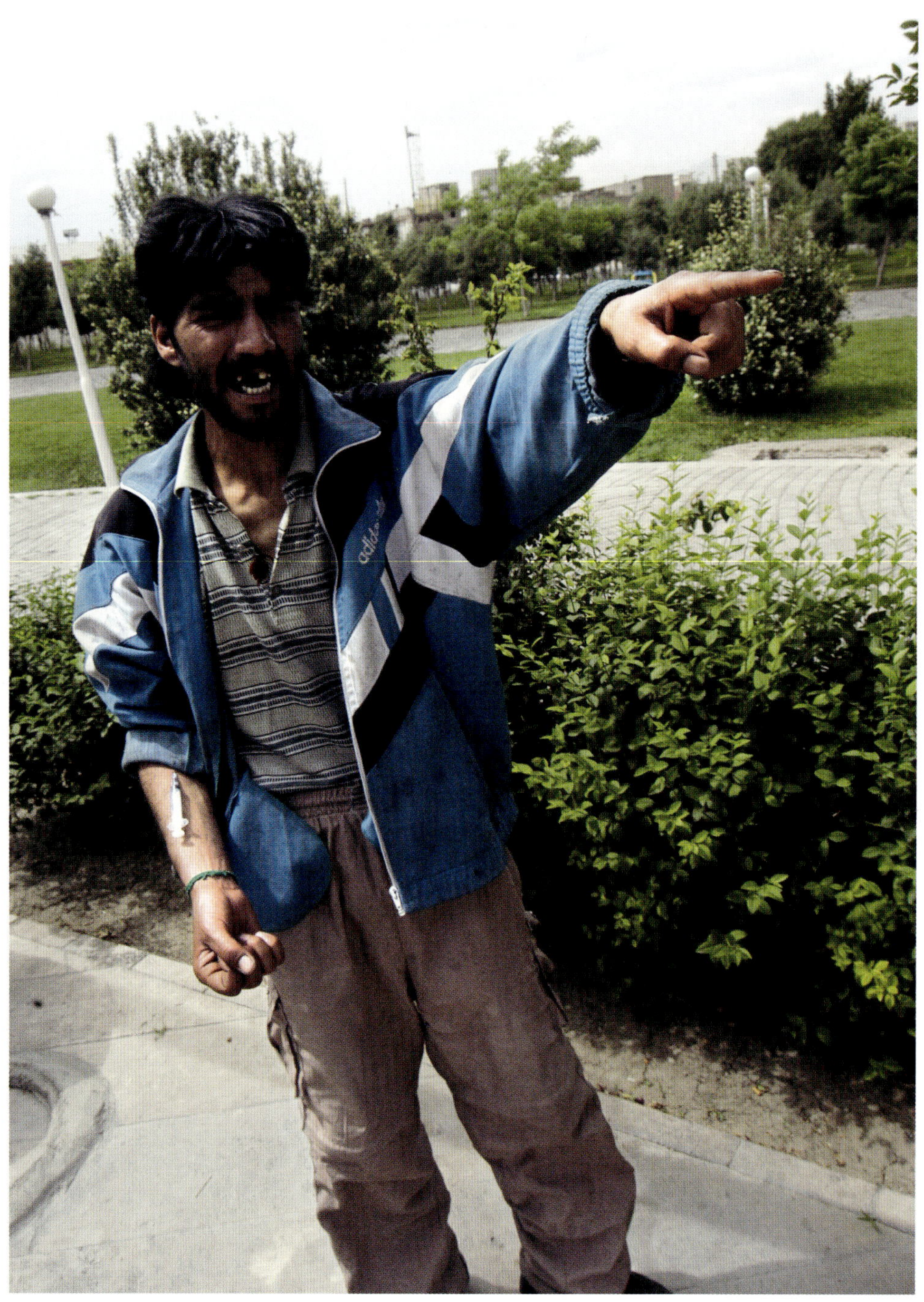

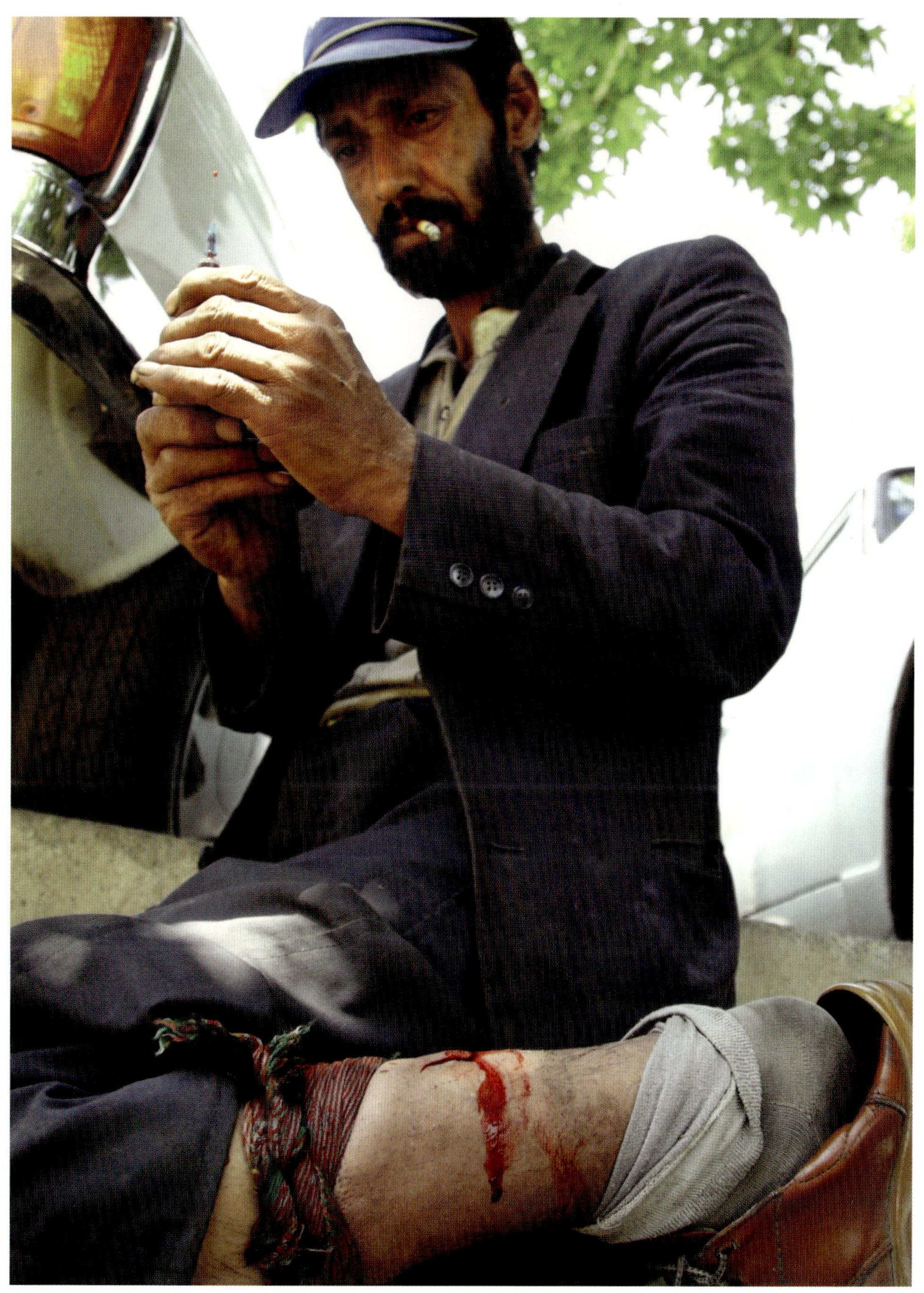

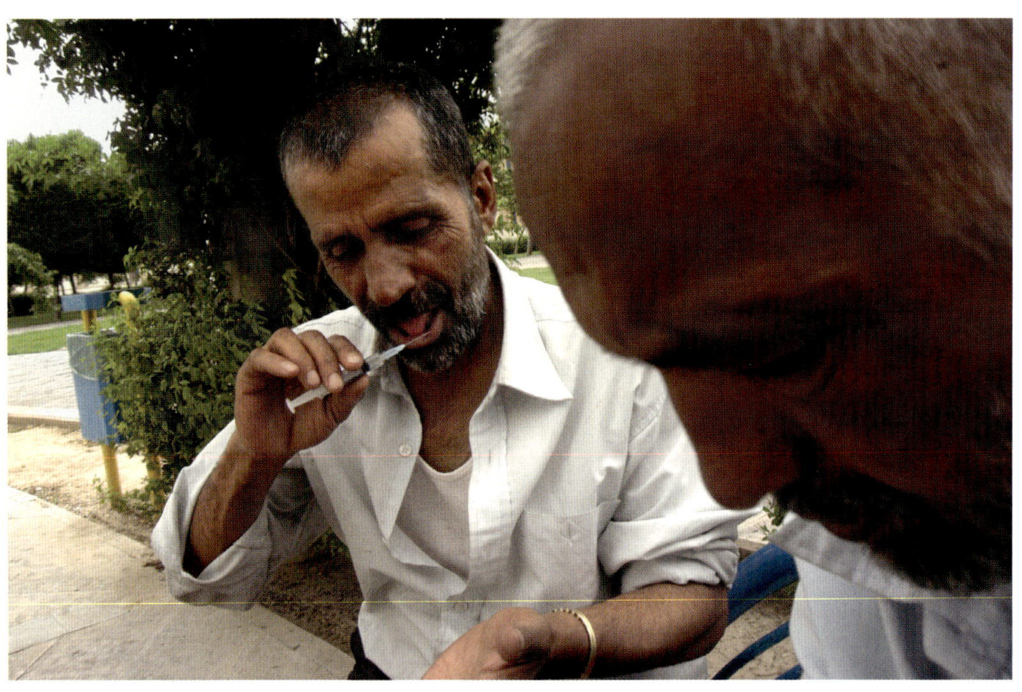

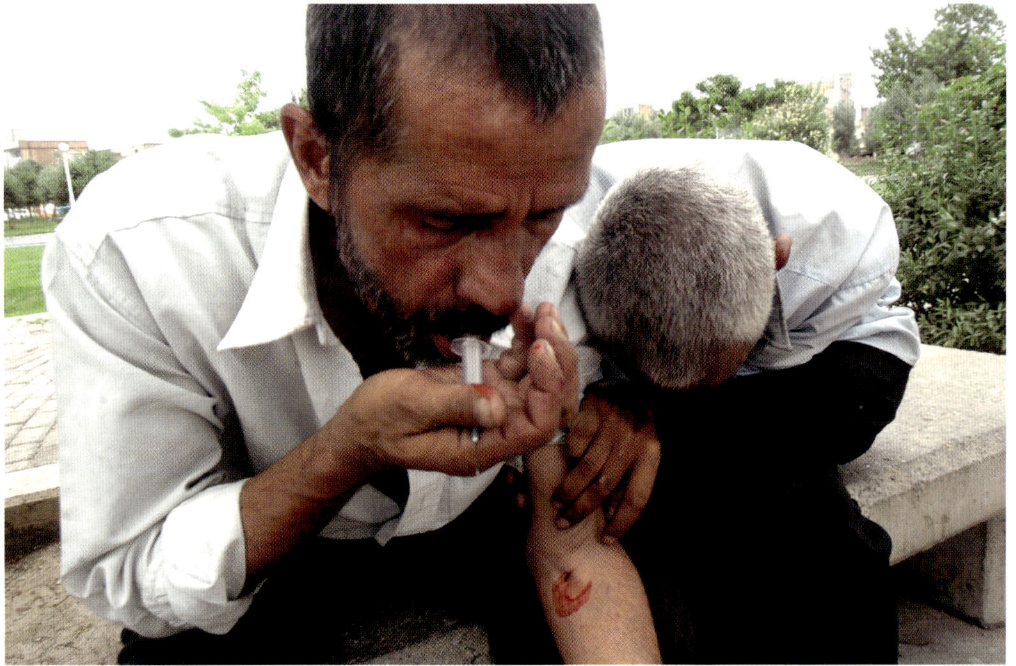

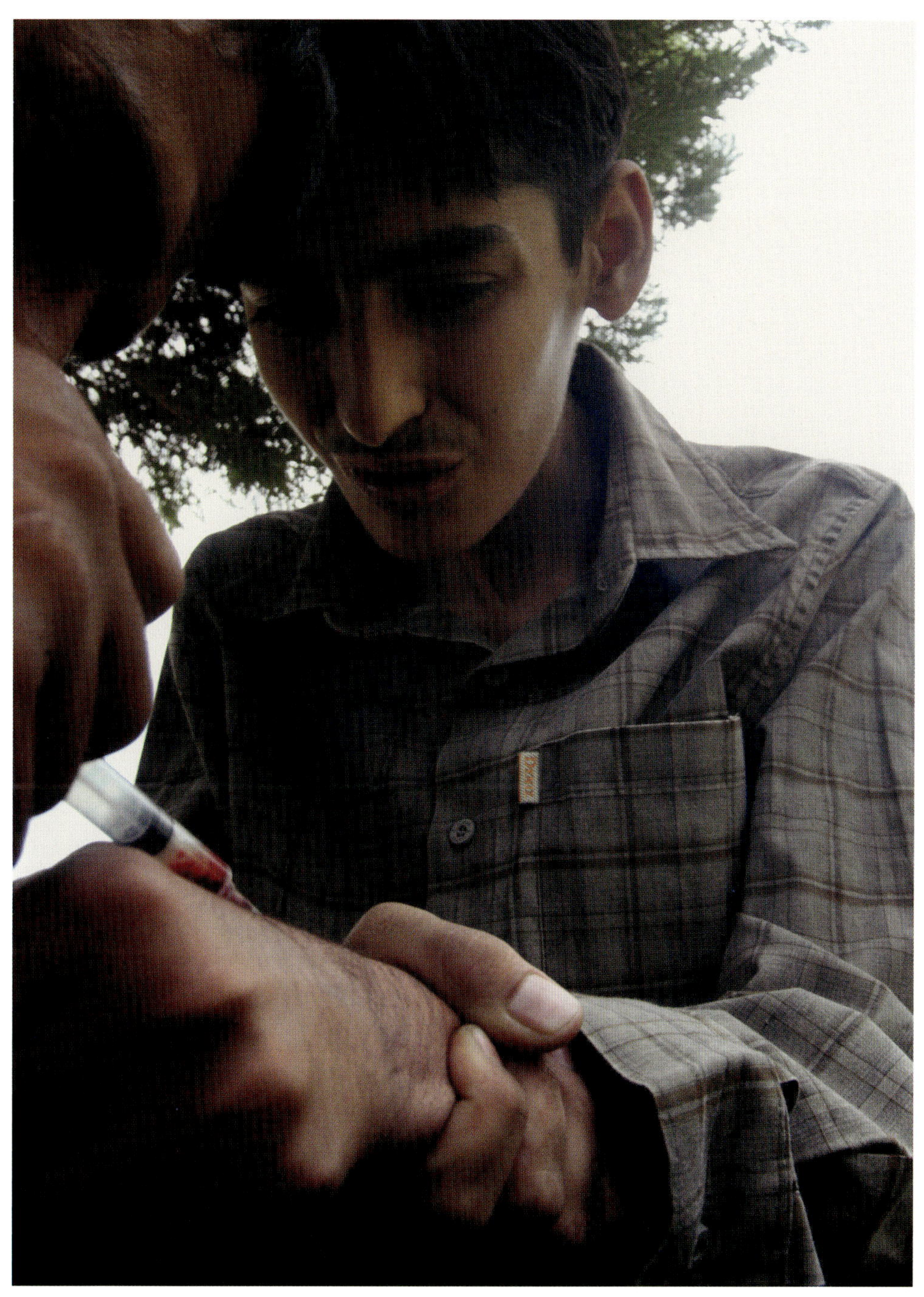

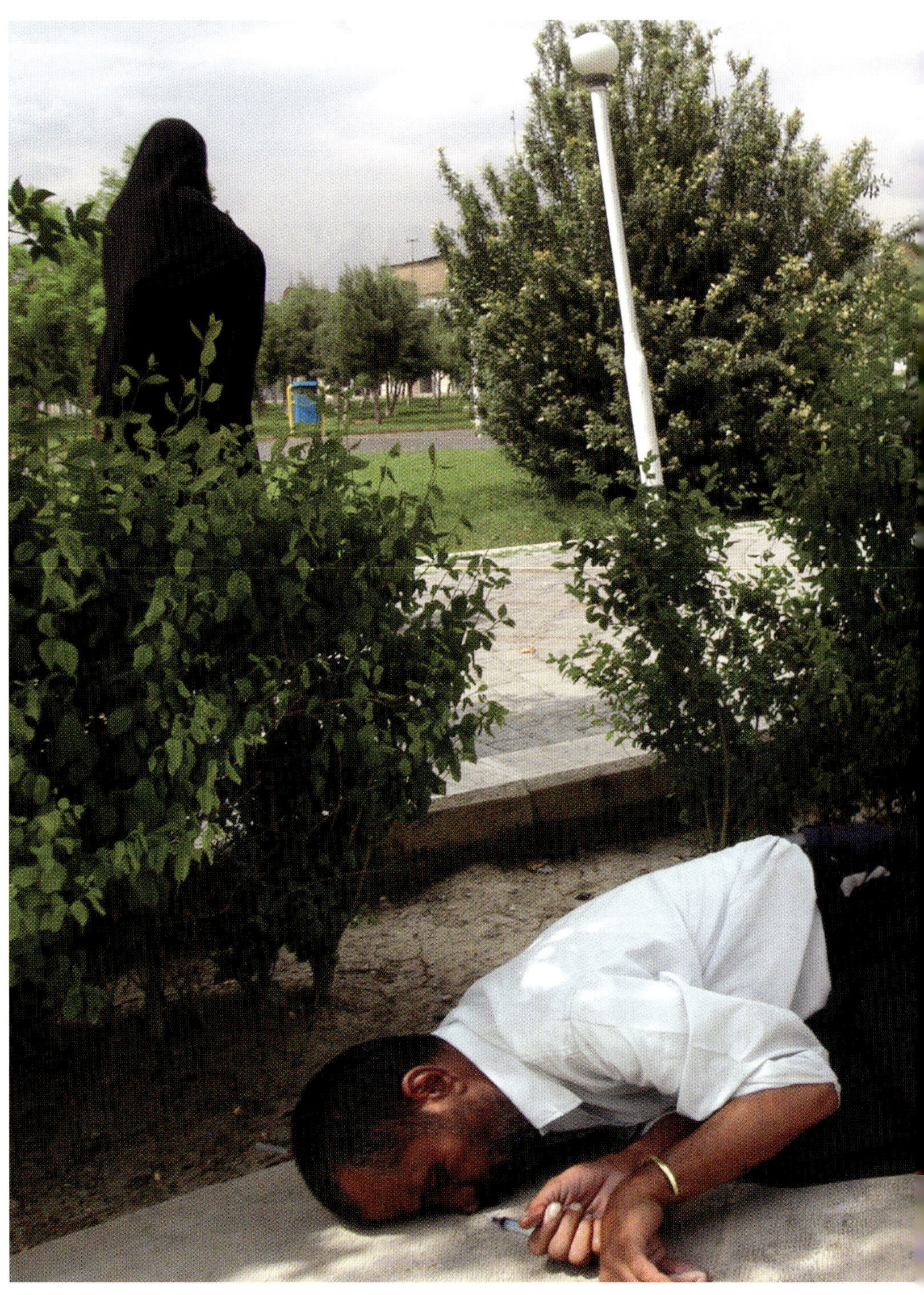

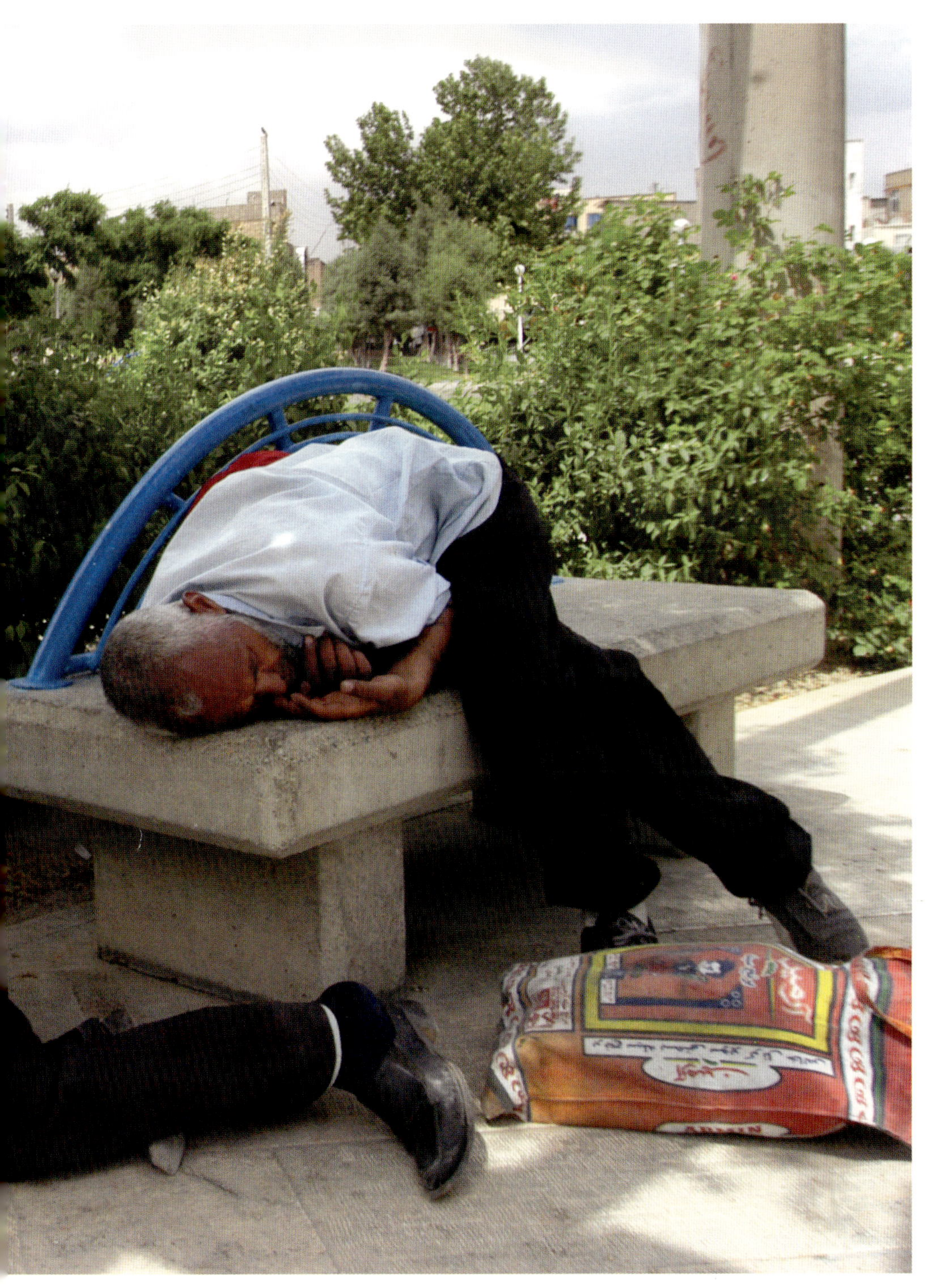

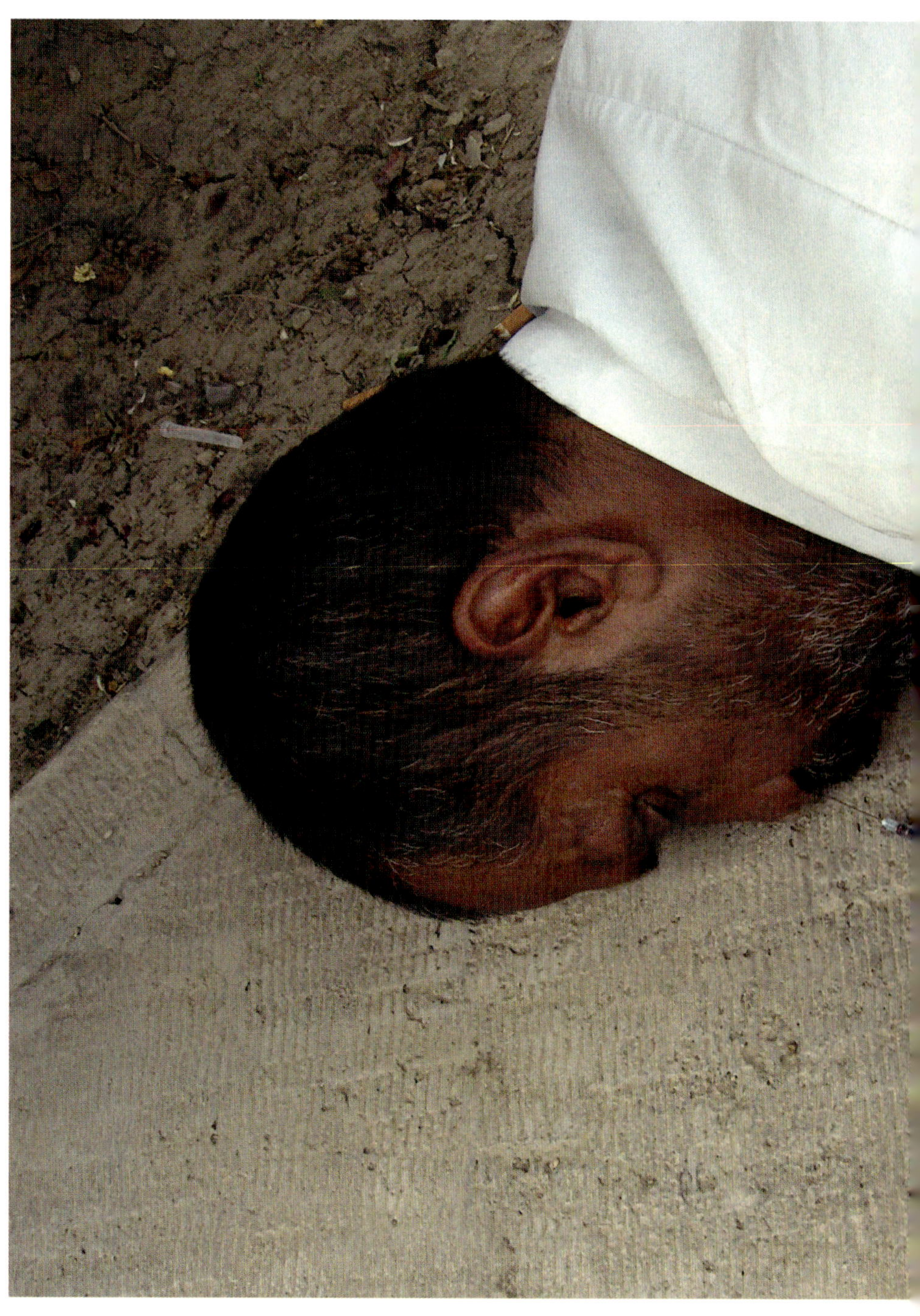

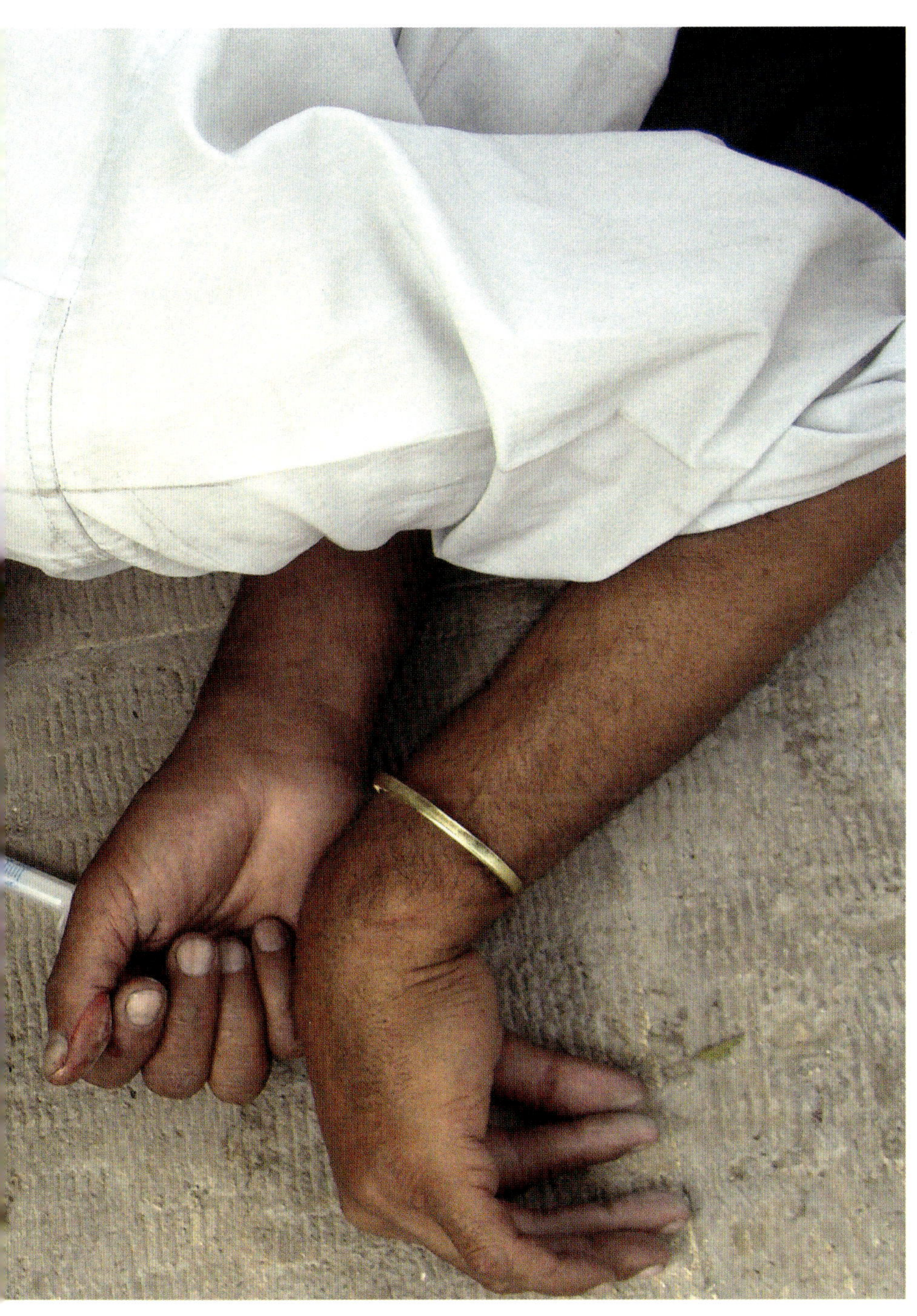

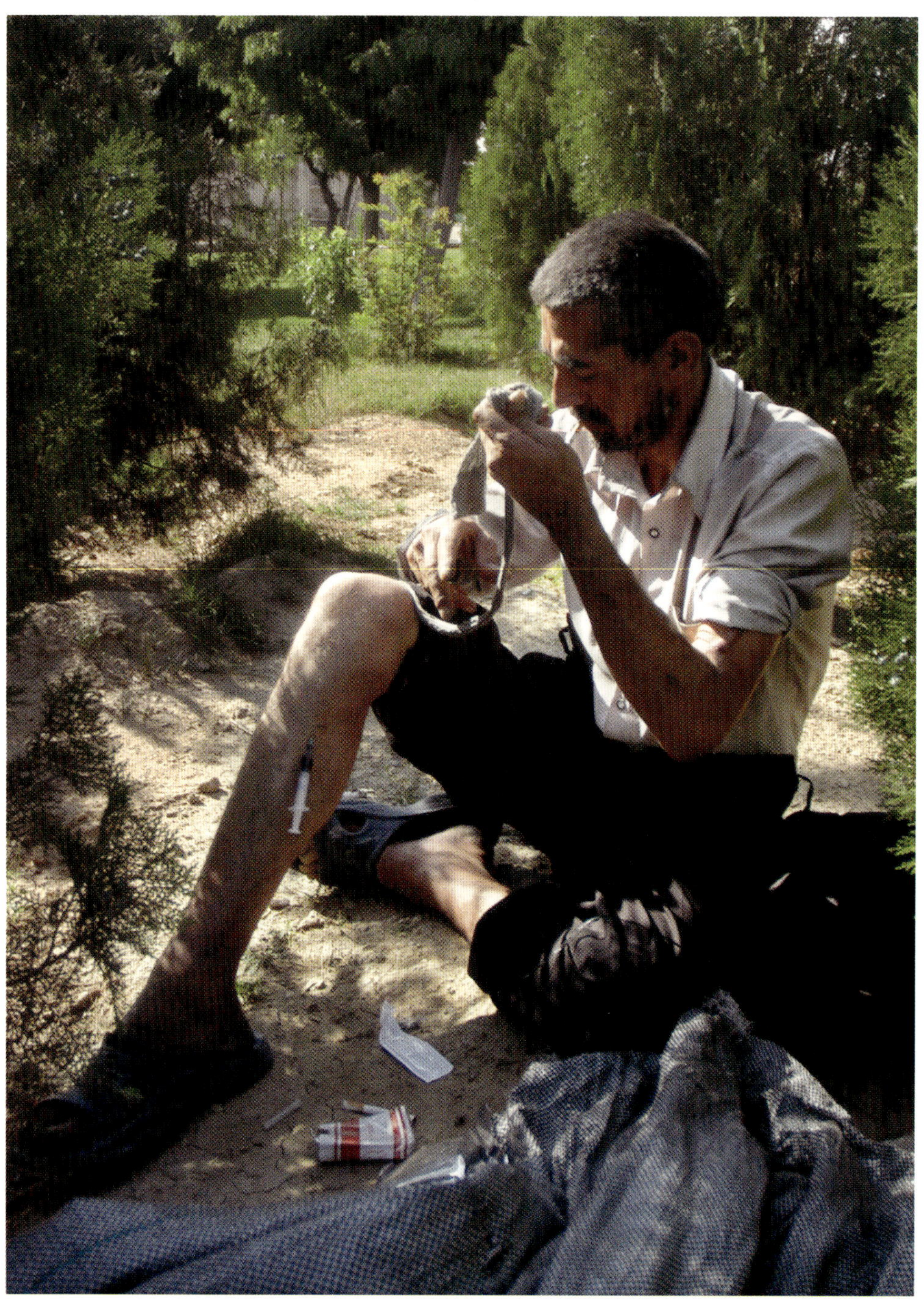

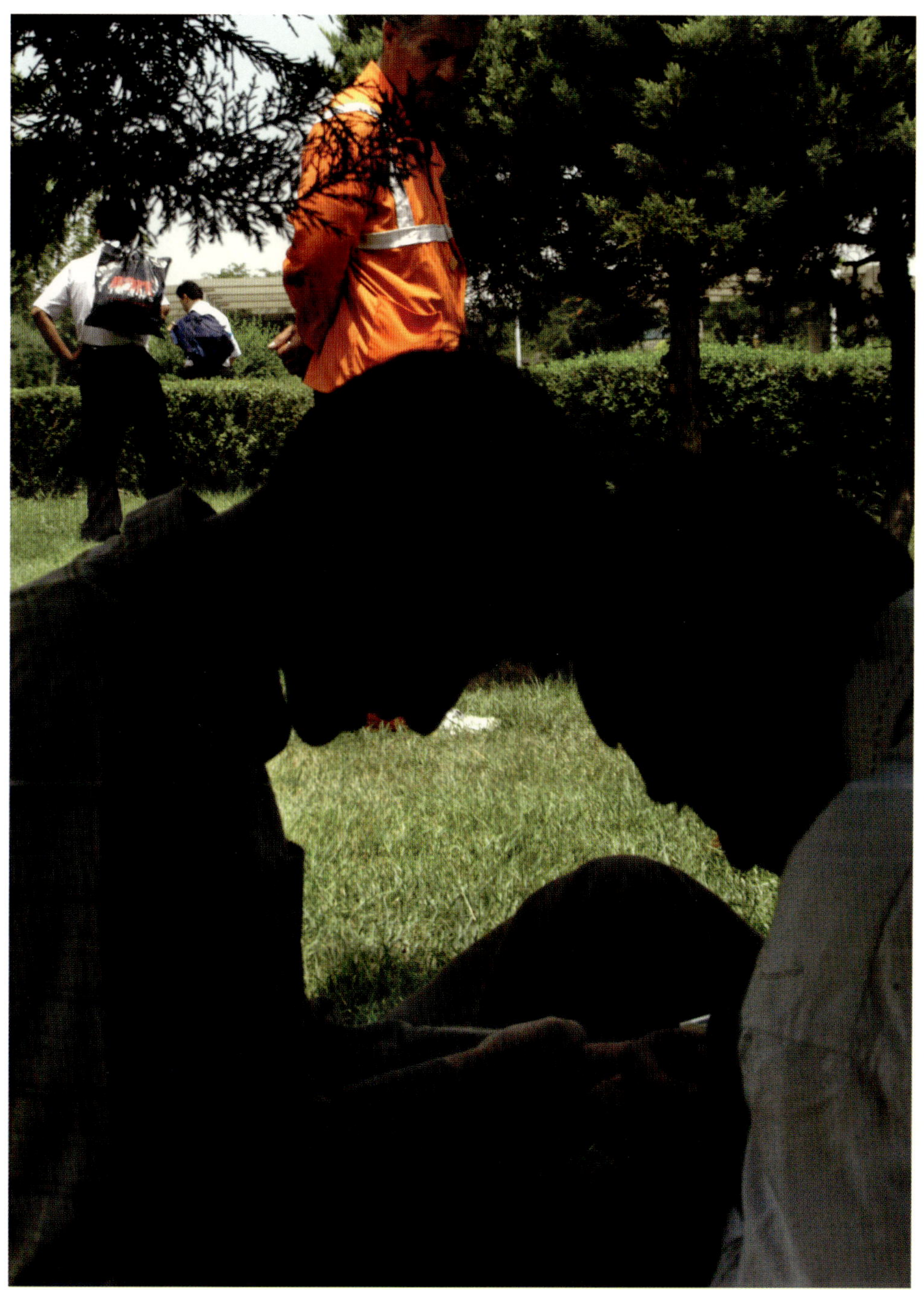

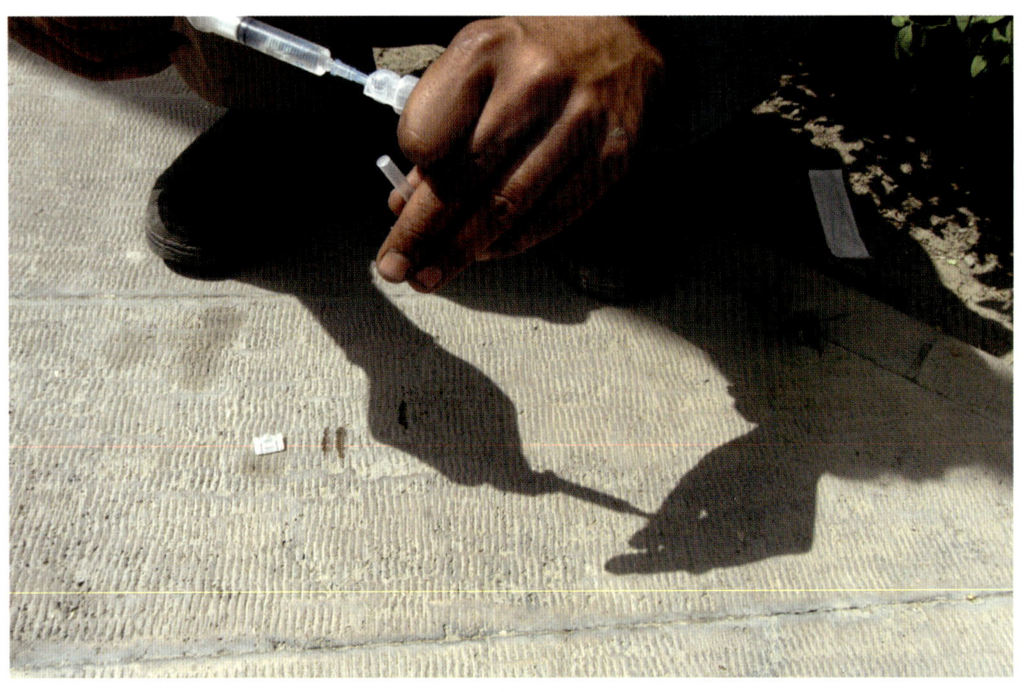

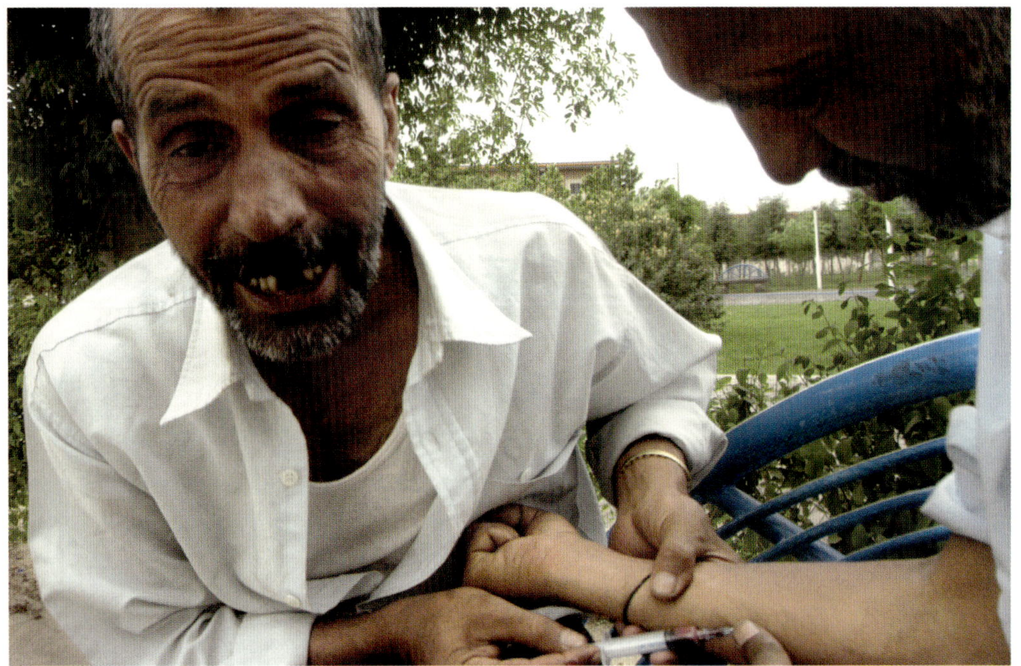

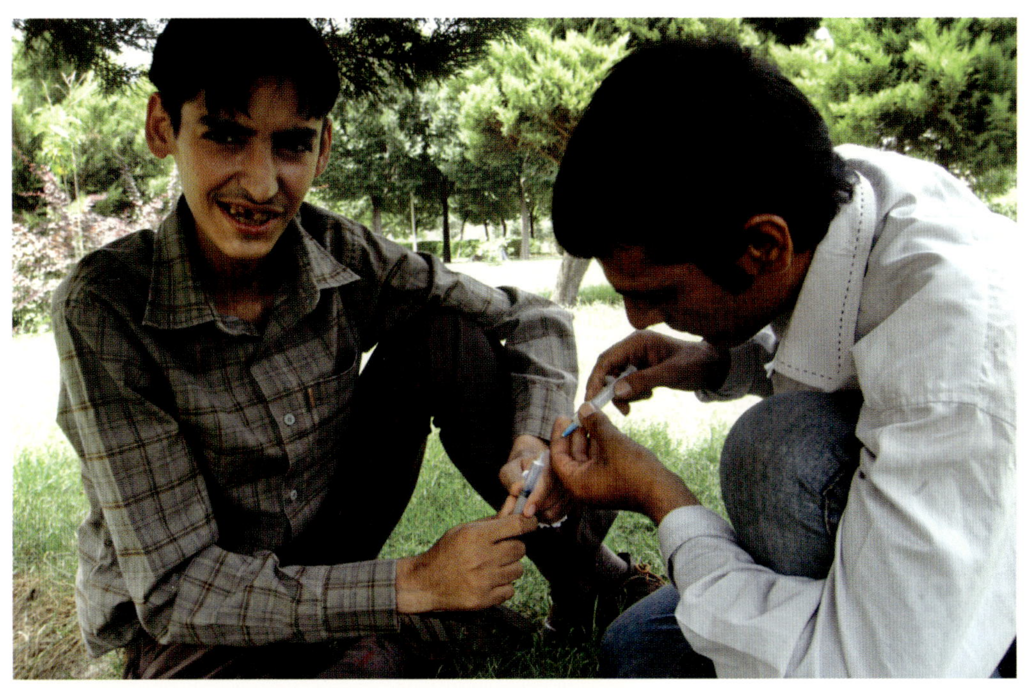

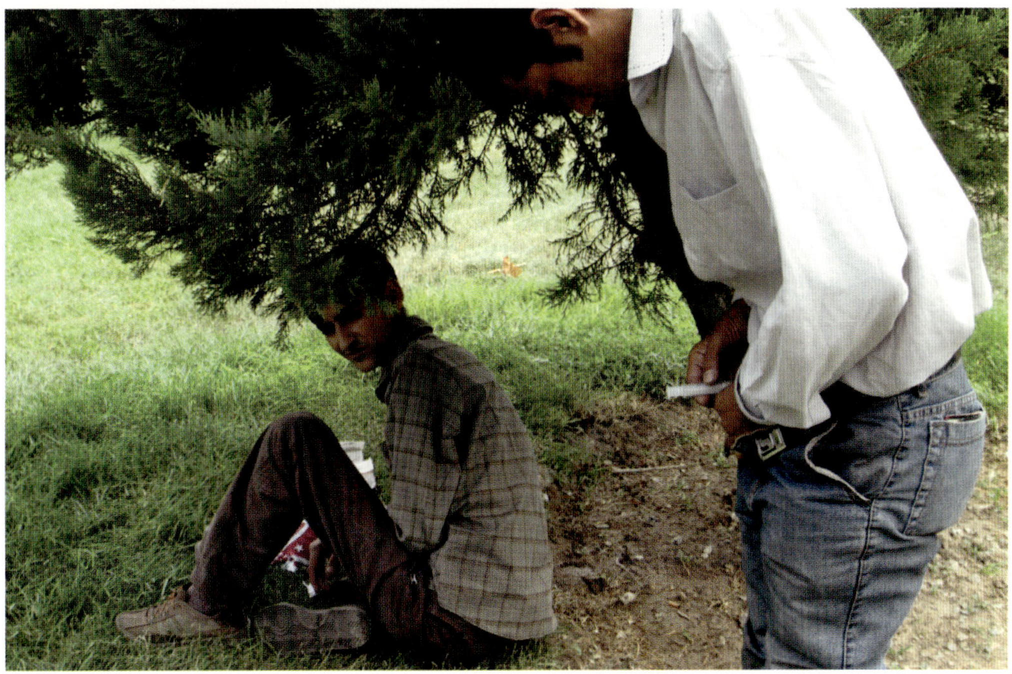

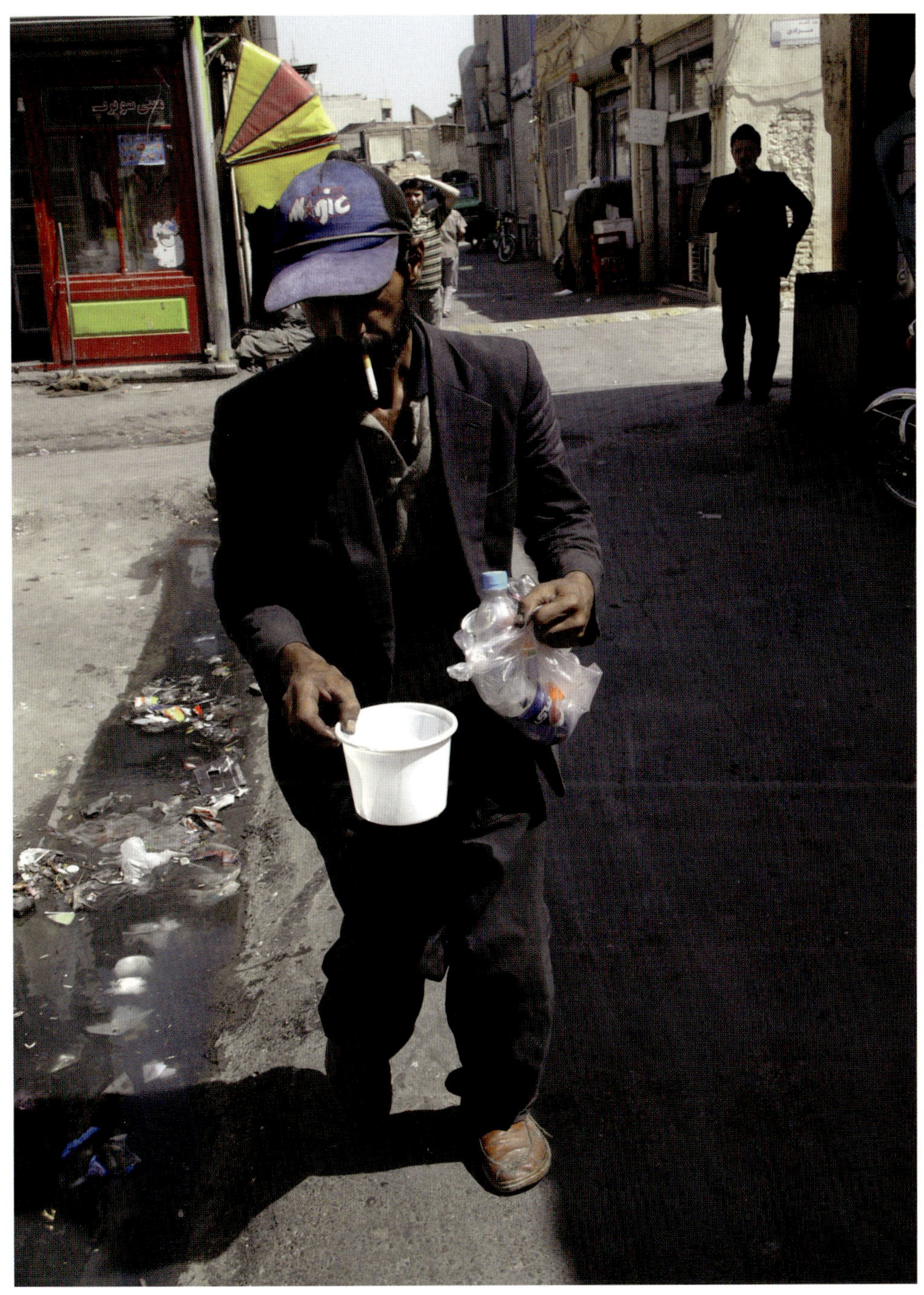
Magic

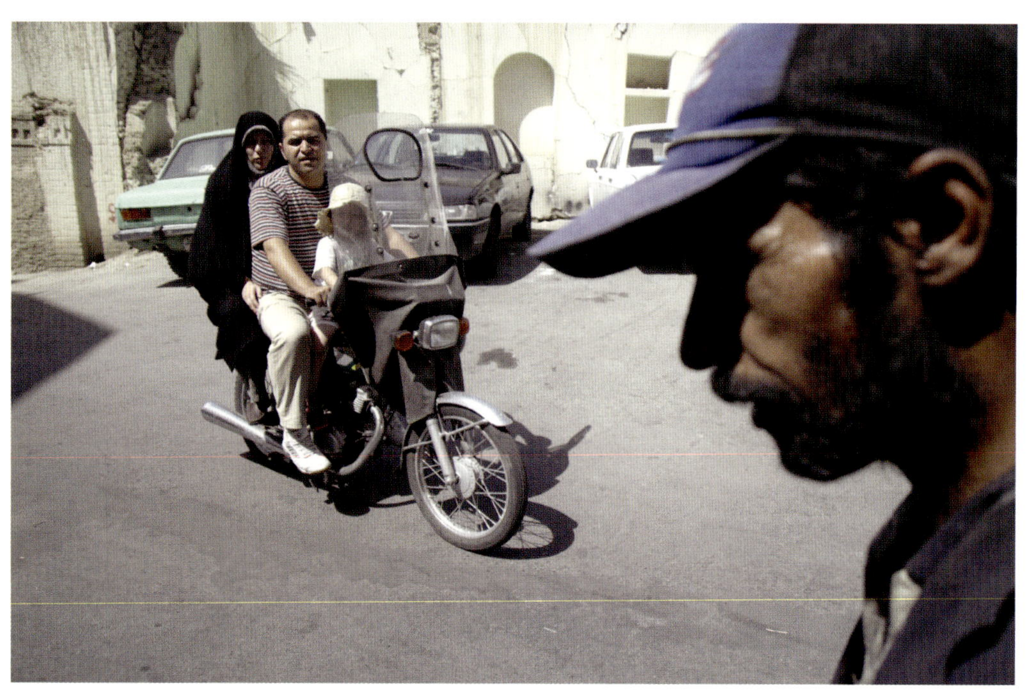

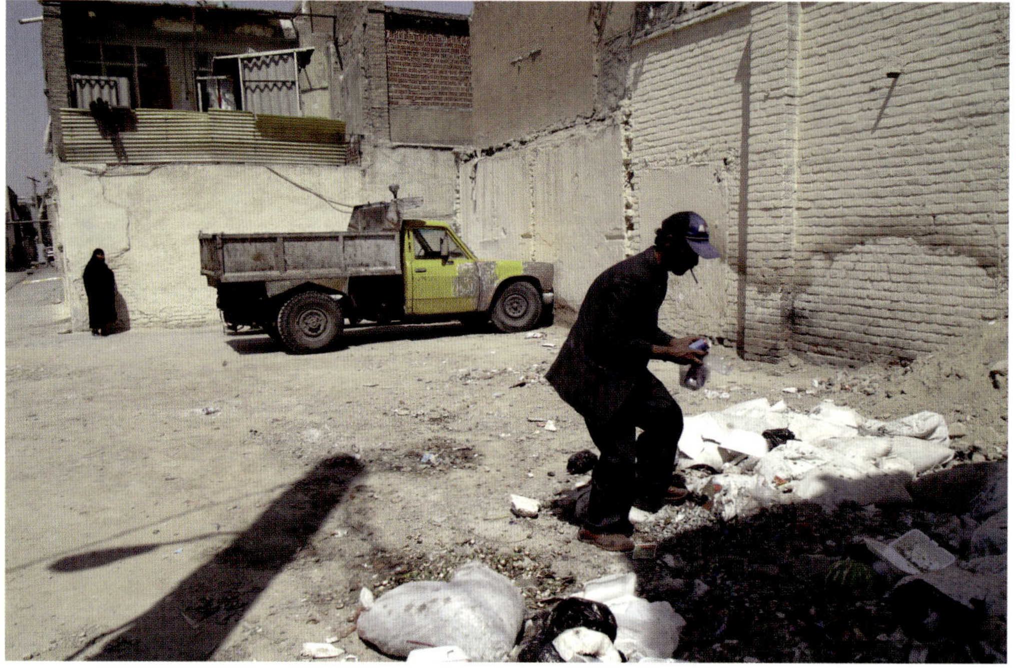

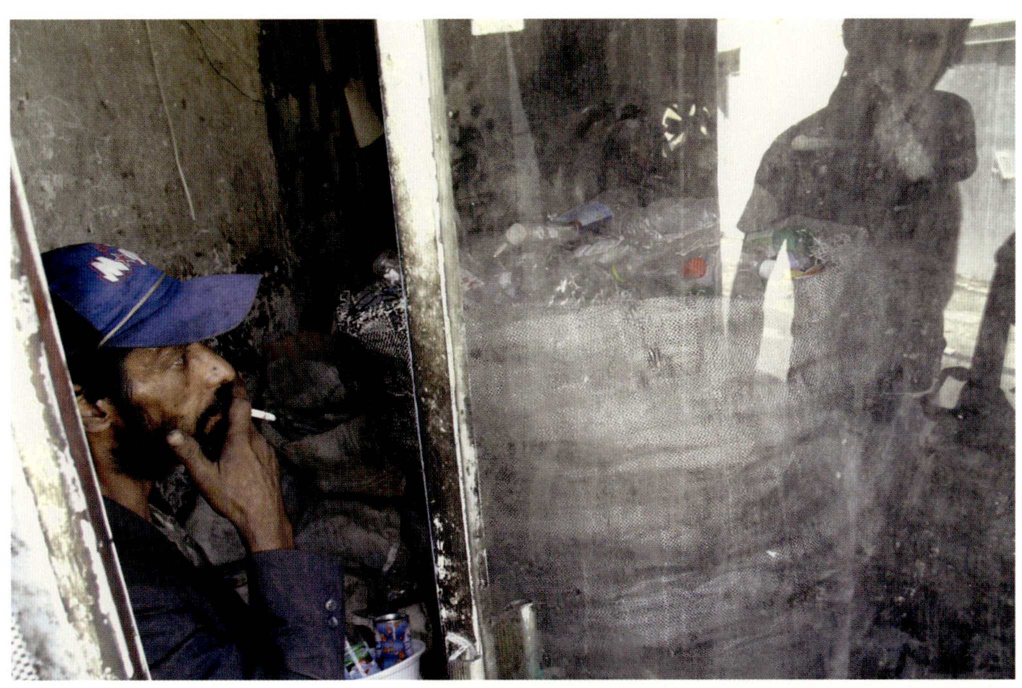

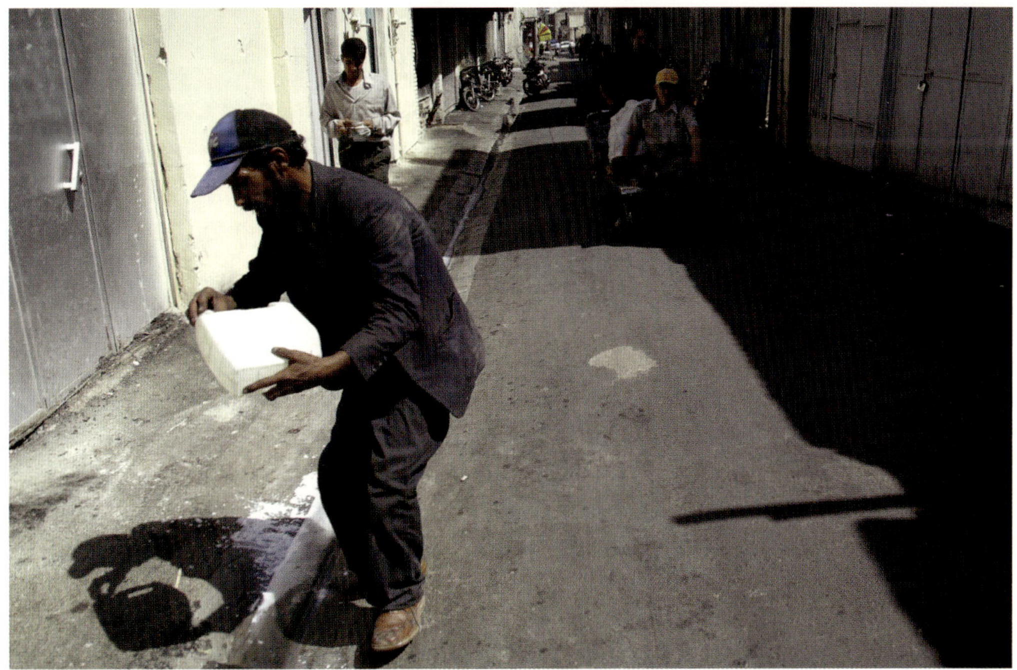

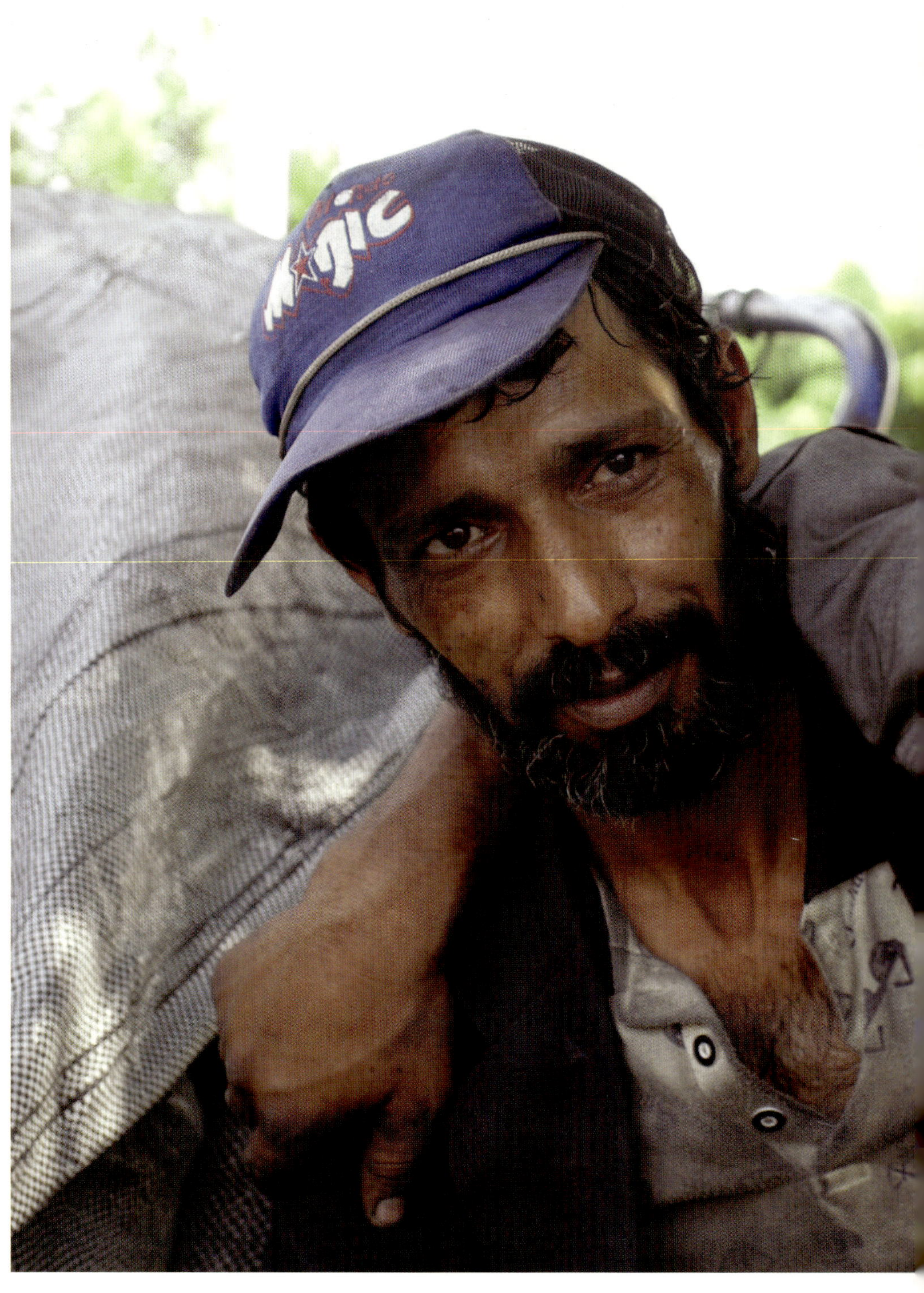

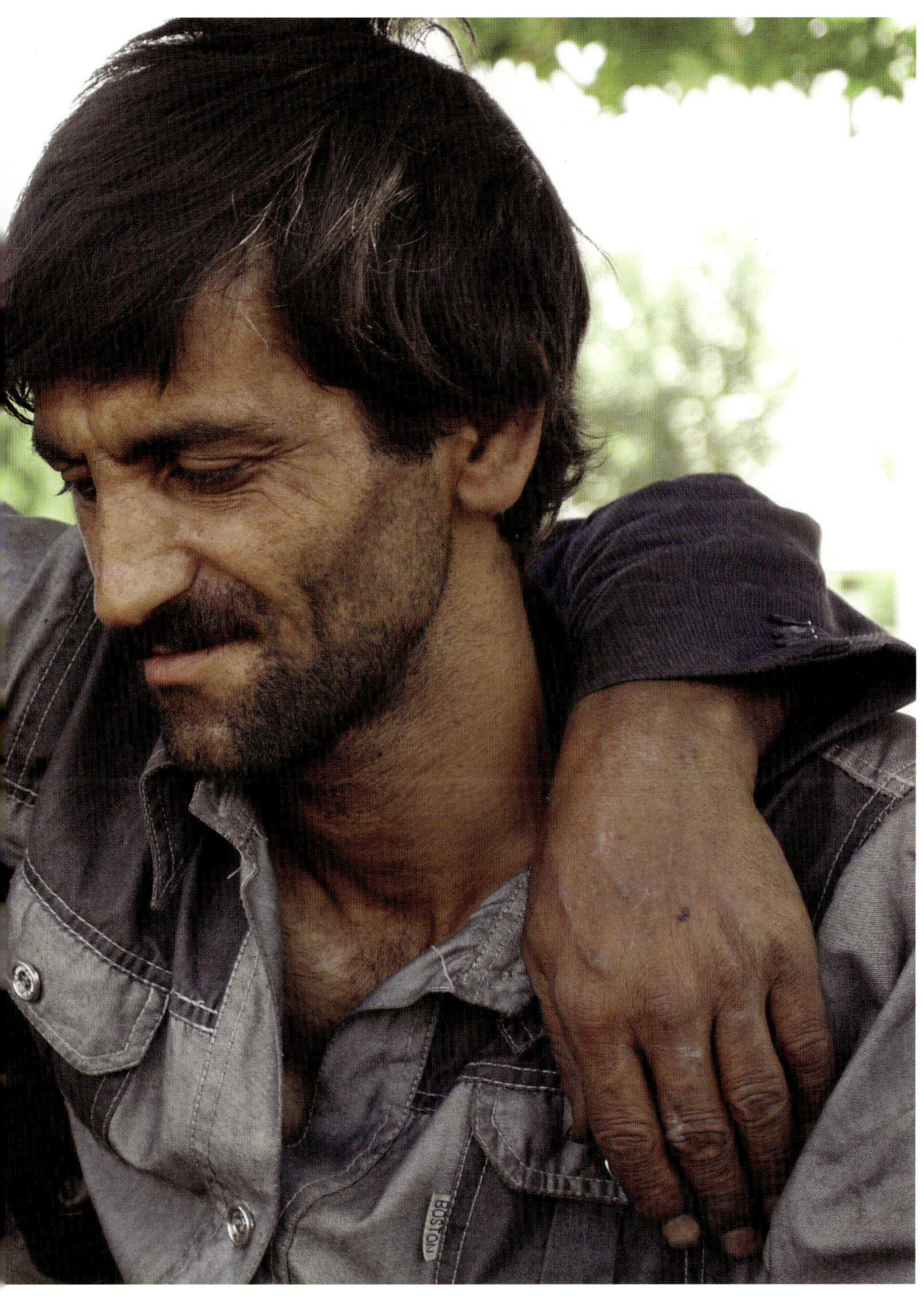
BOSTON

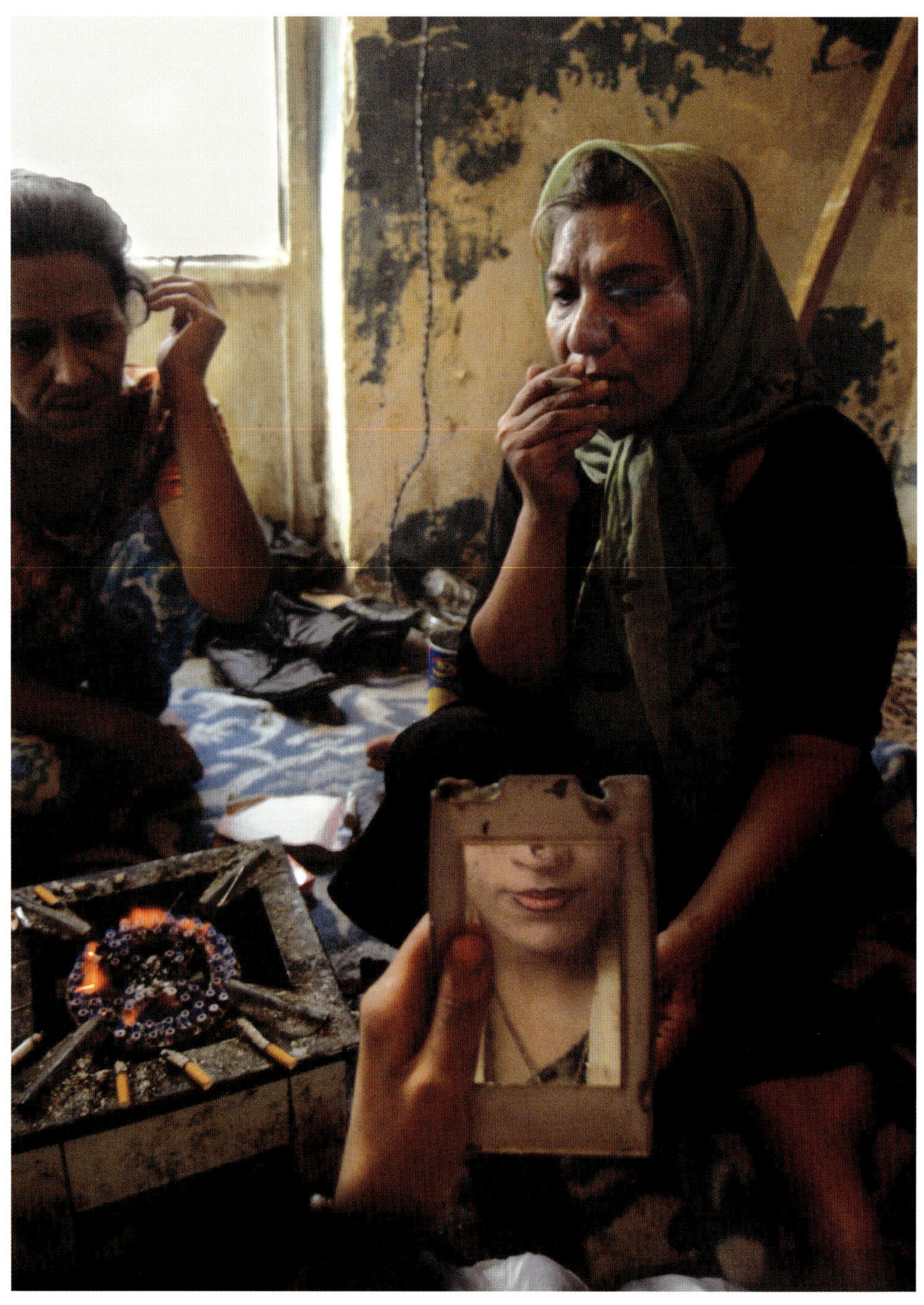

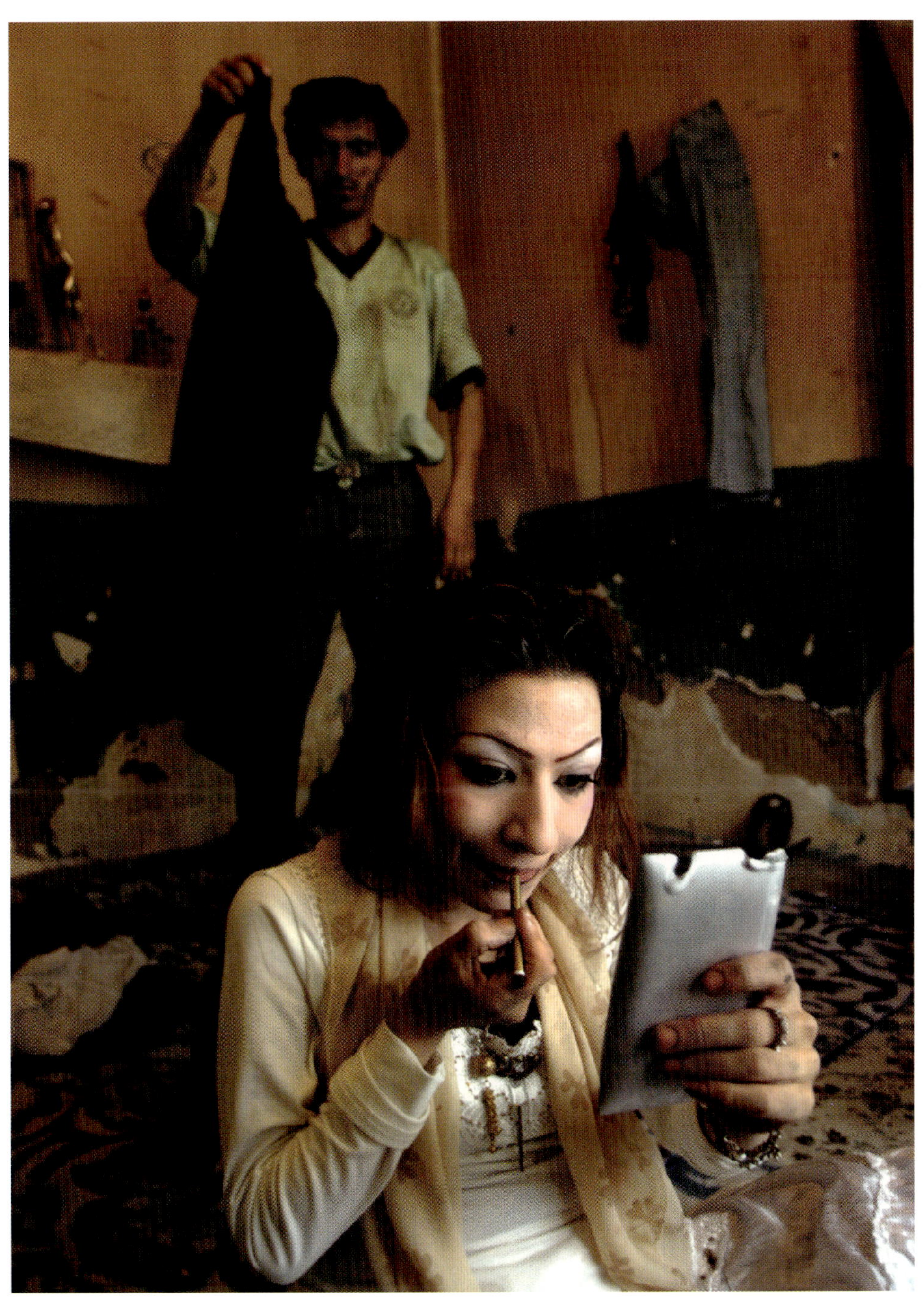

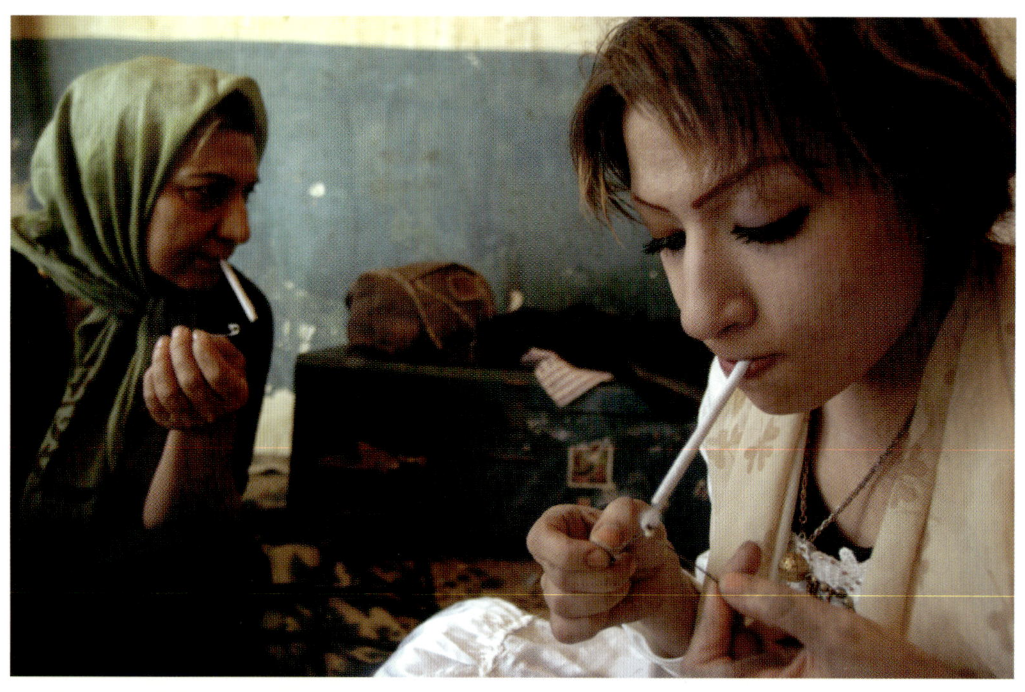

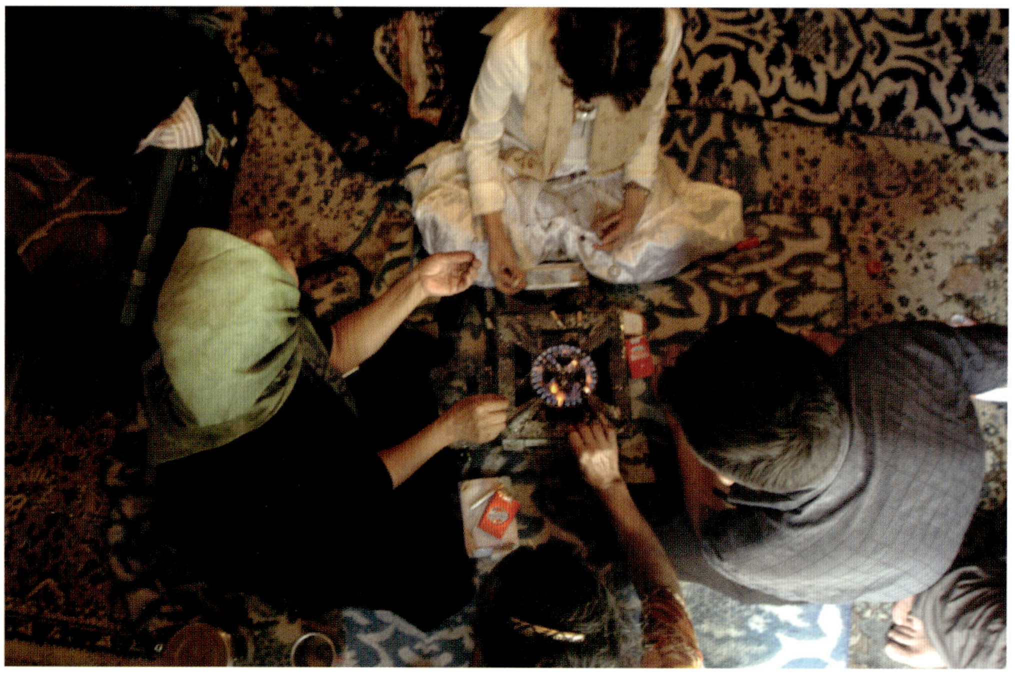

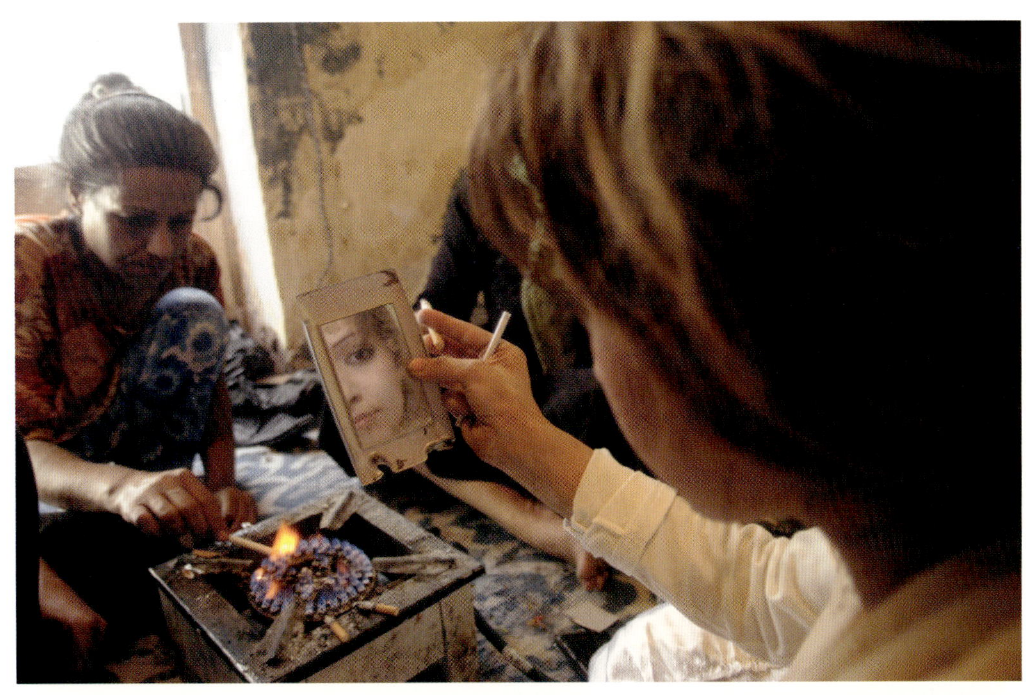

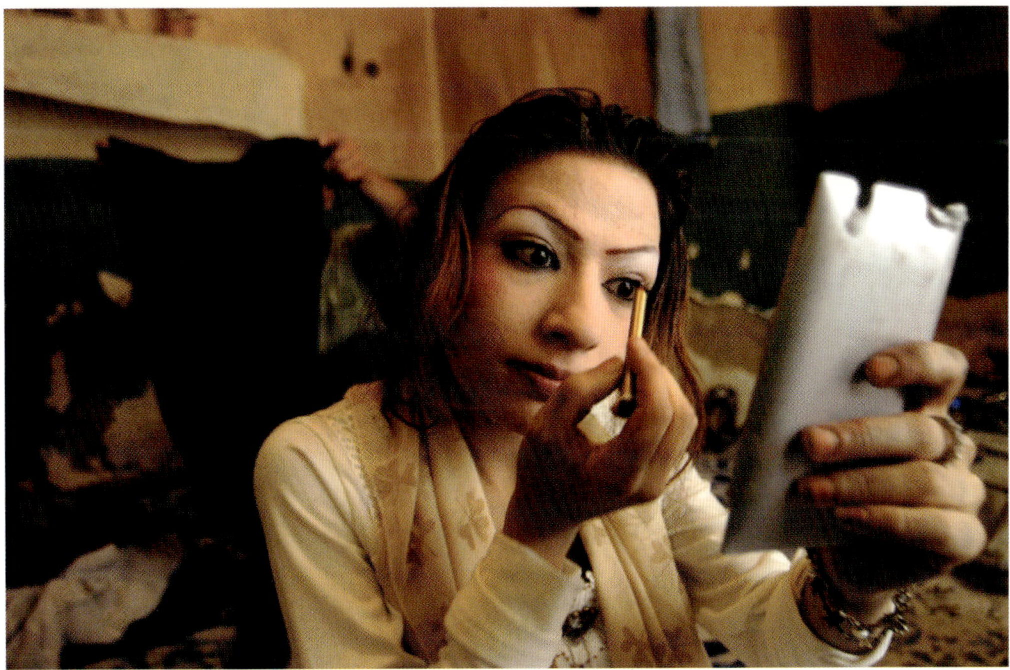

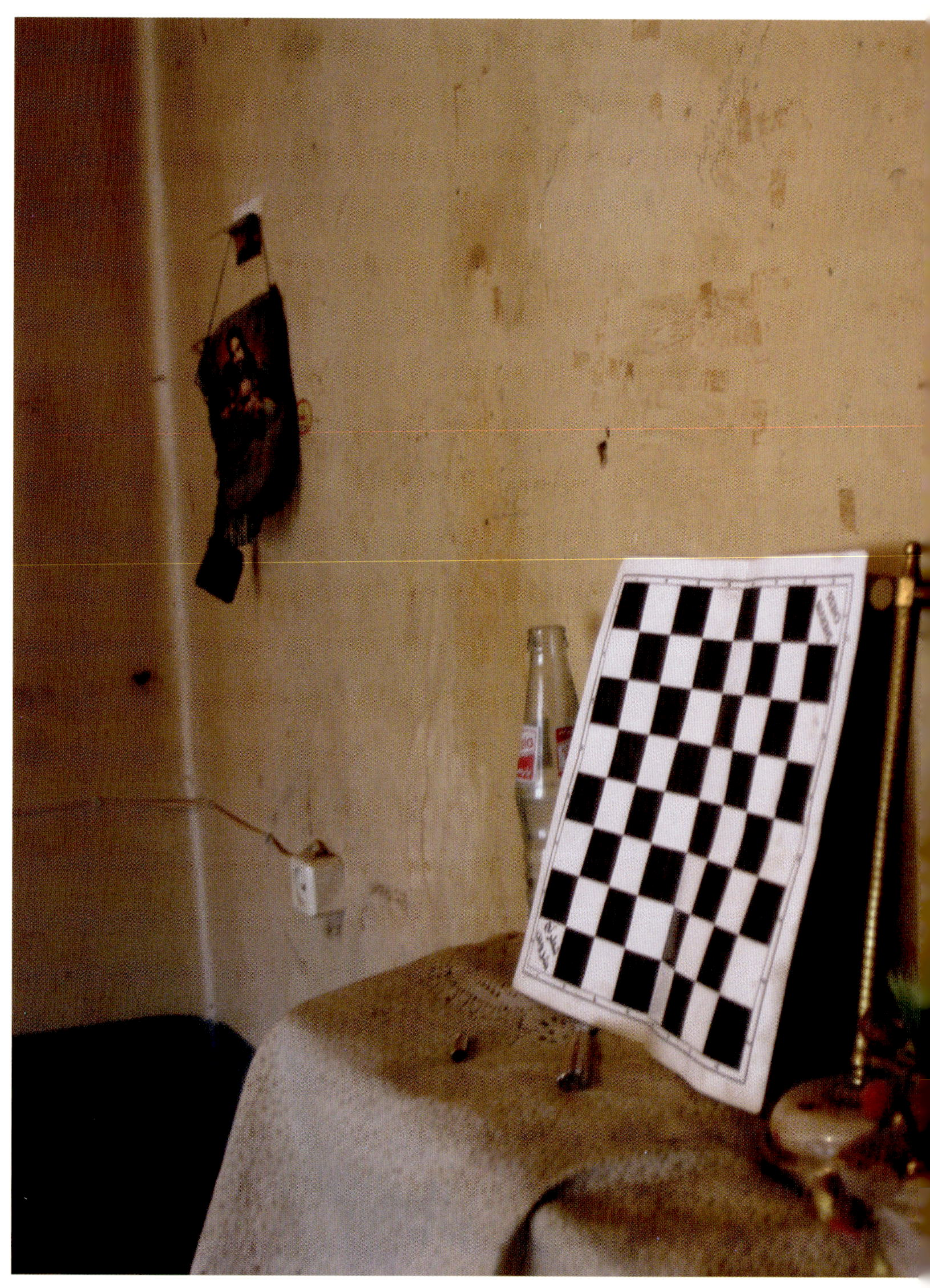

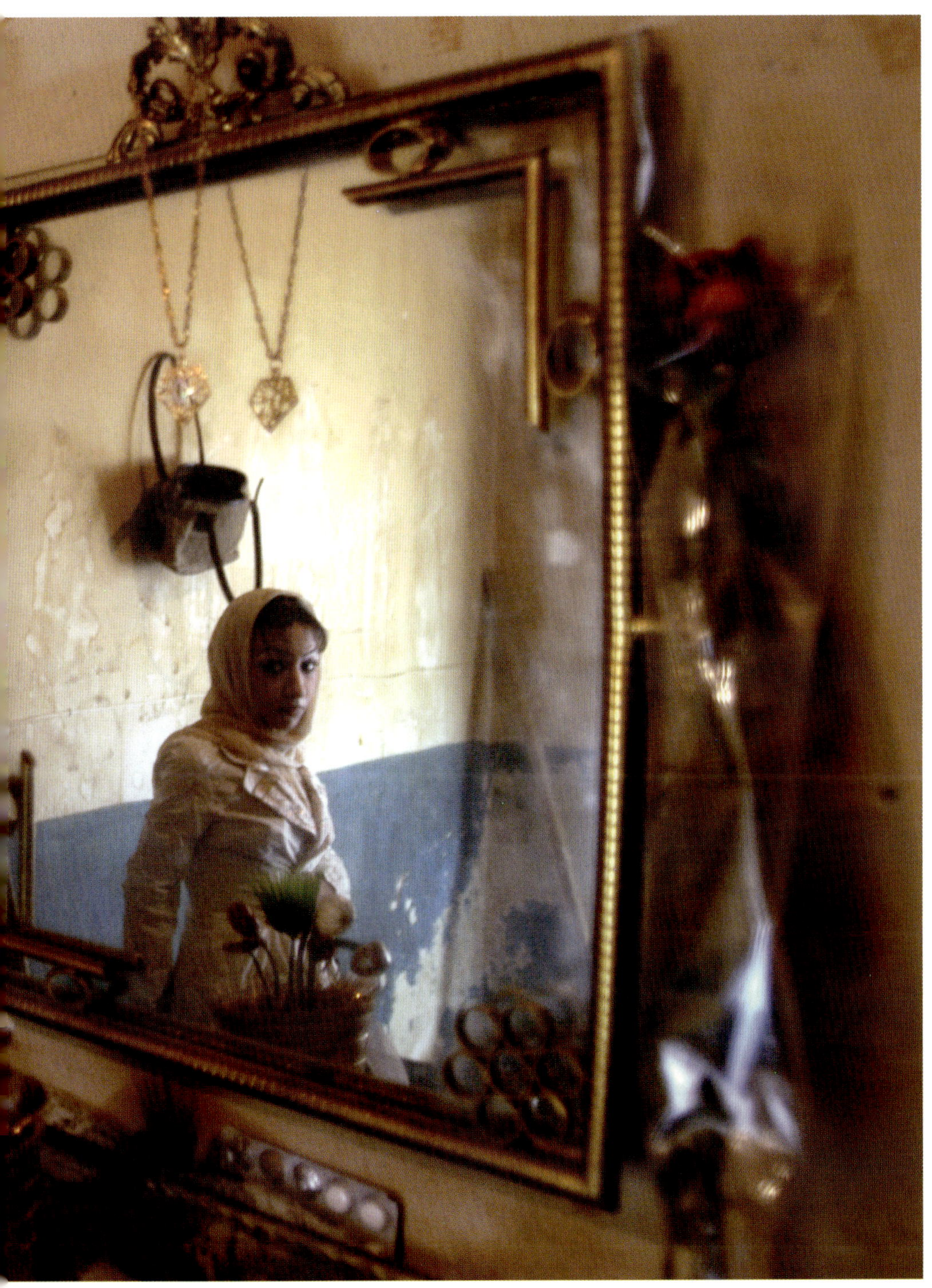

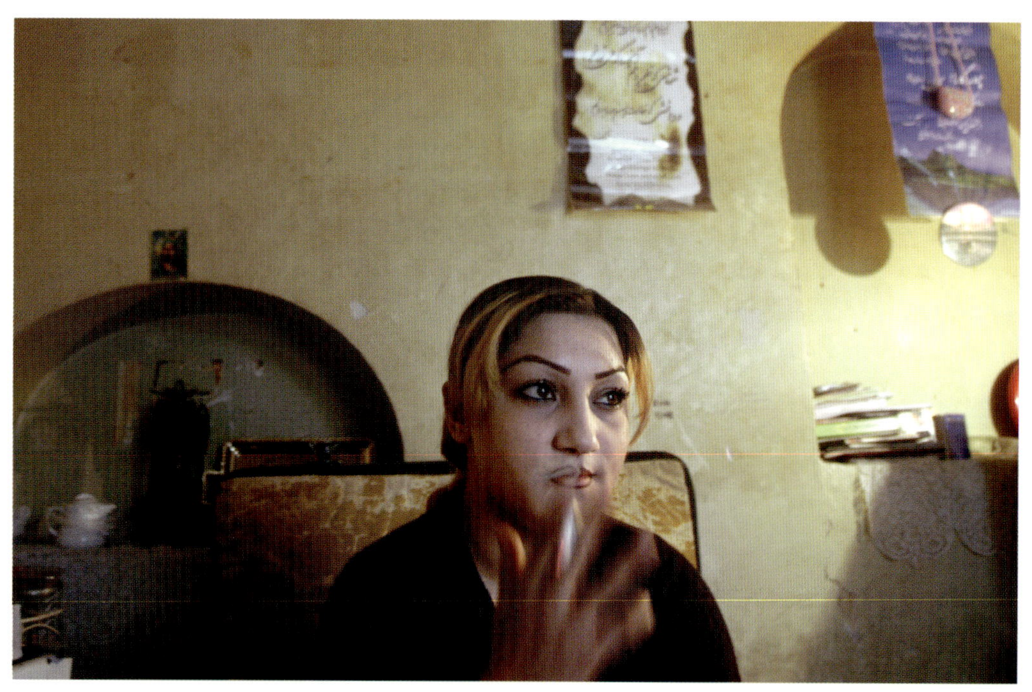

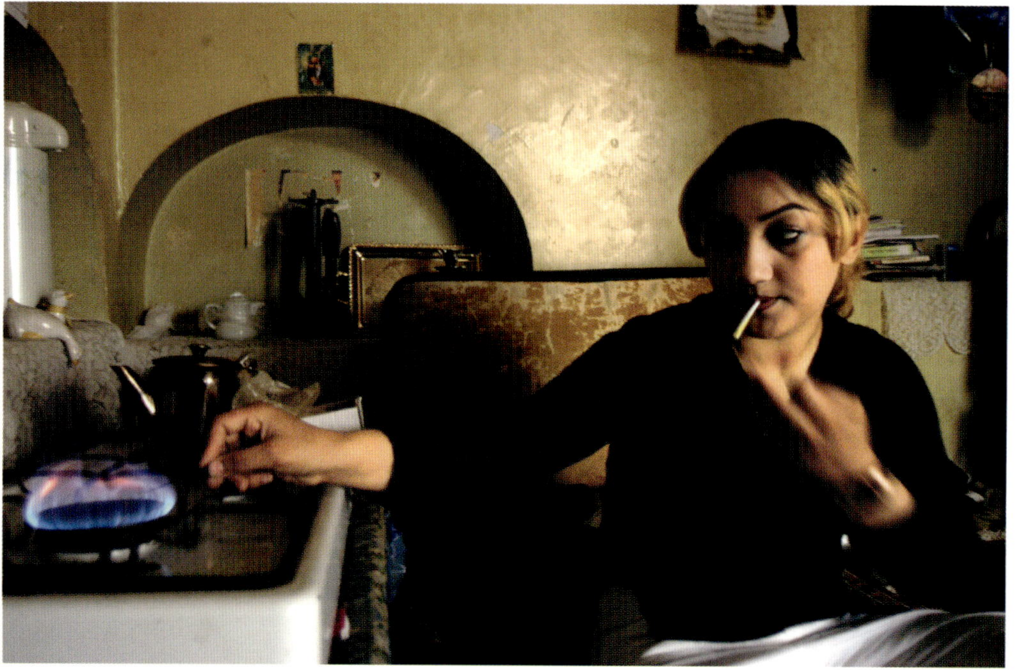

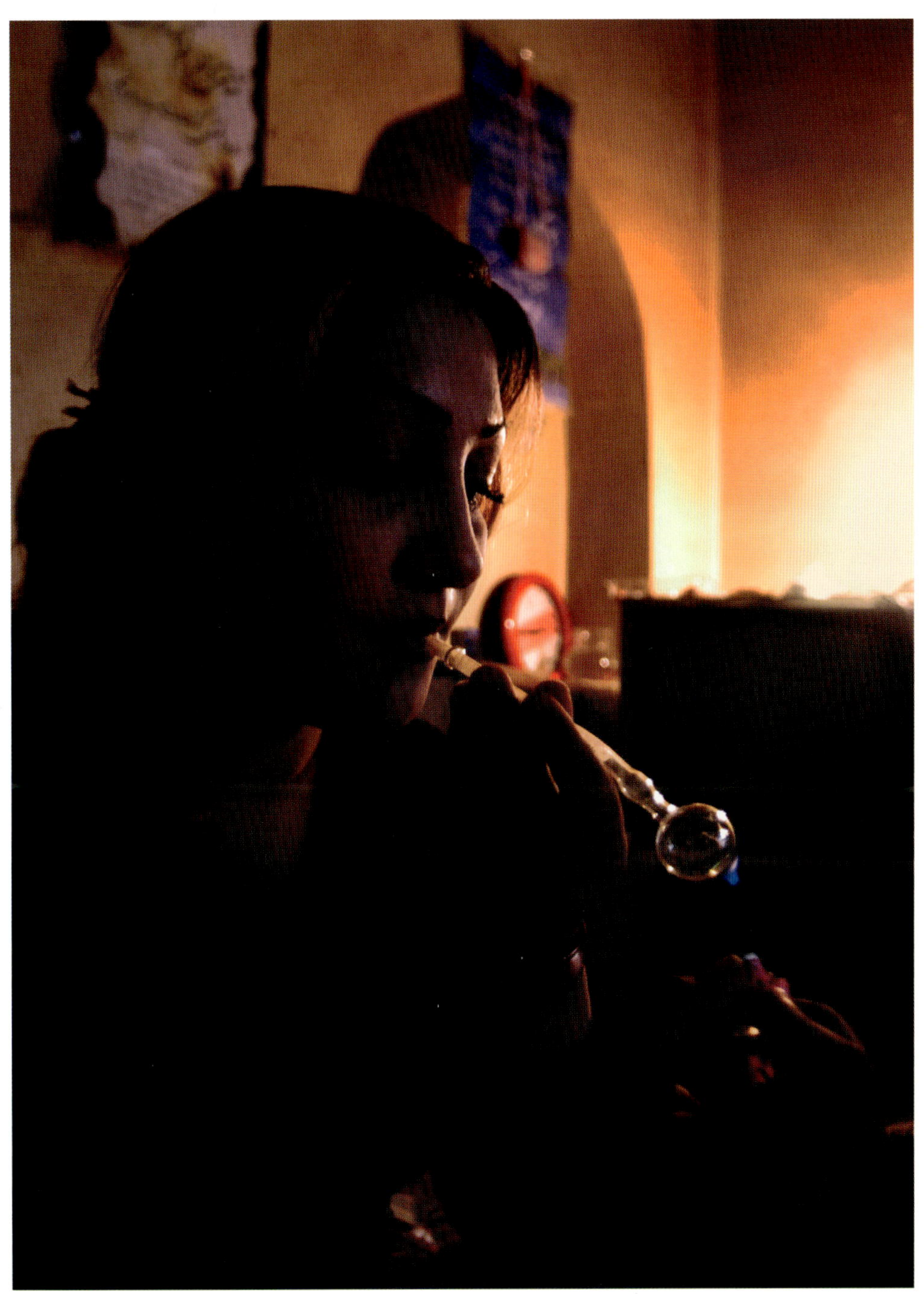

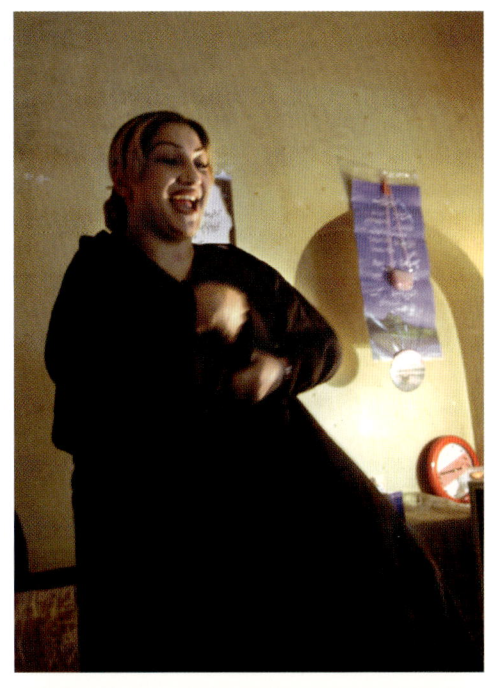
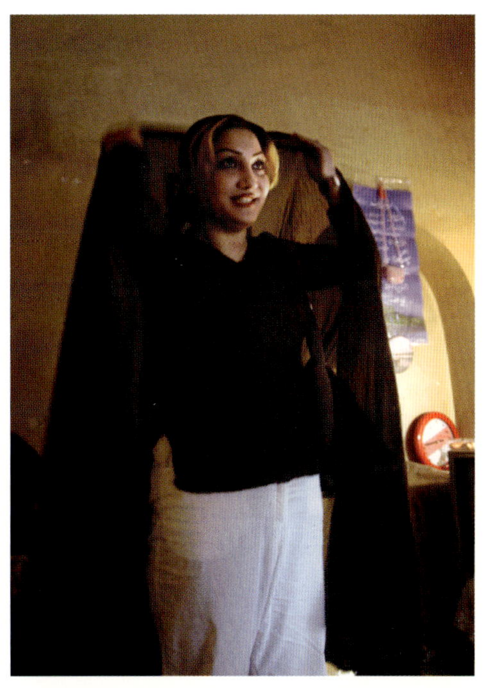
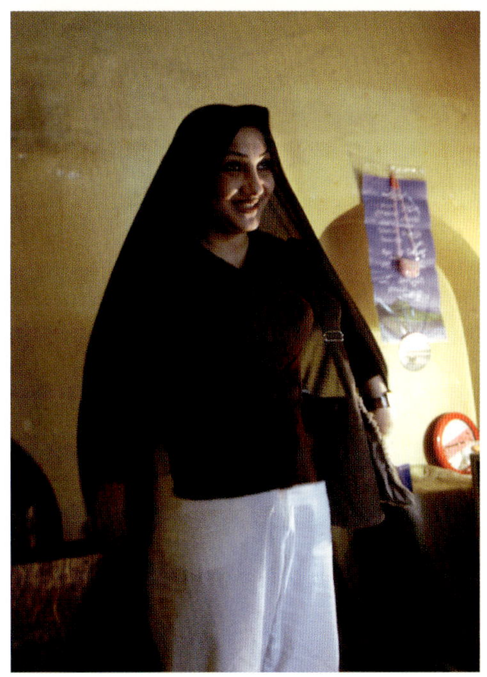
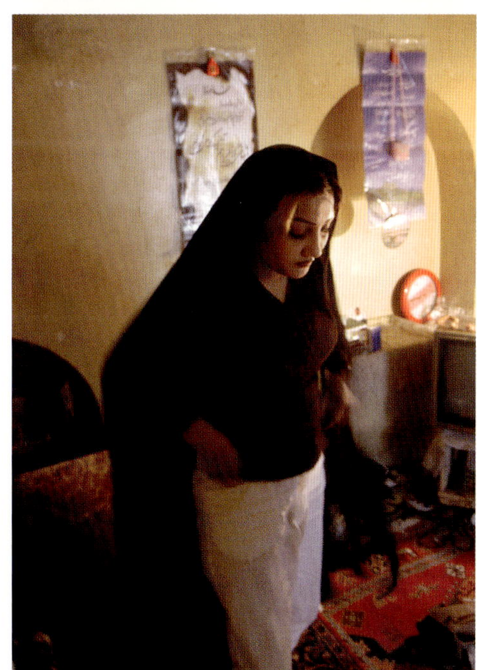

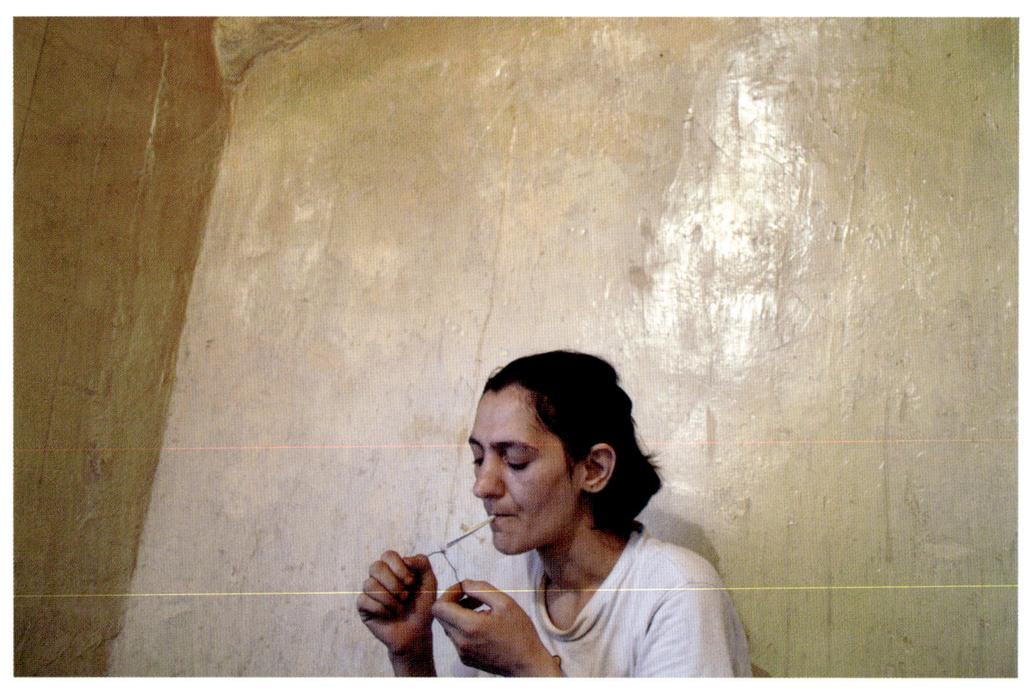

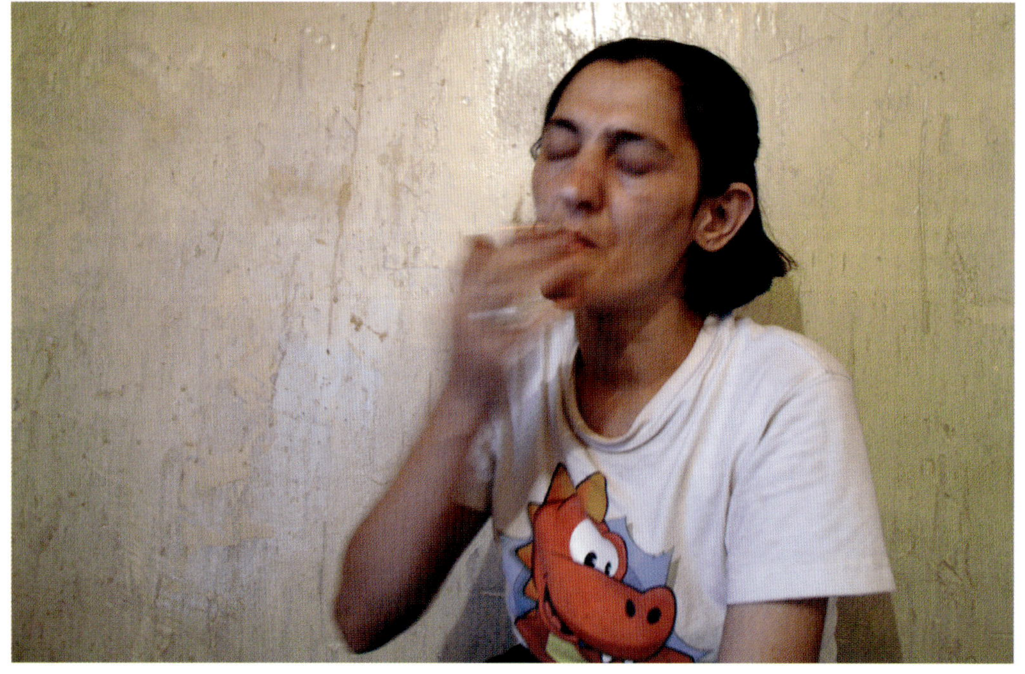

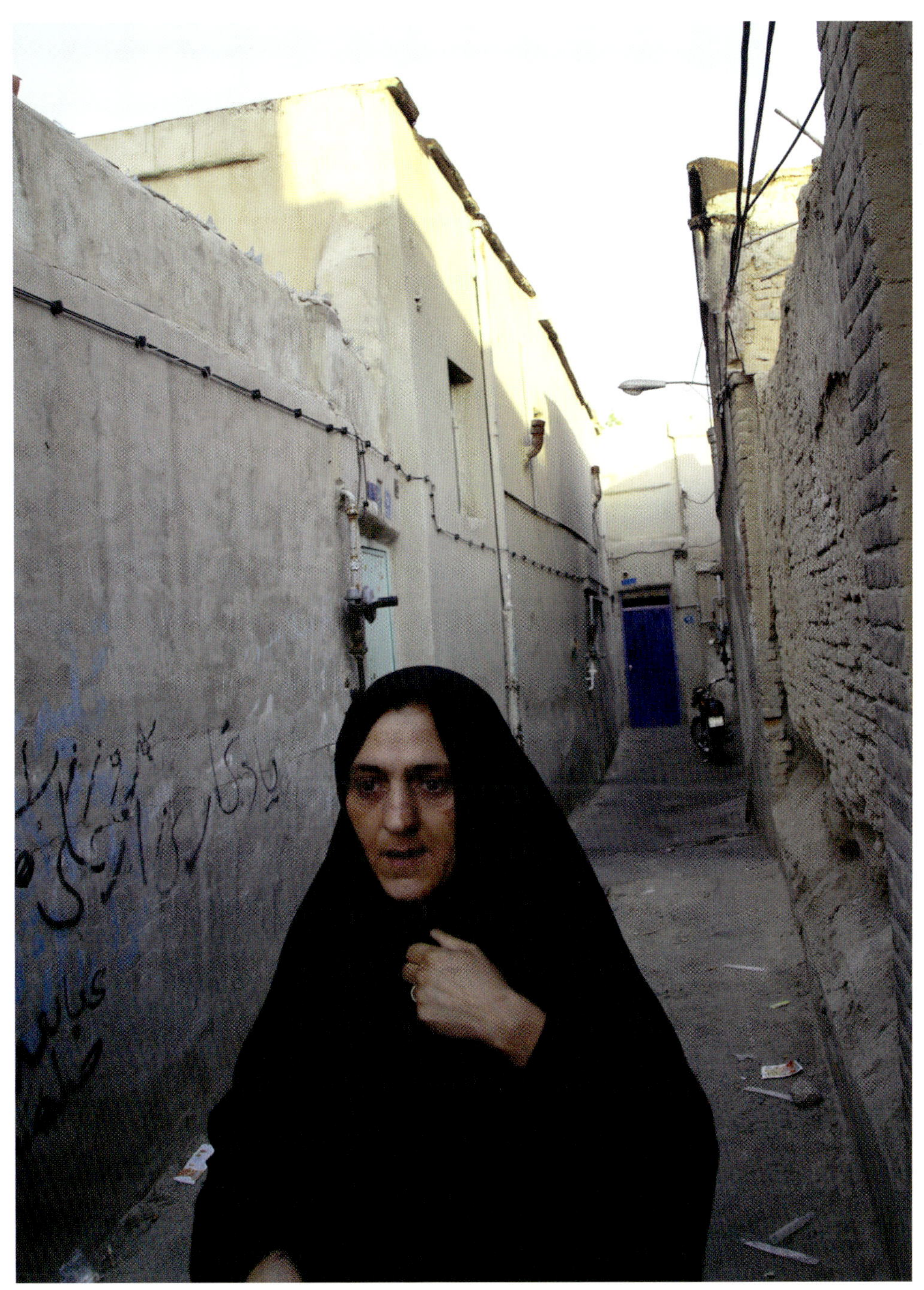

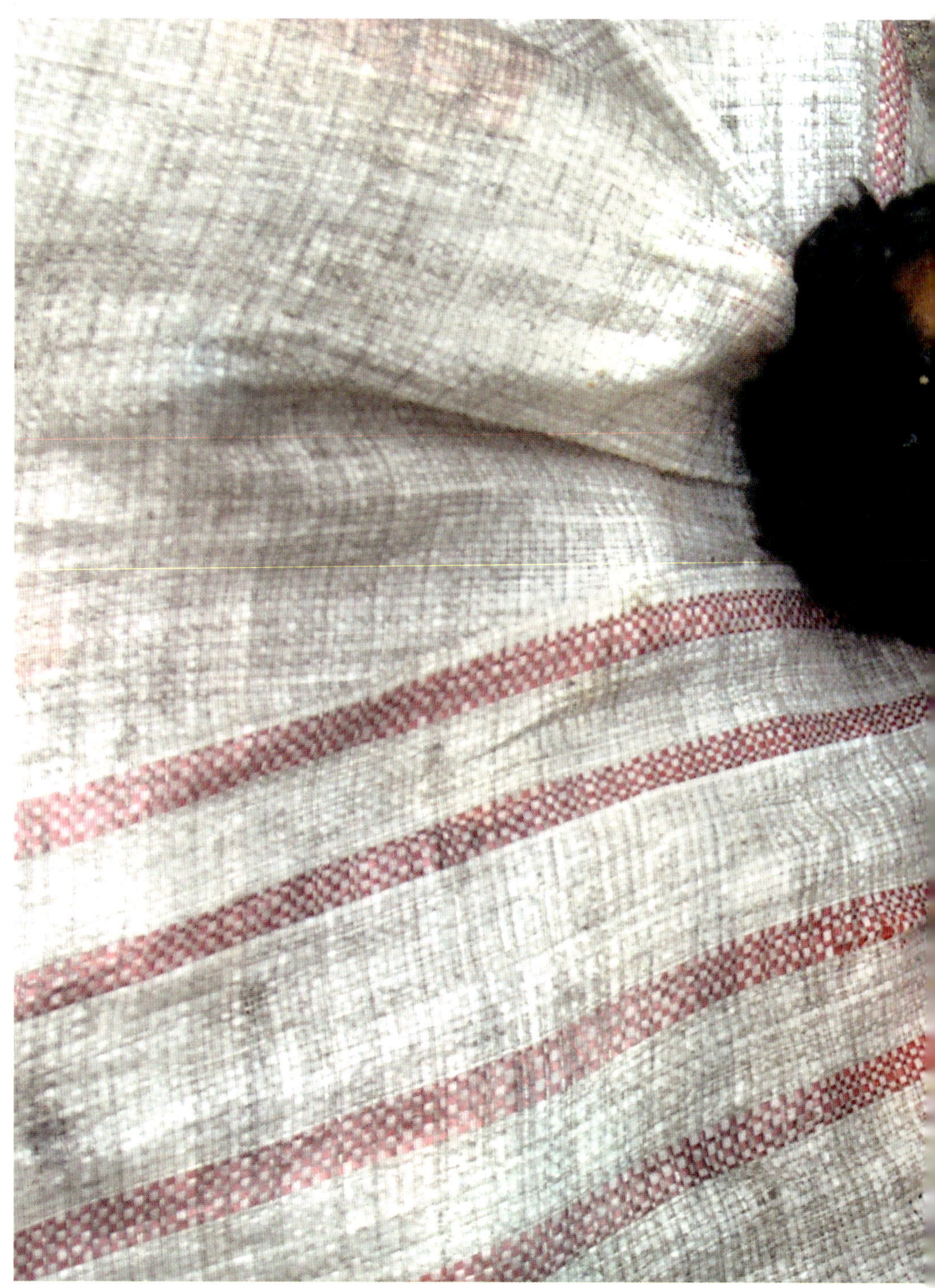

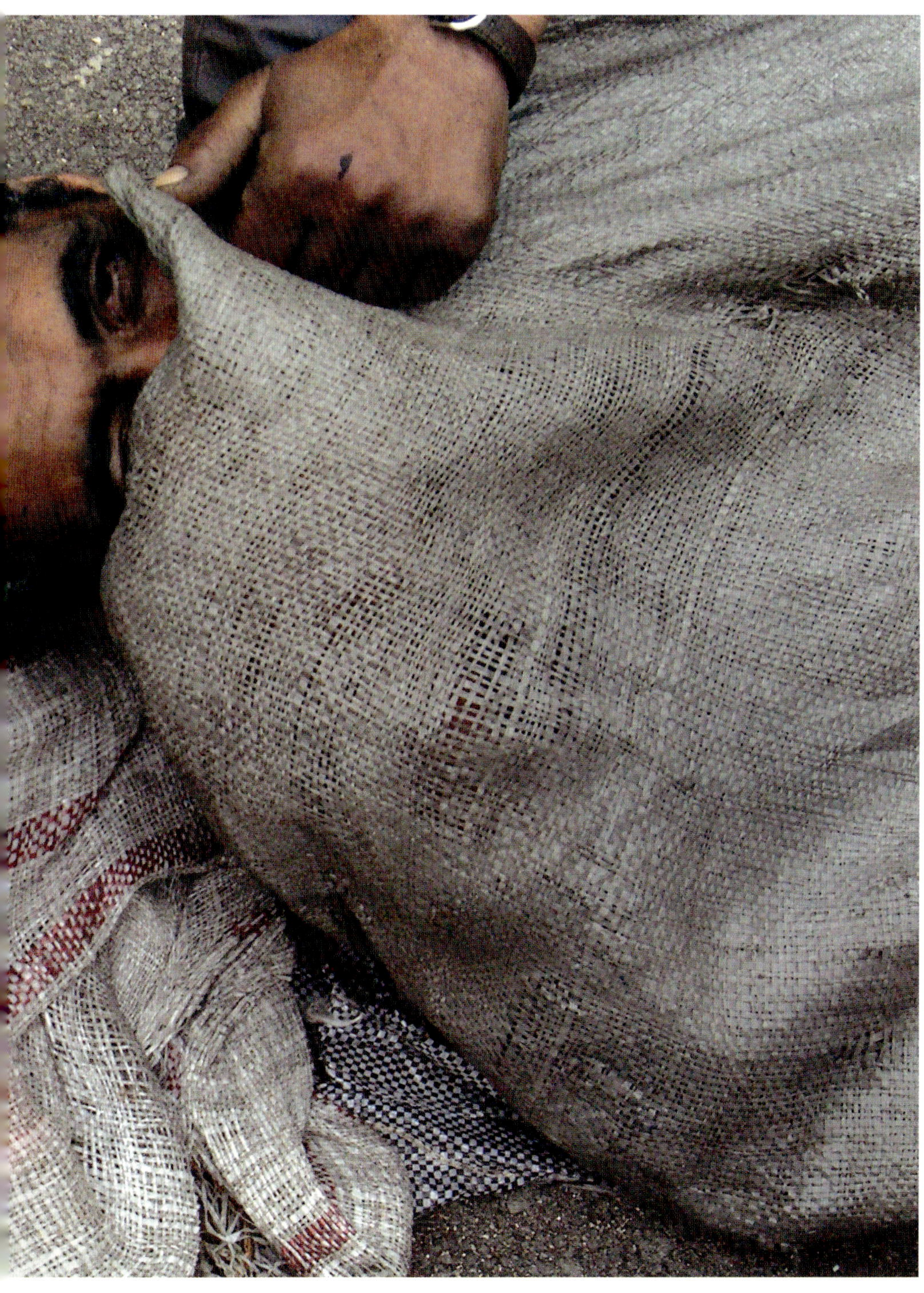

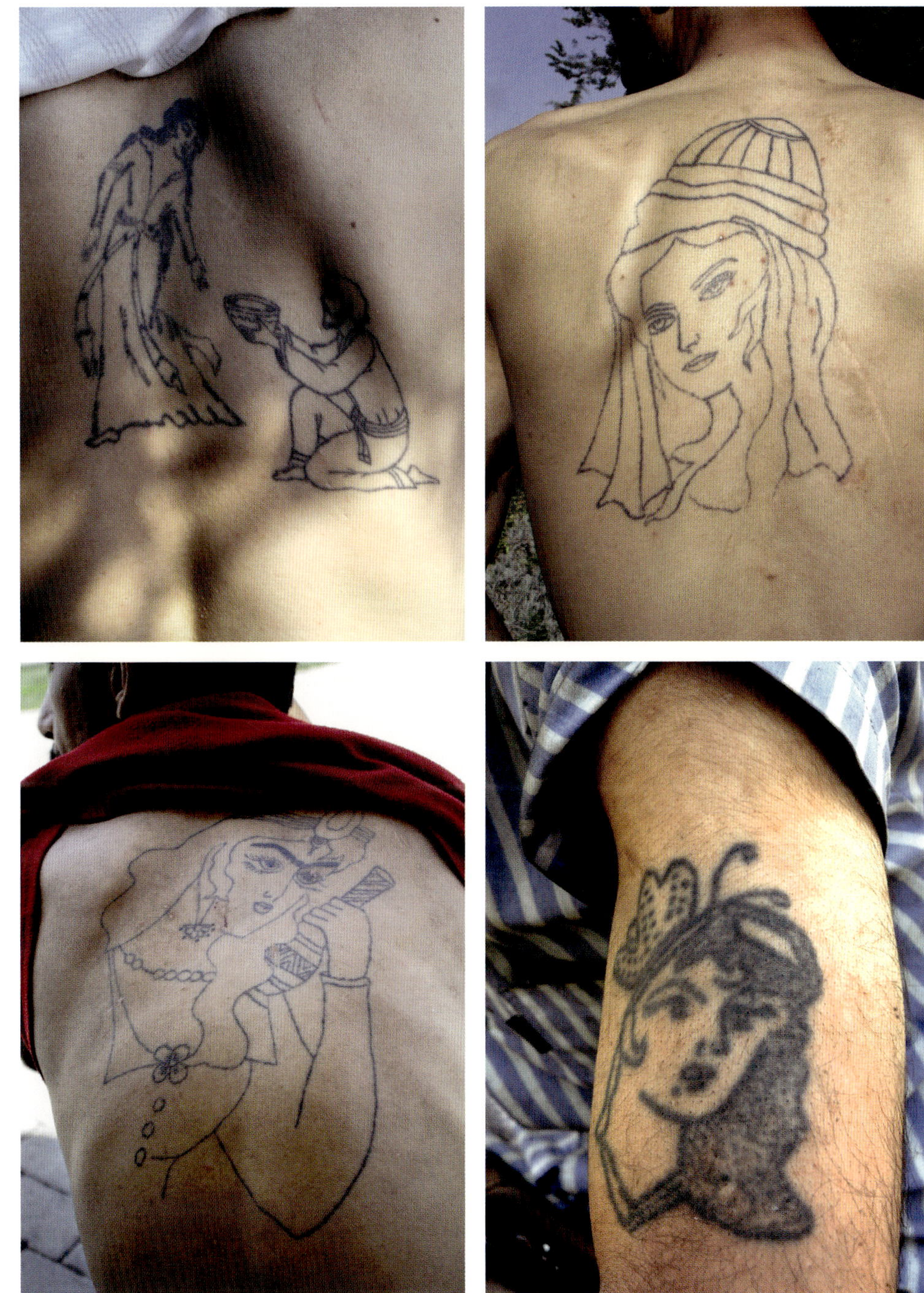

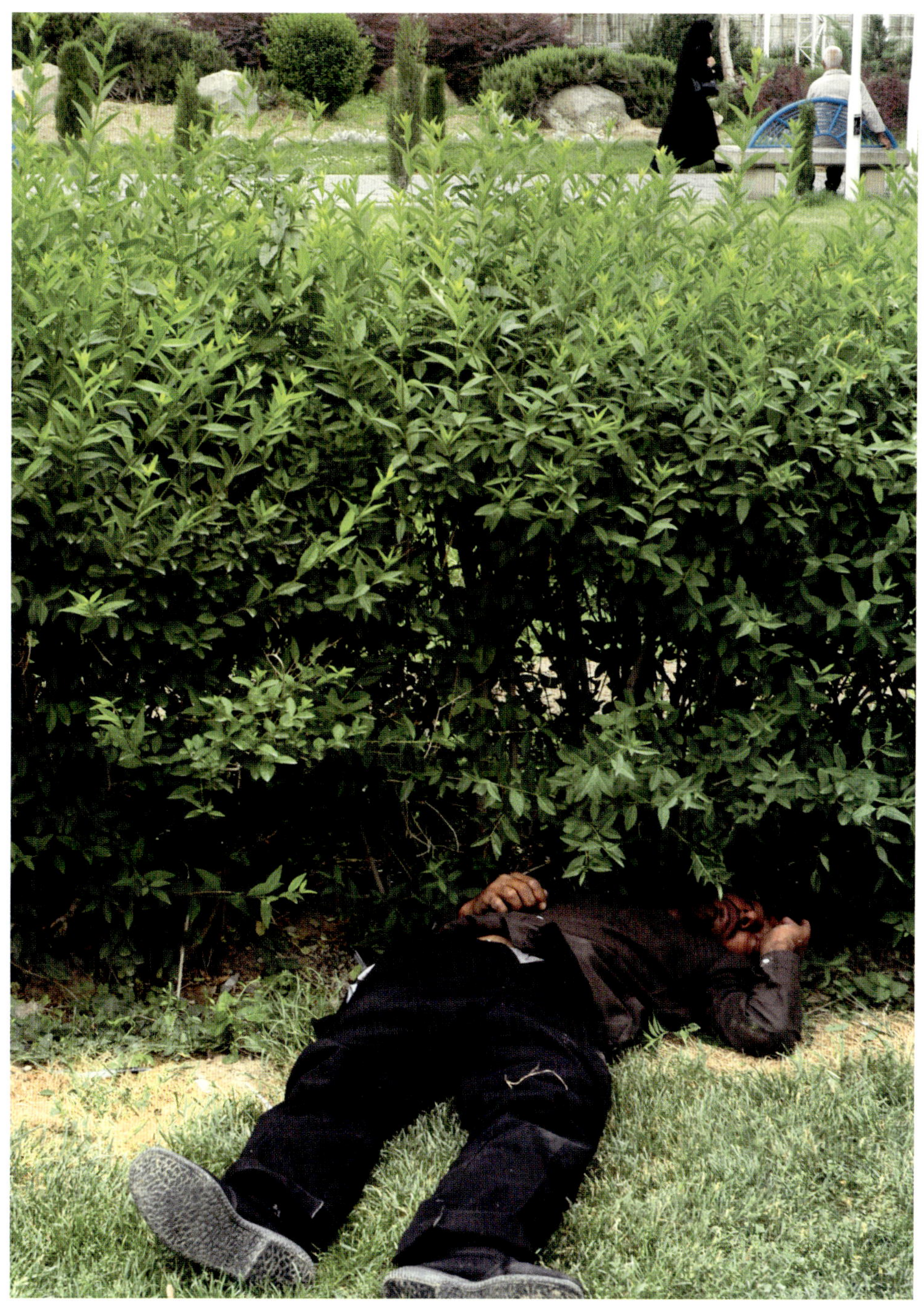

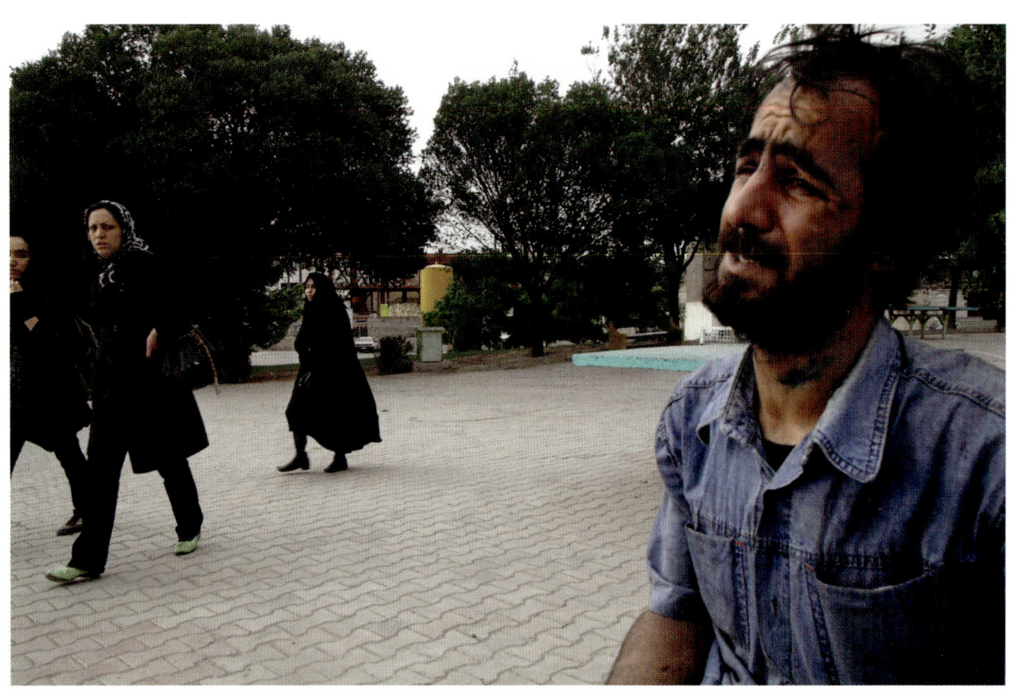

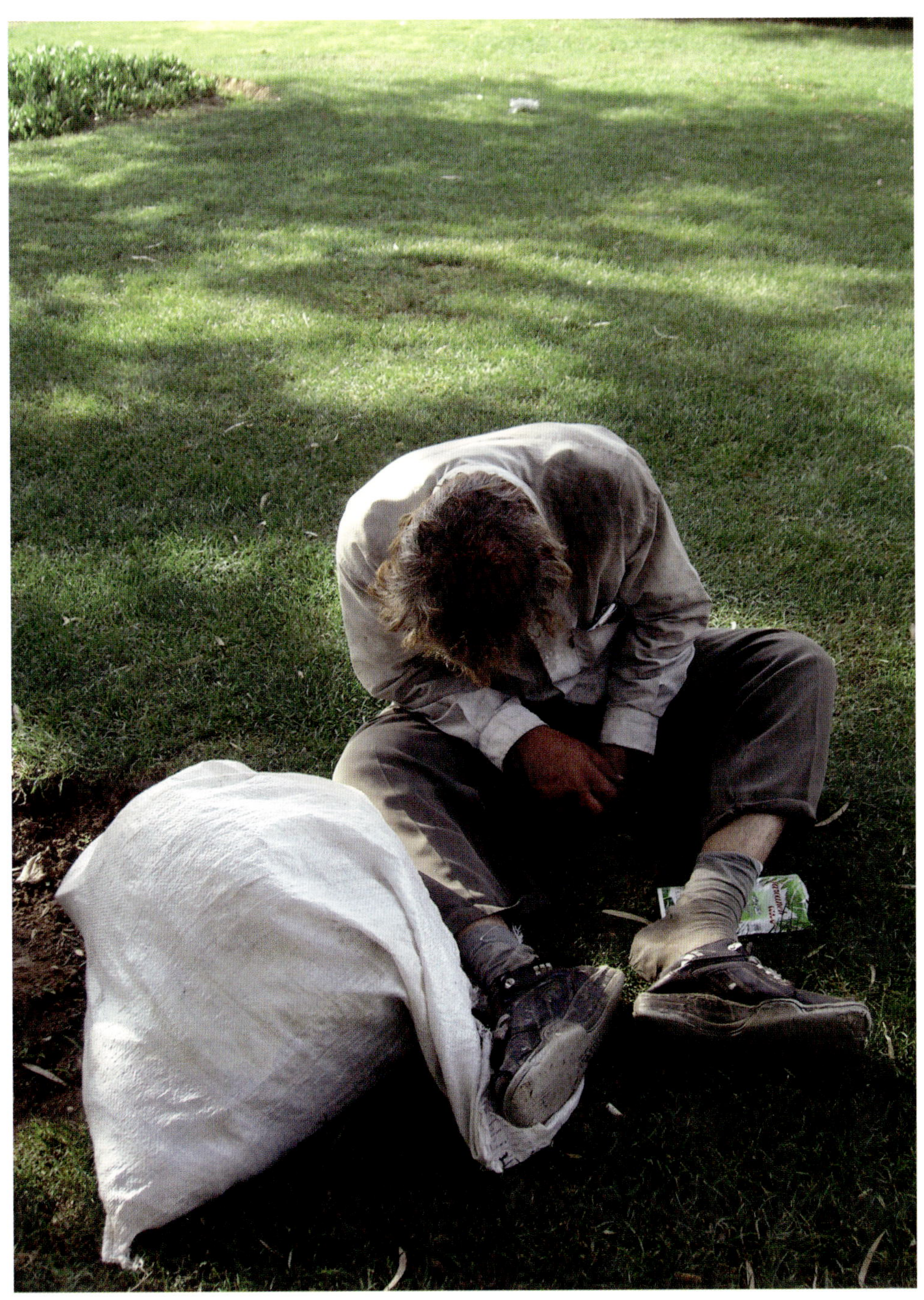

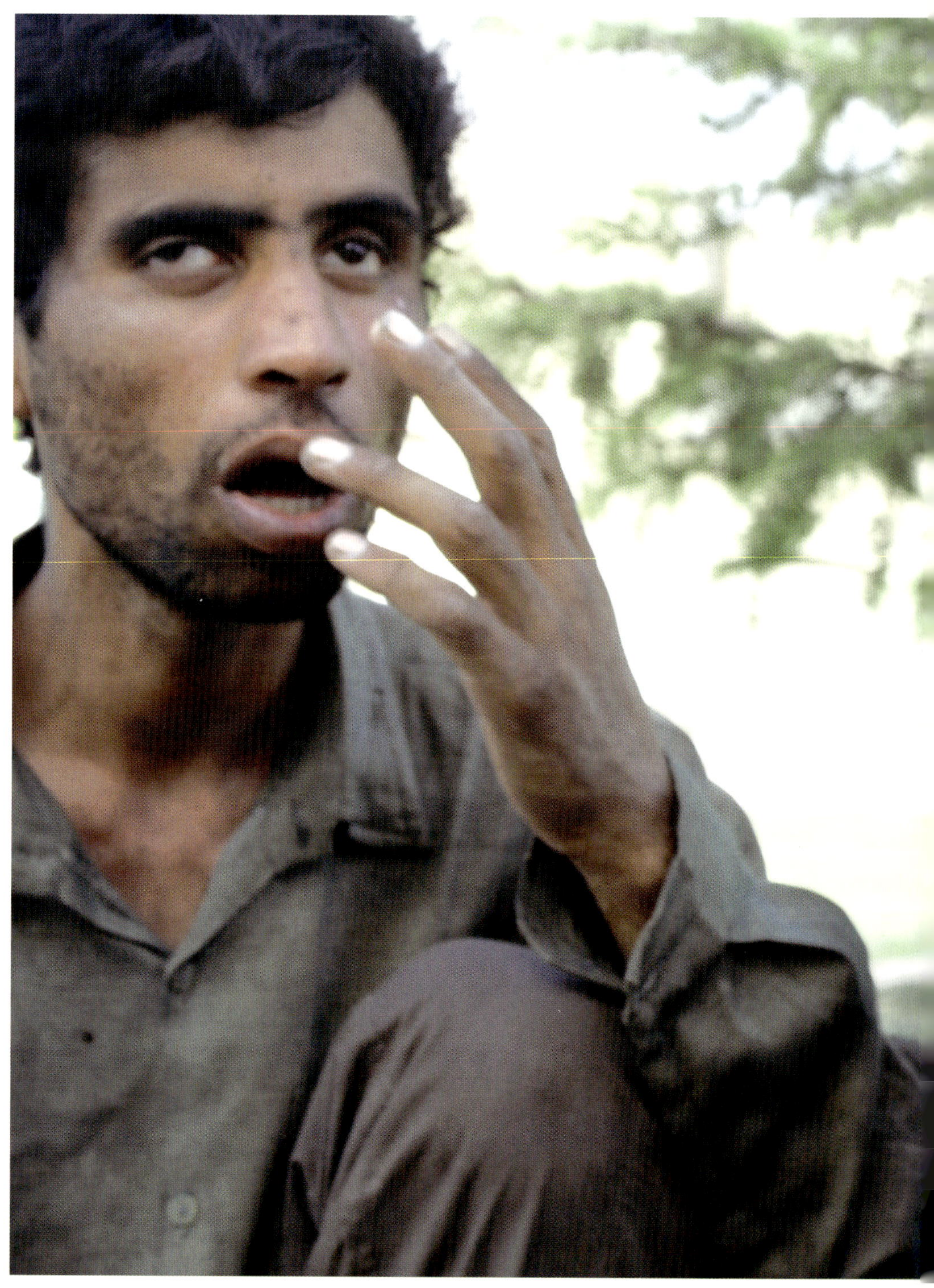

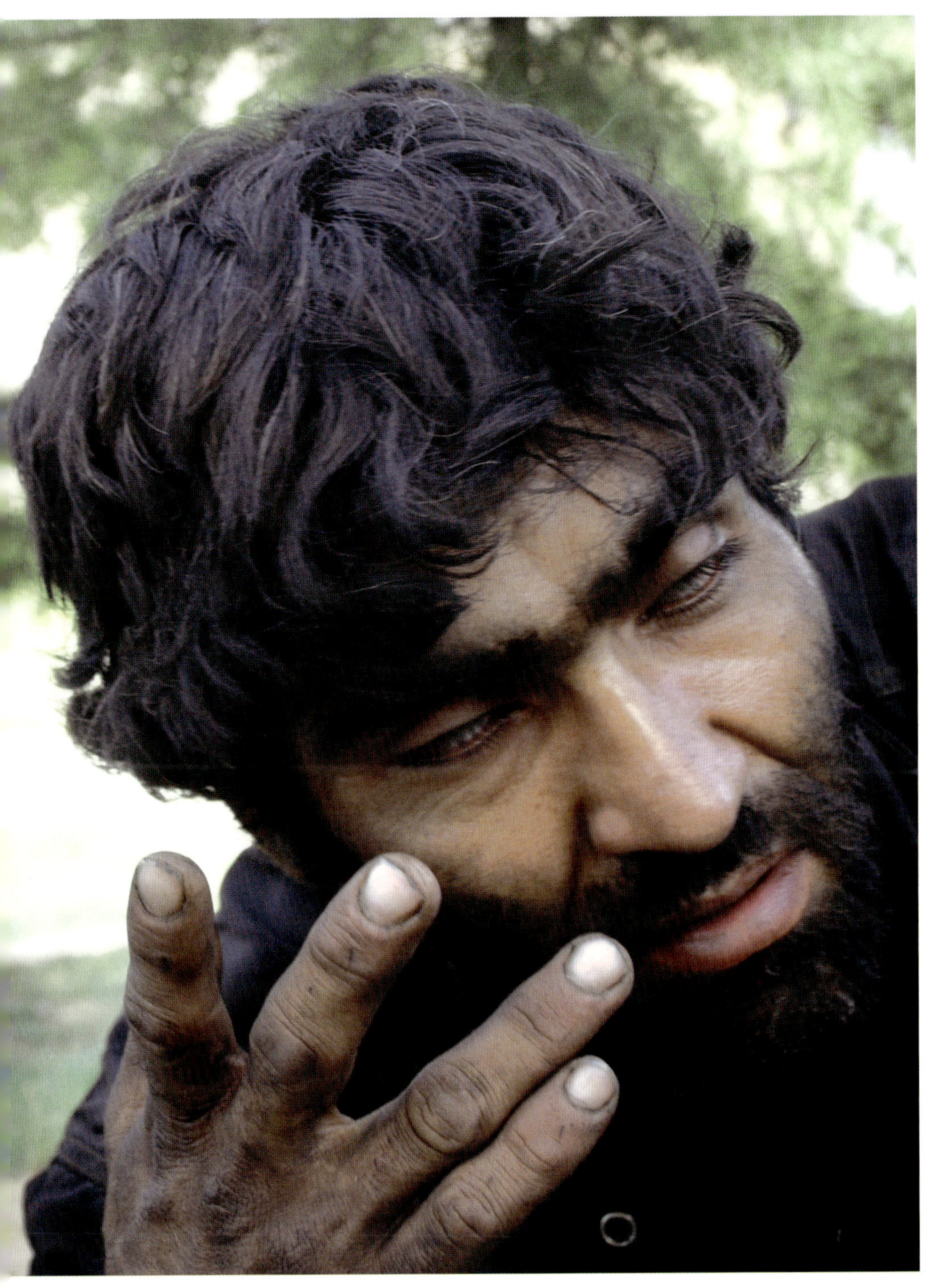

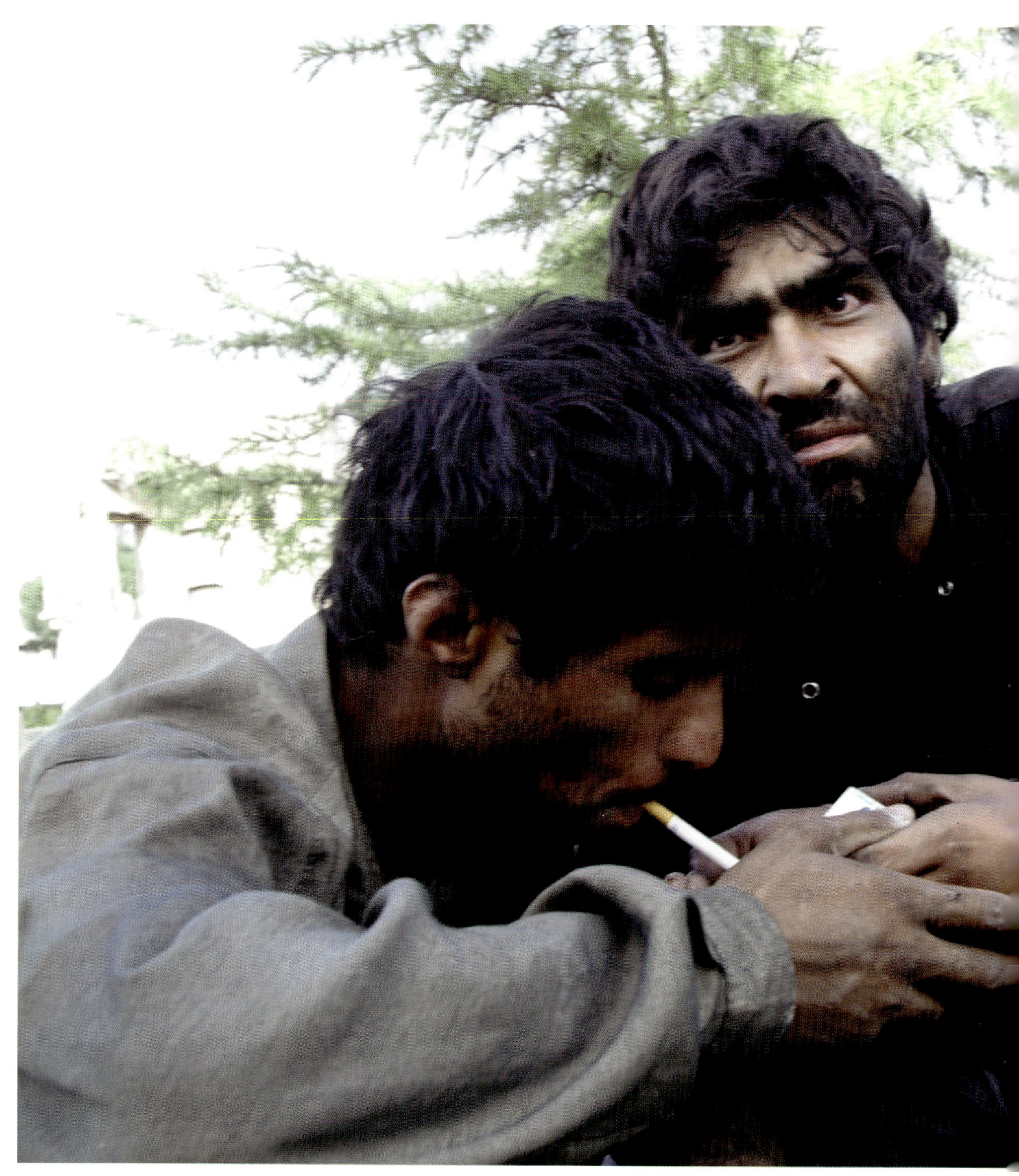

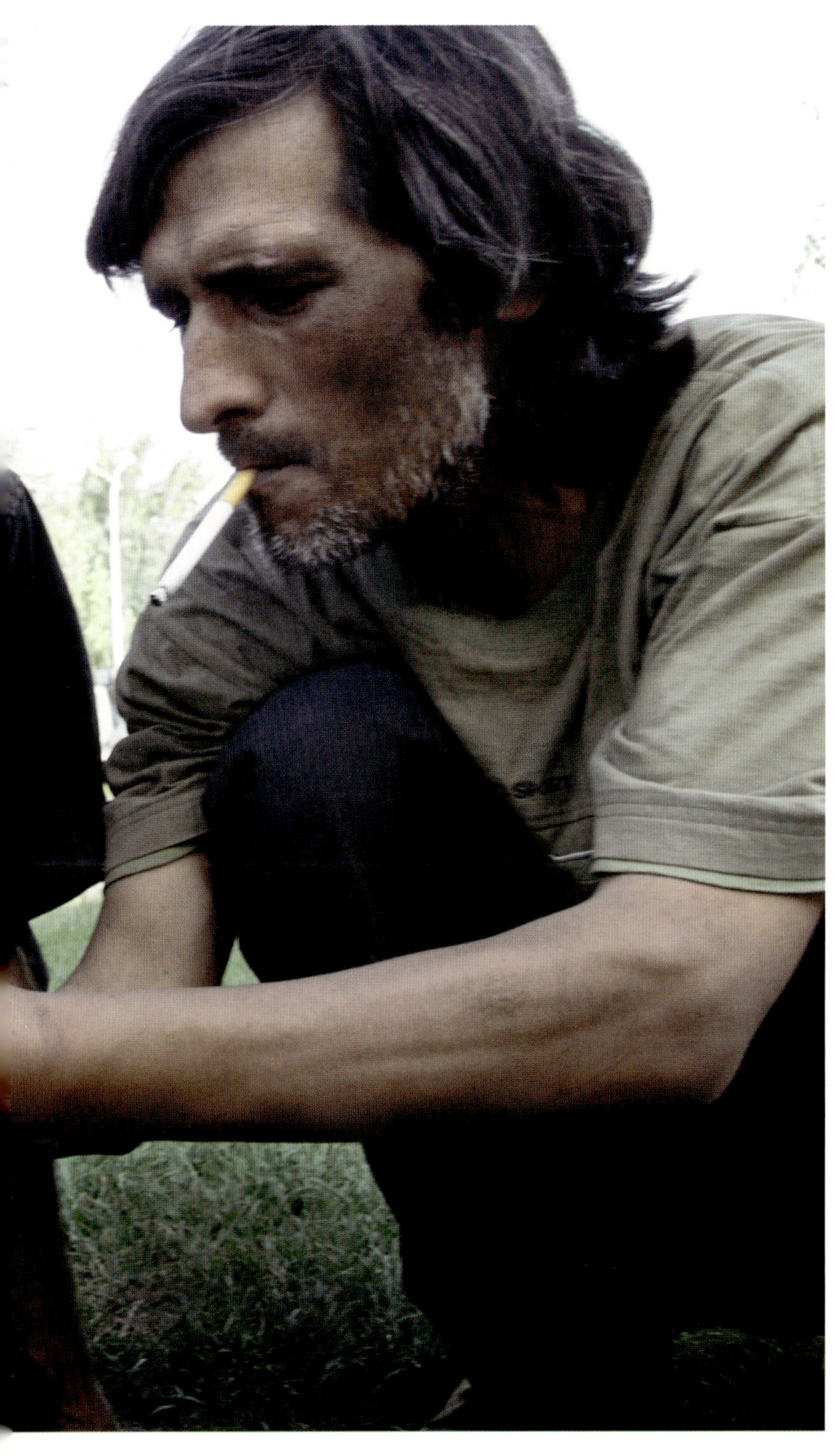

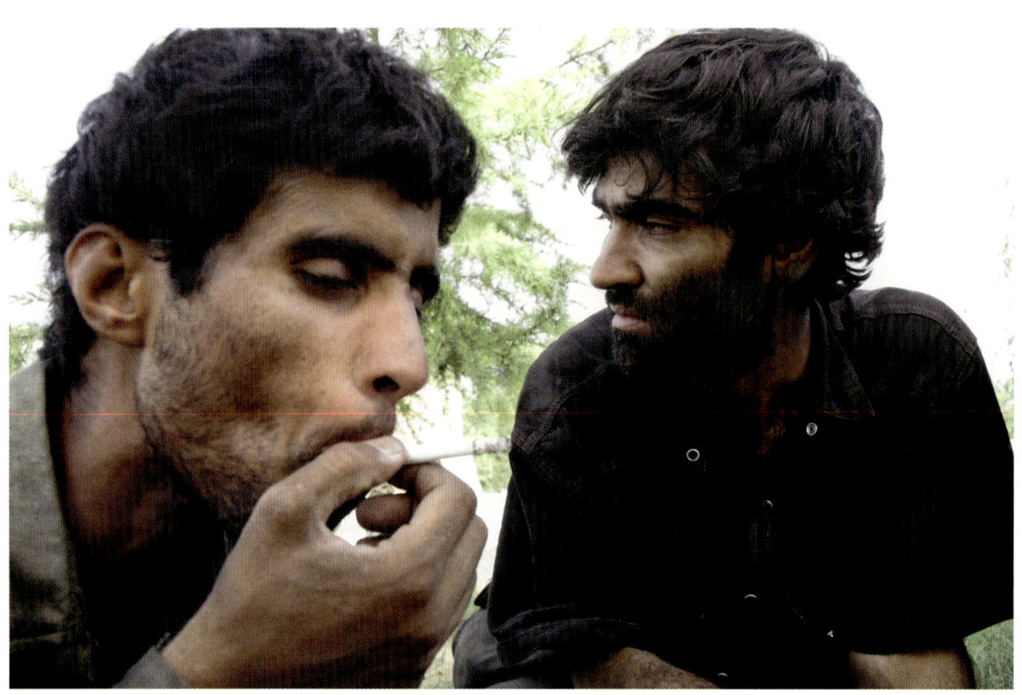

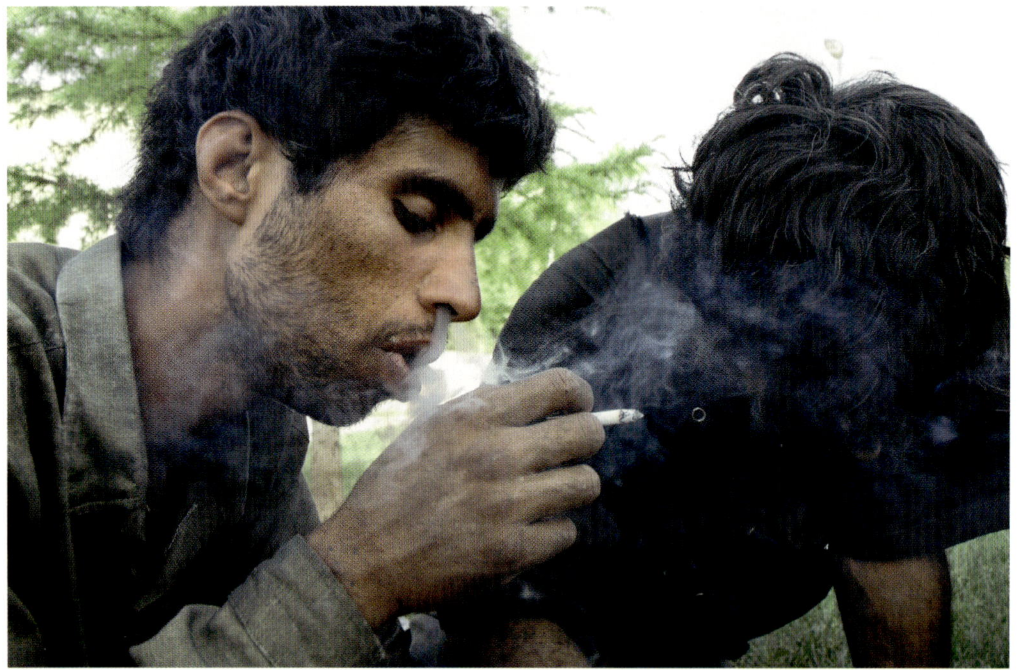

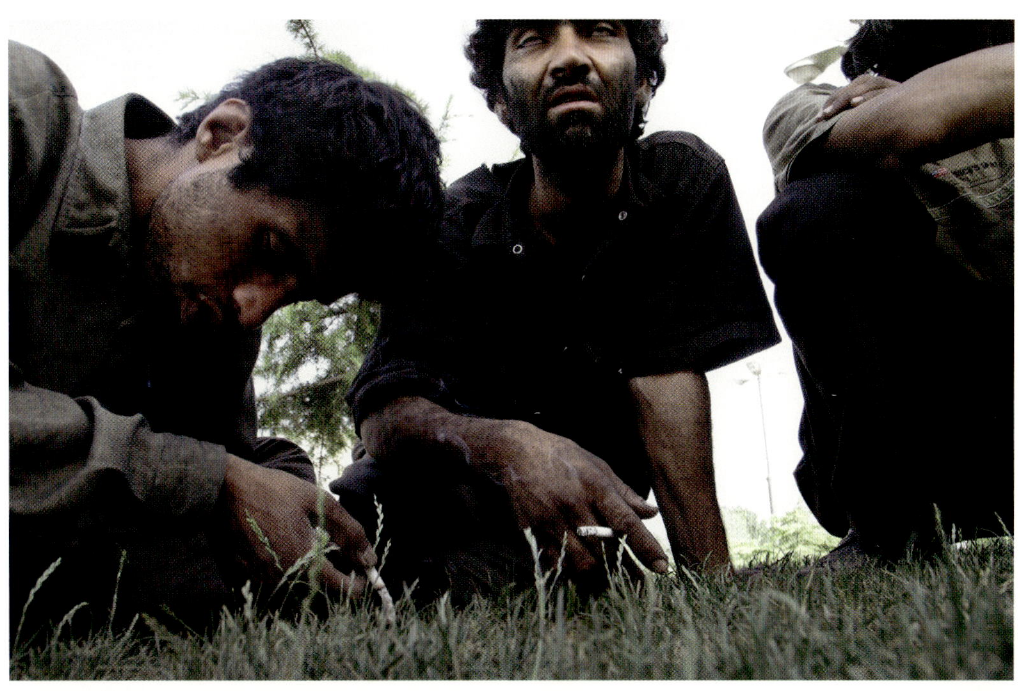

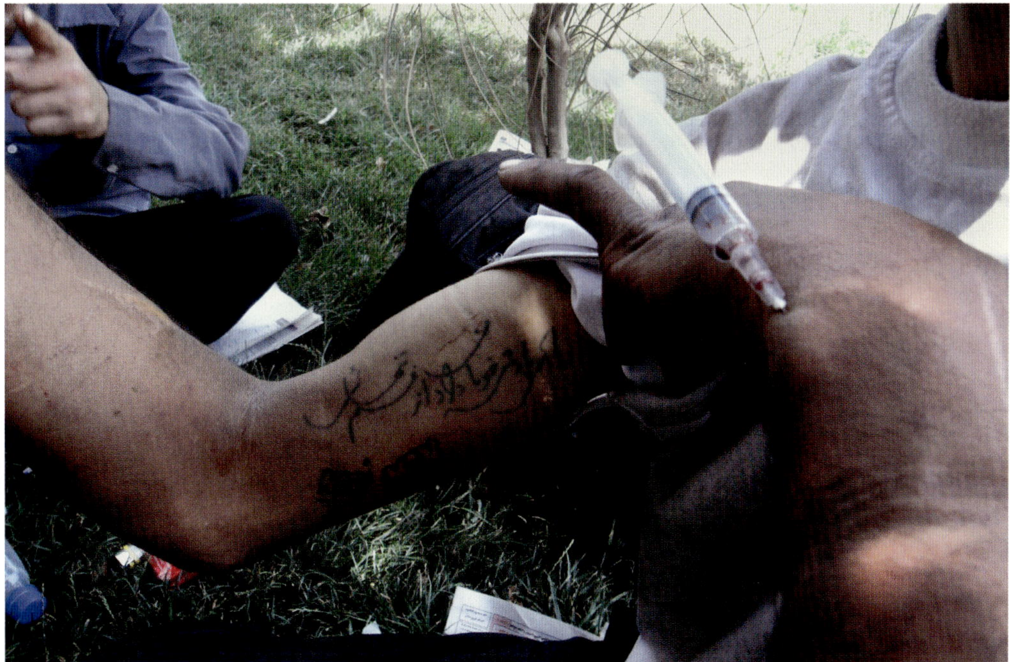

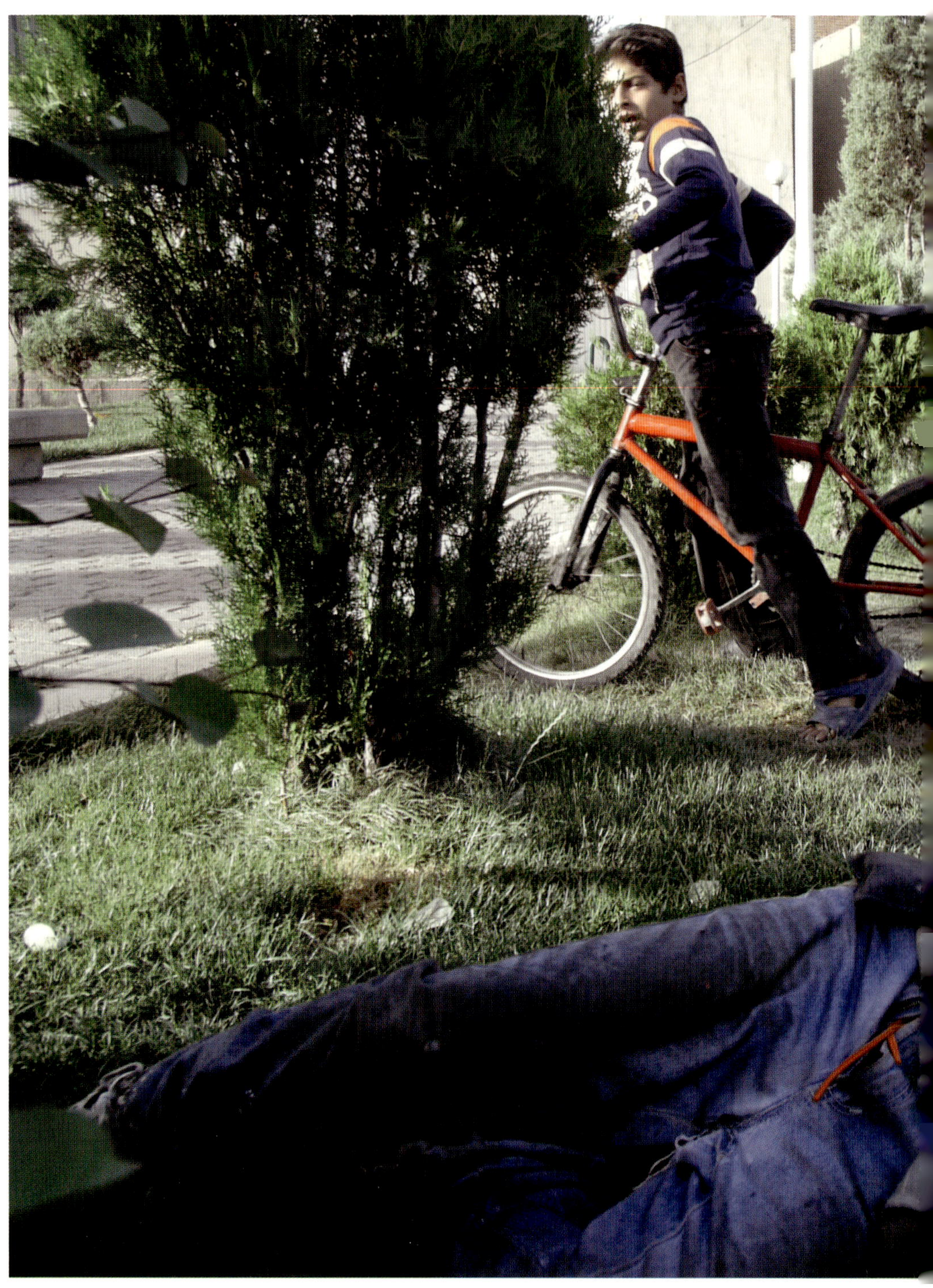

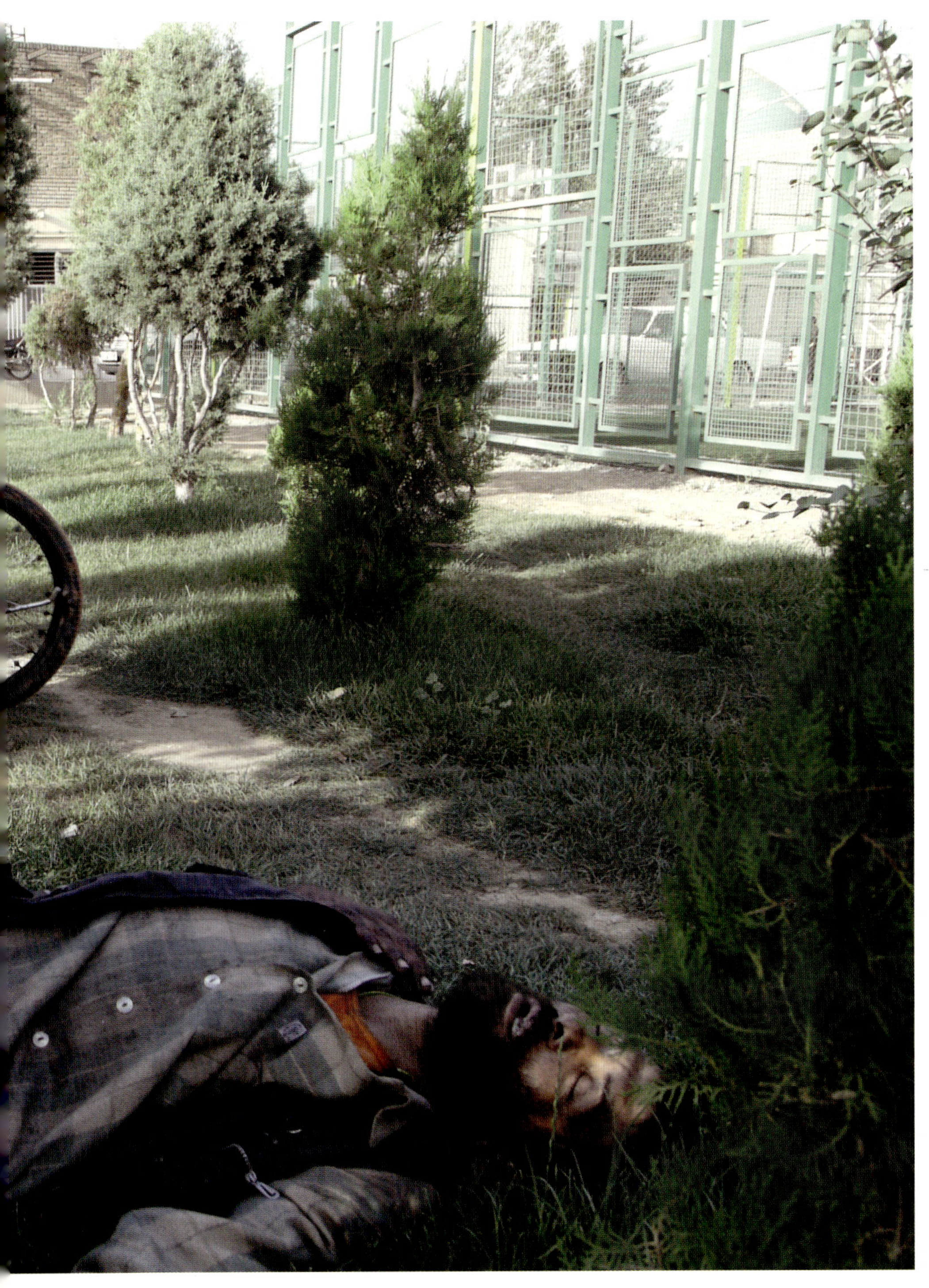

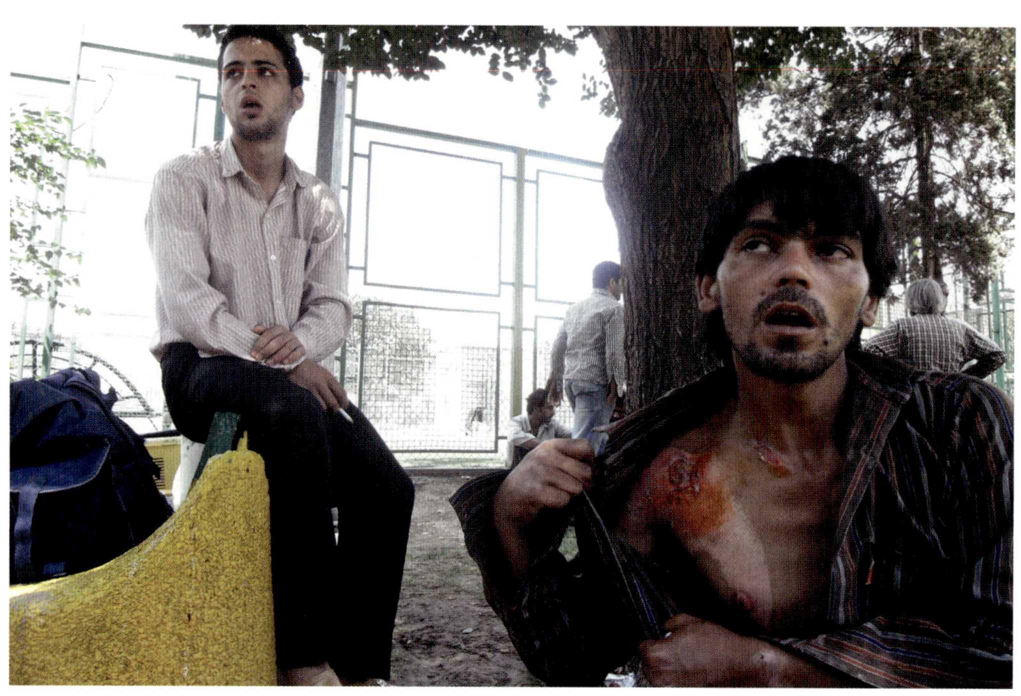

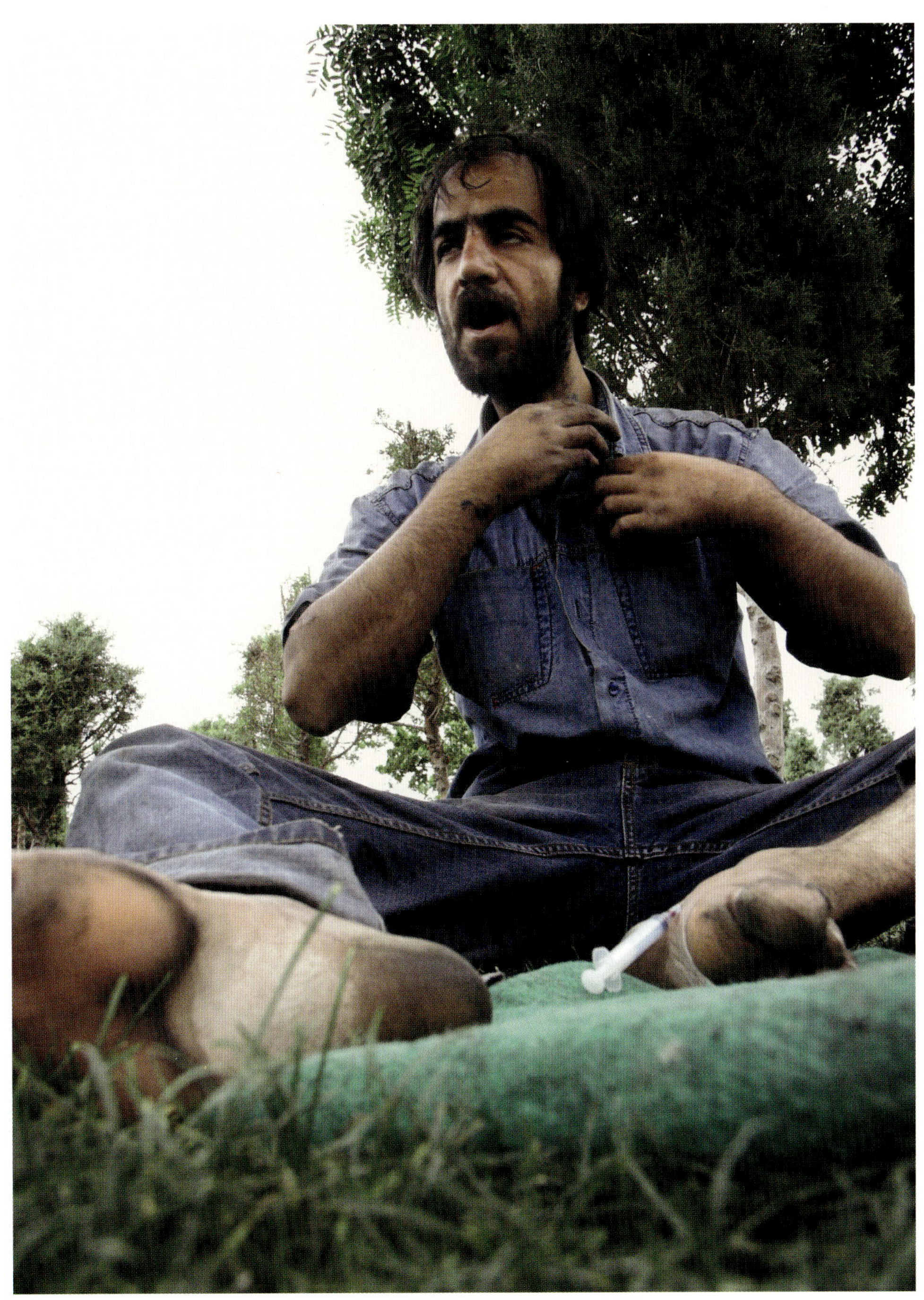

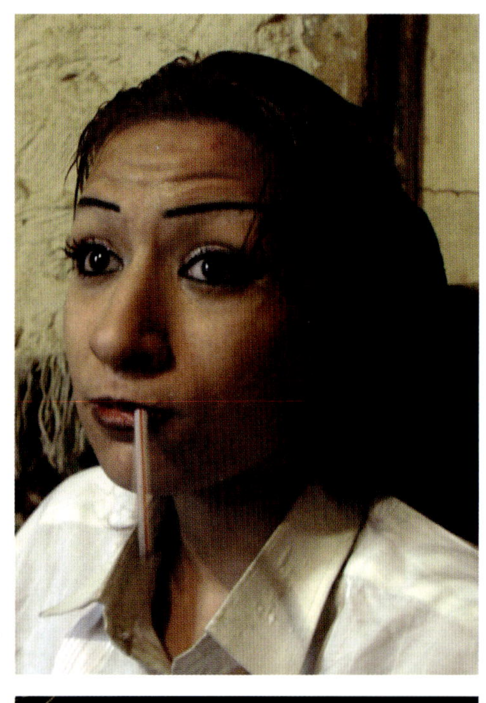

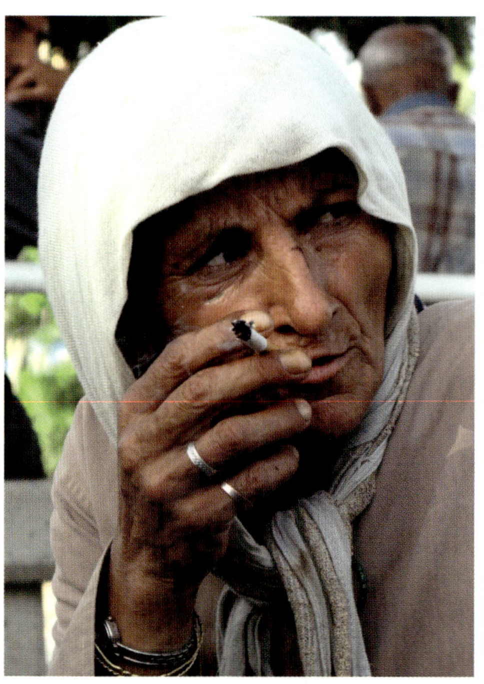

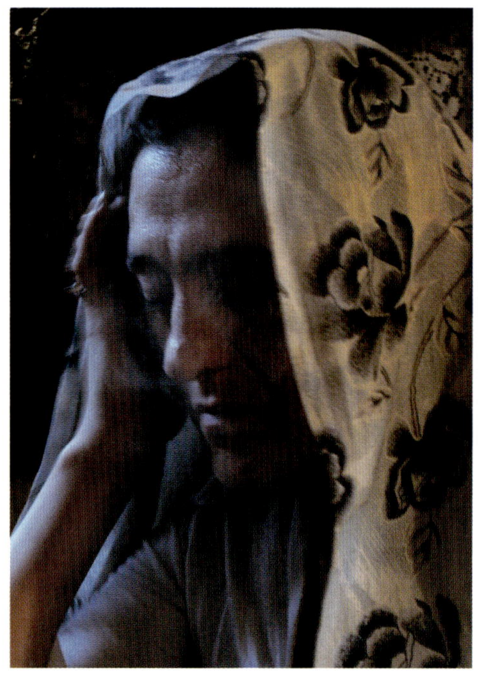

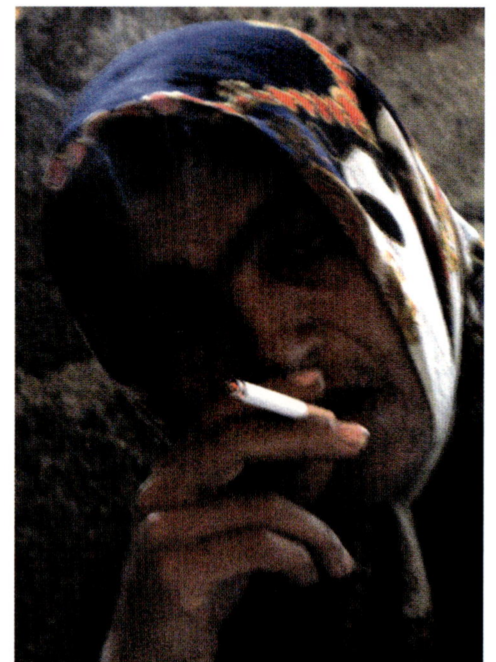

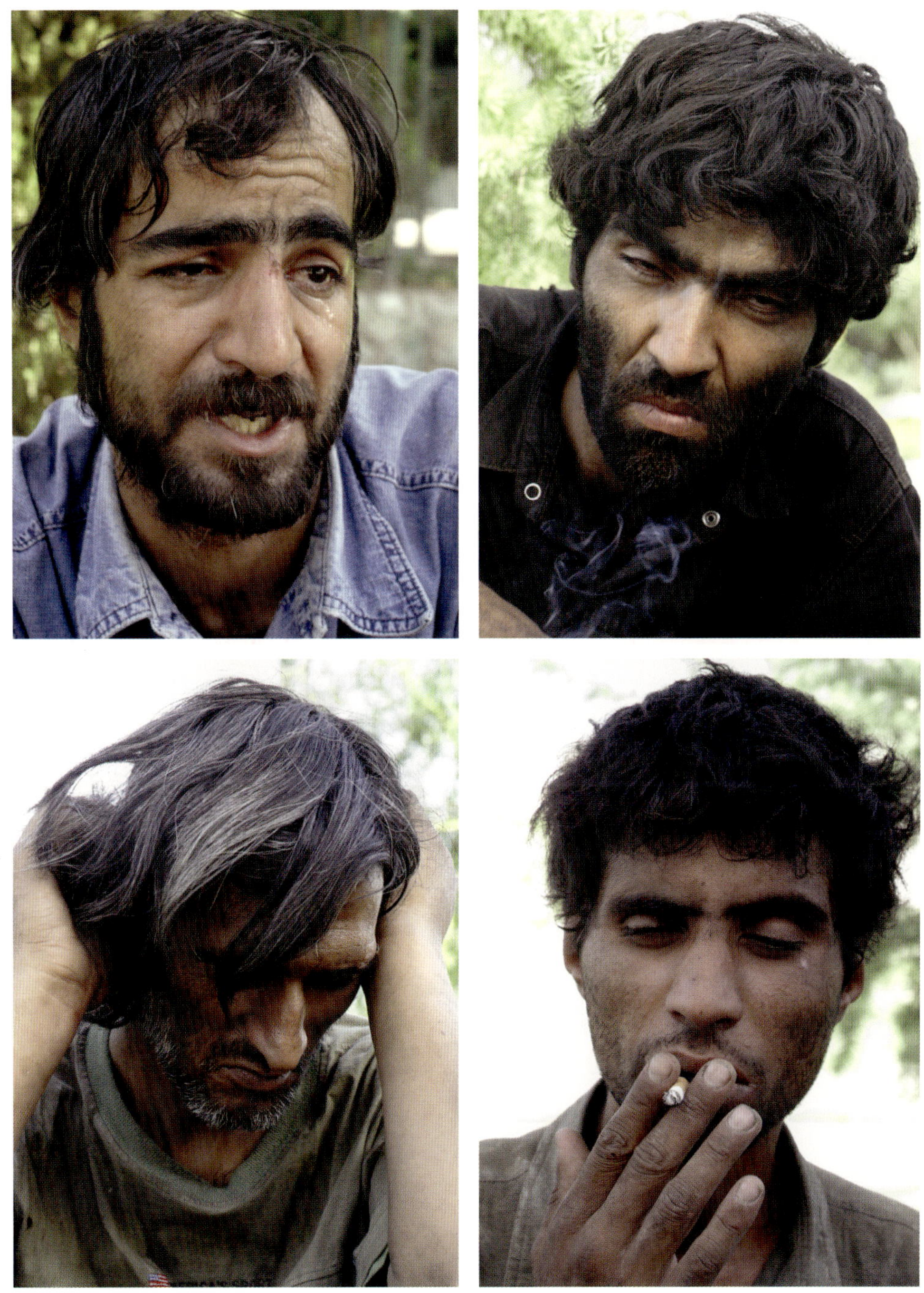

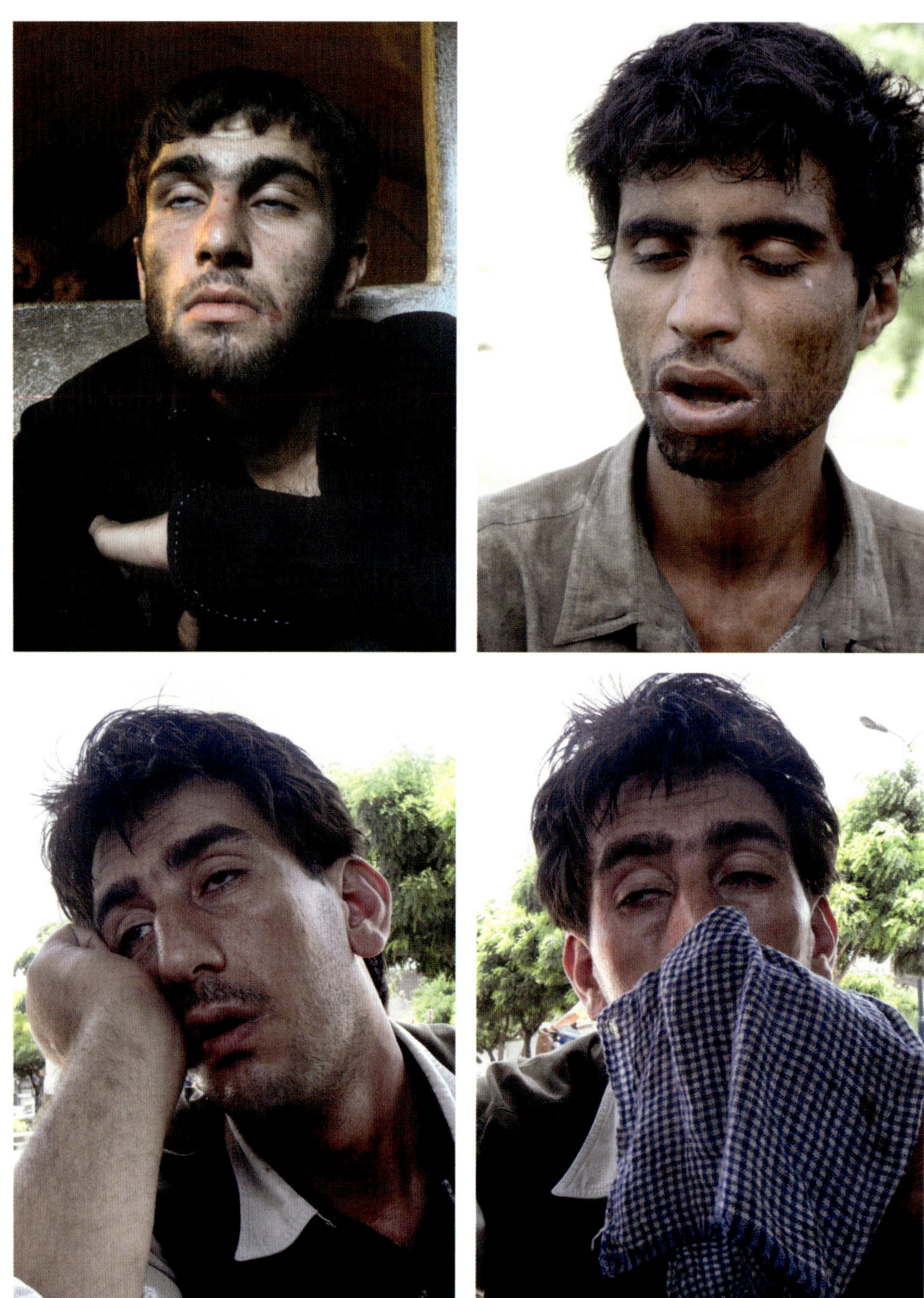

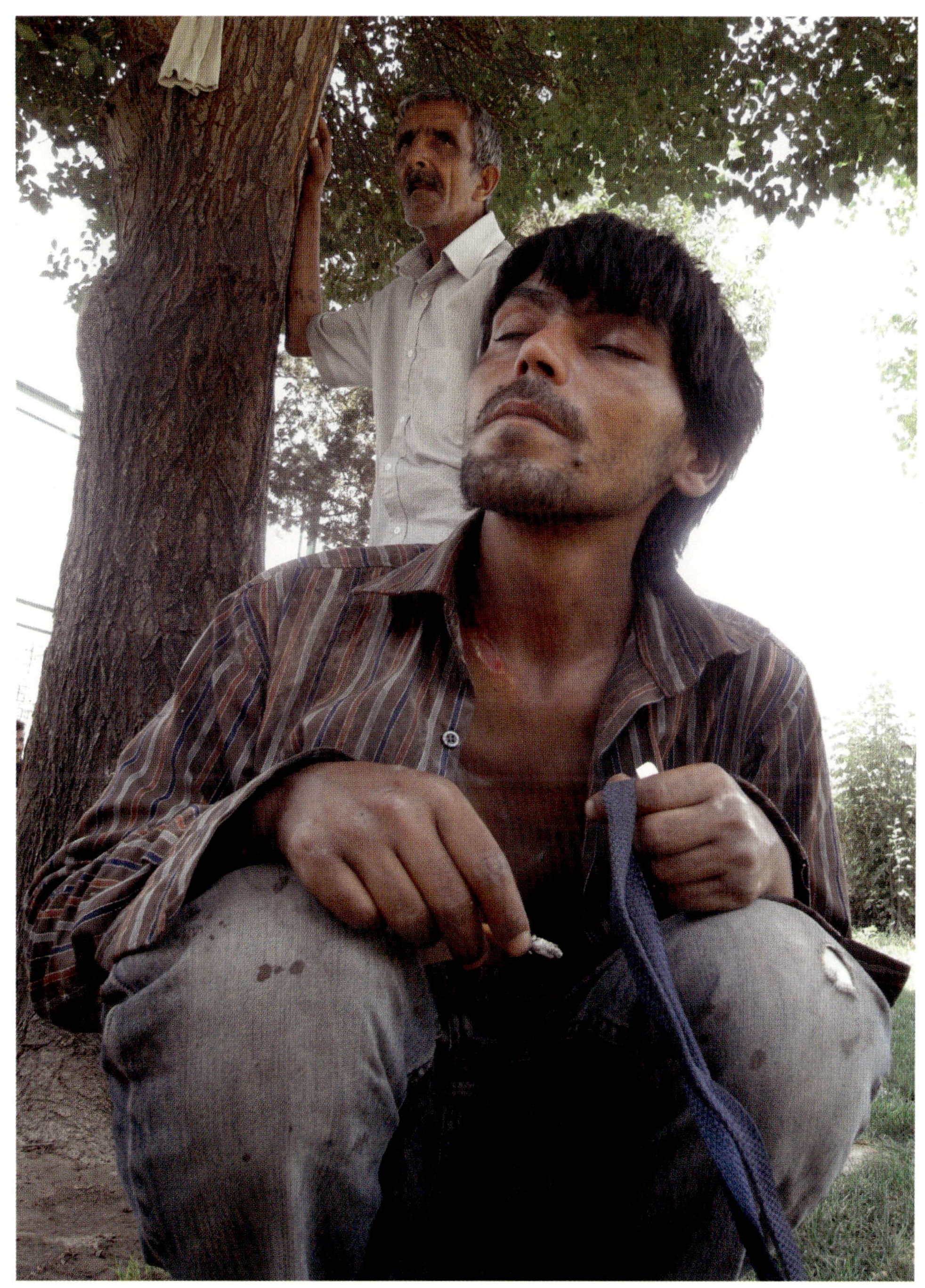

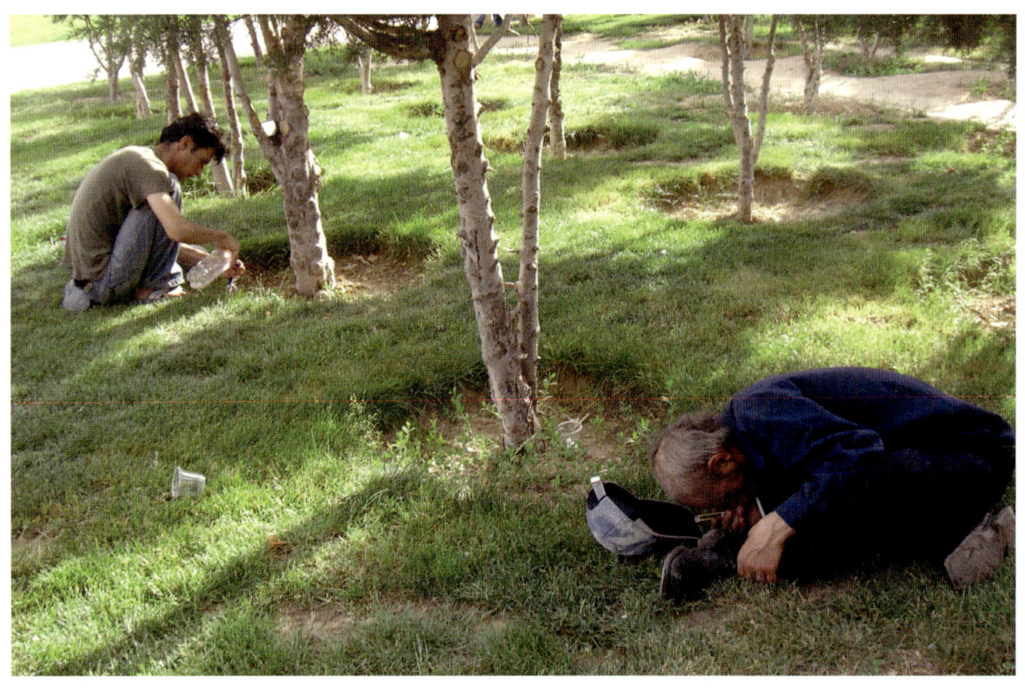

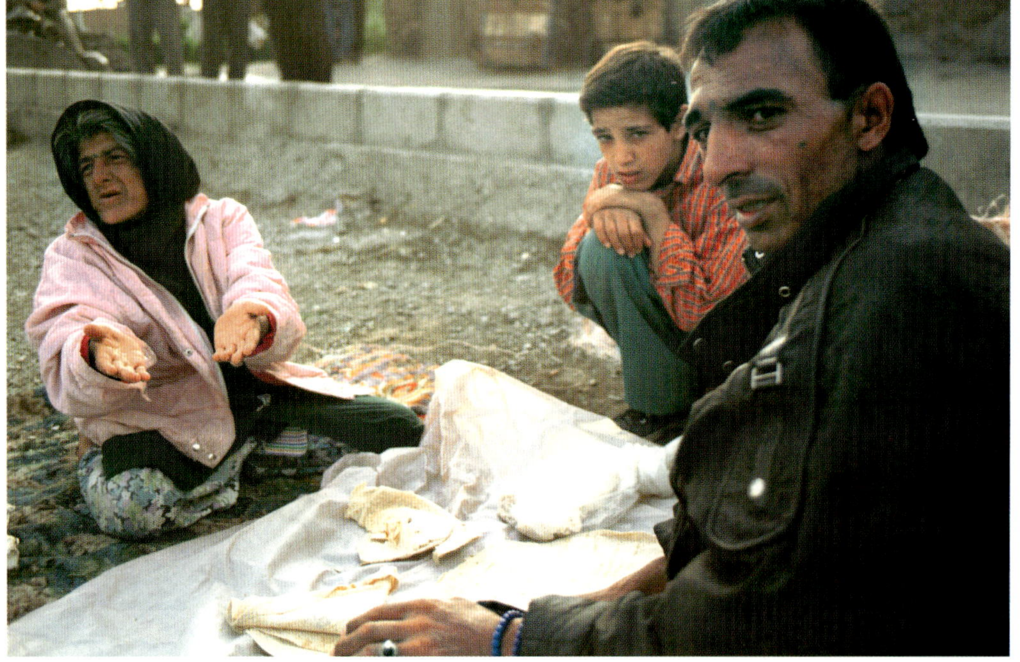

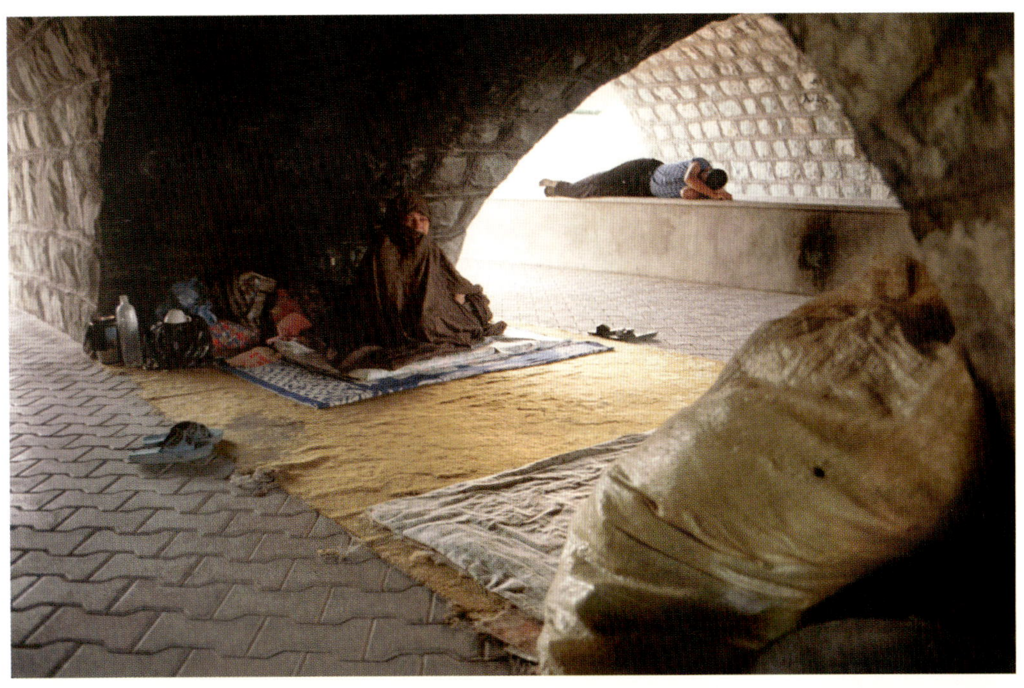

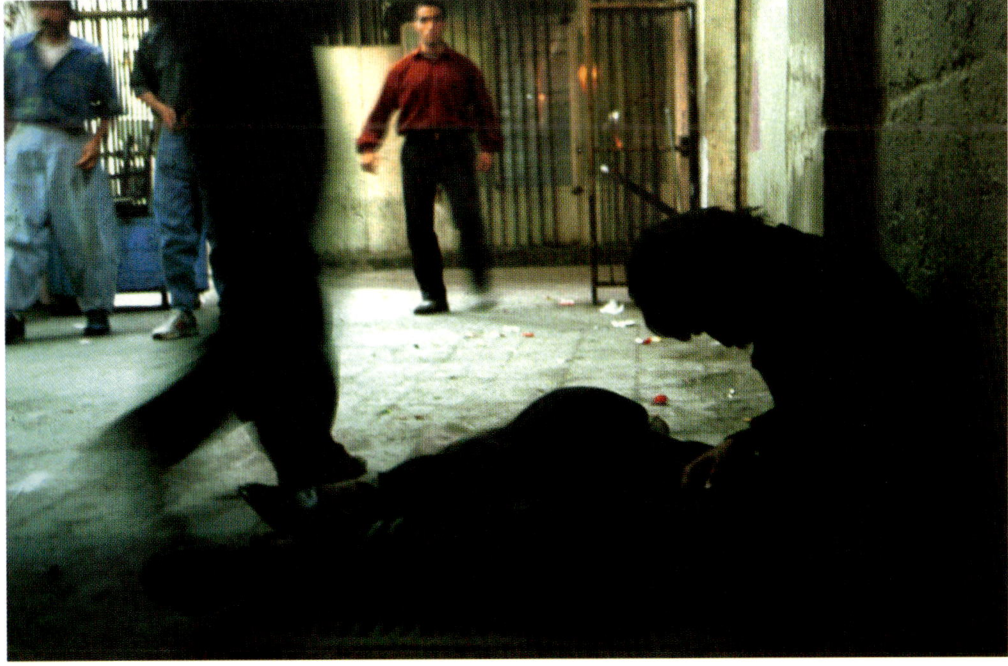

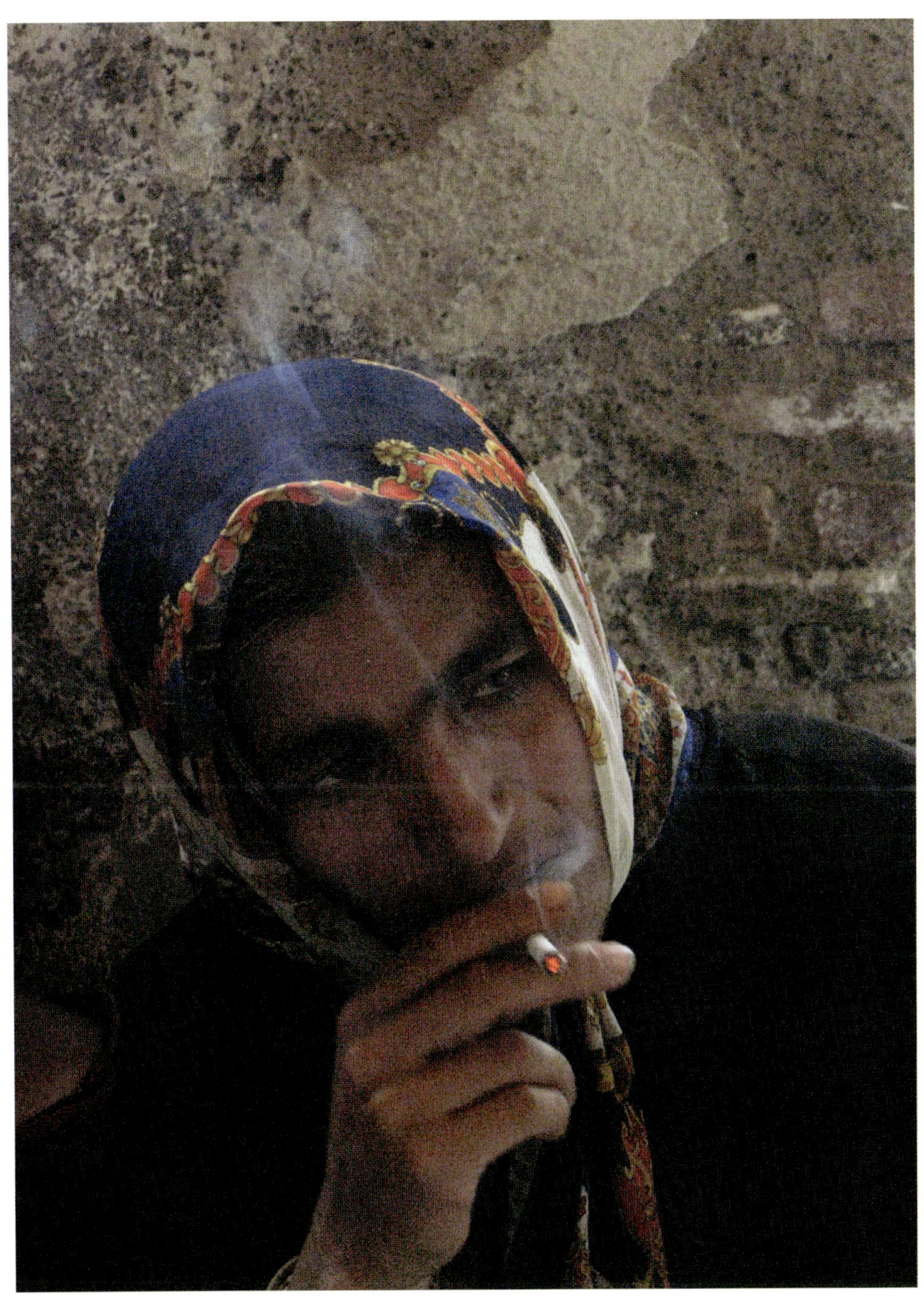

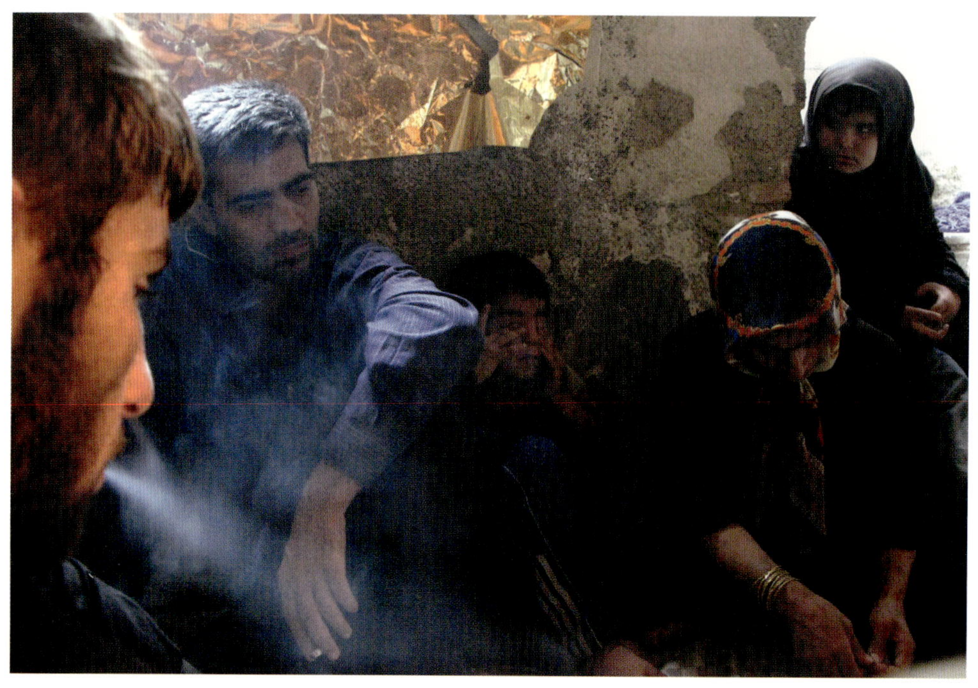

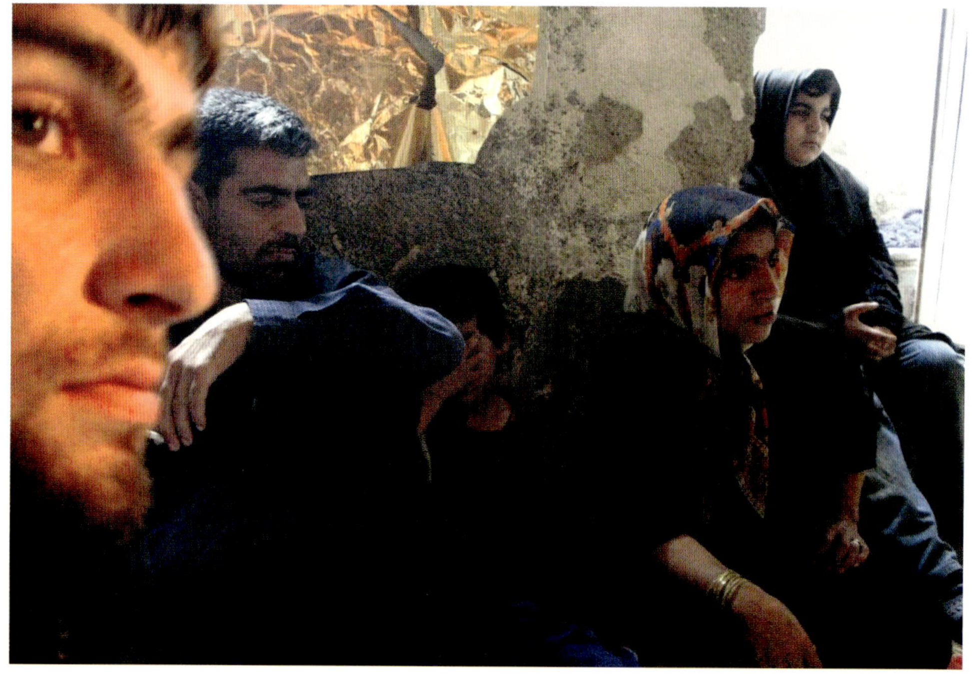

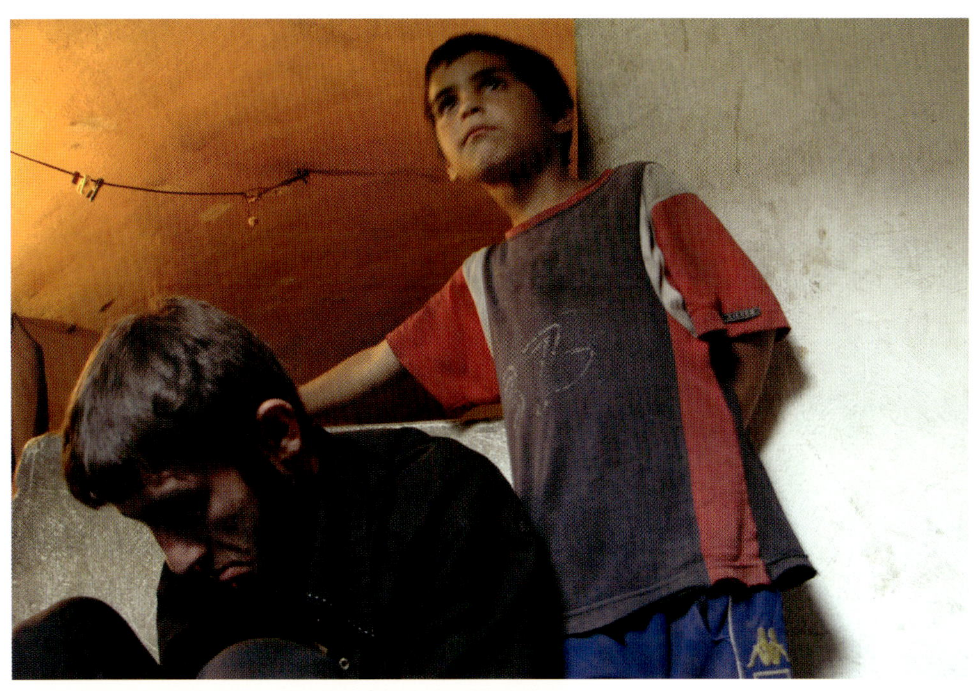

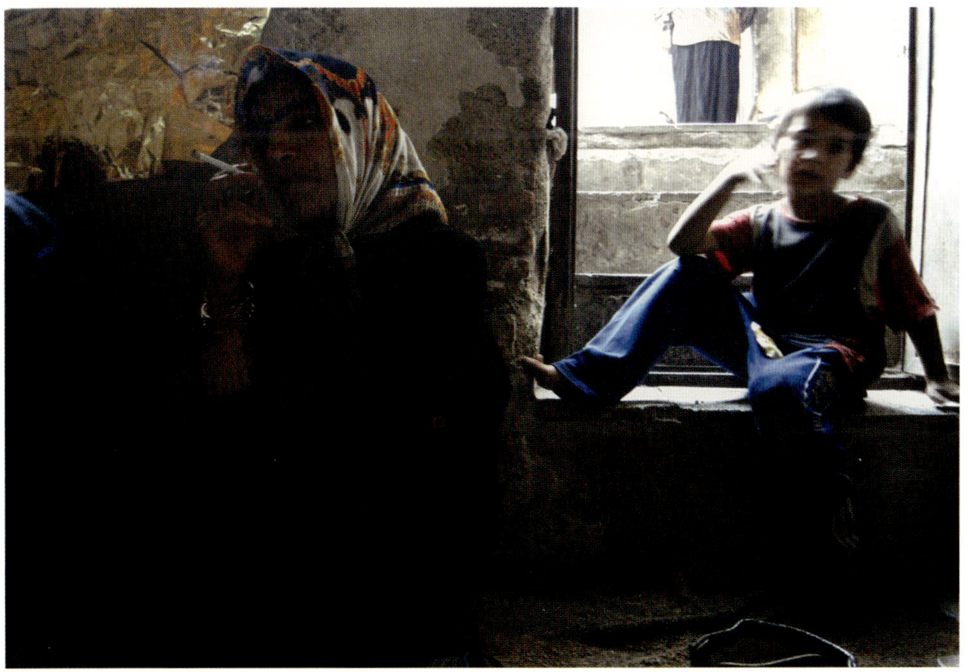

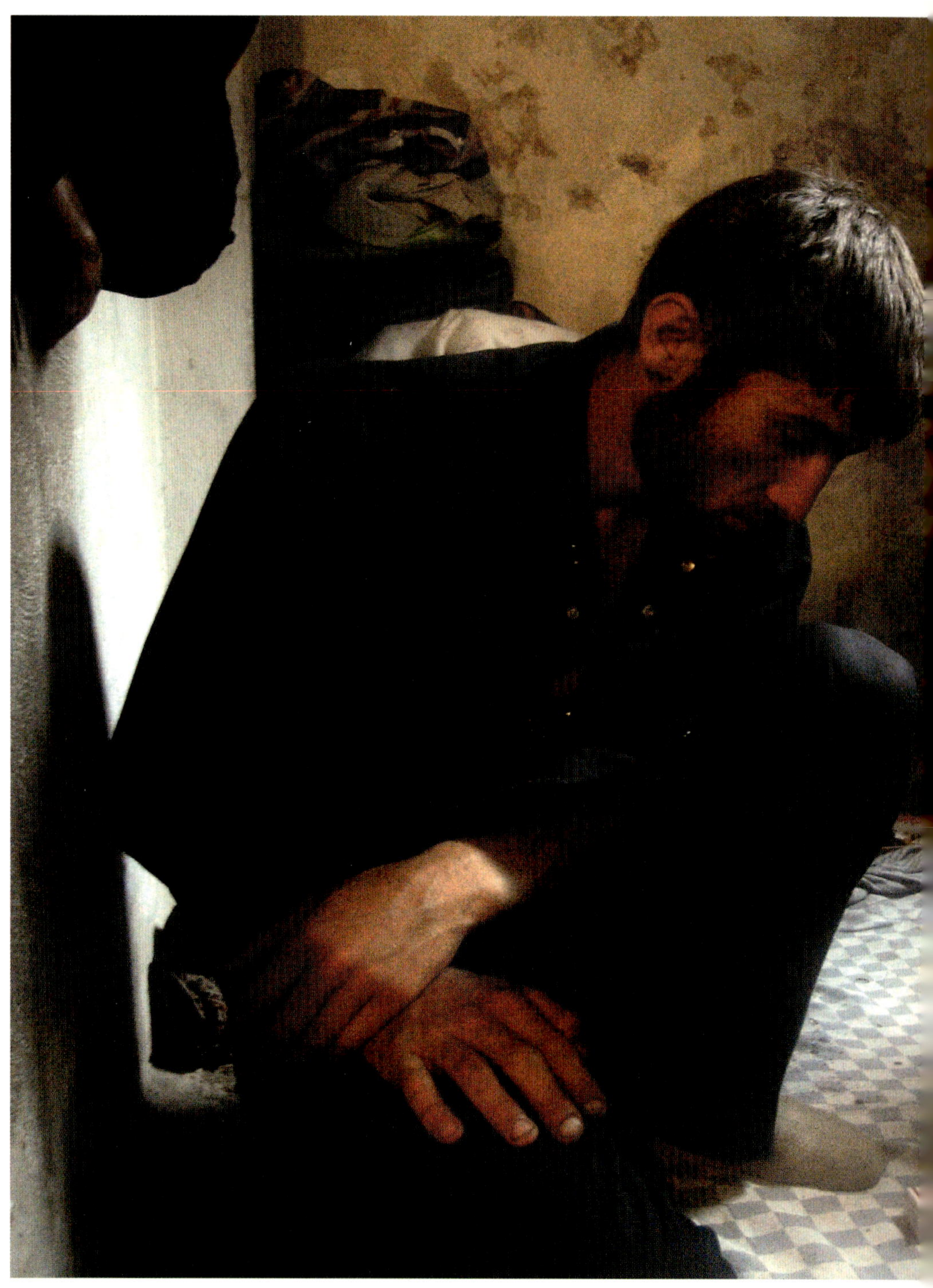

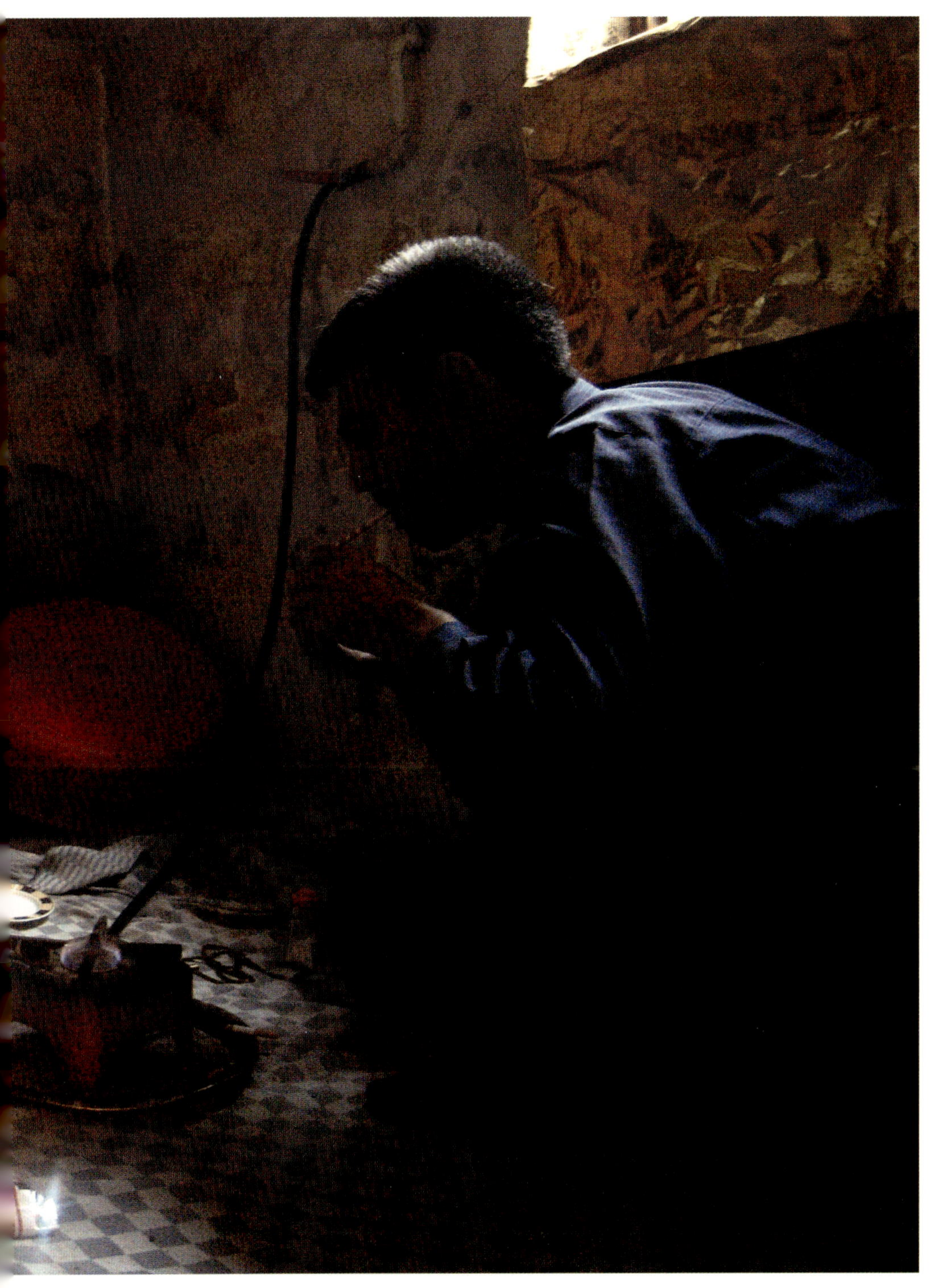

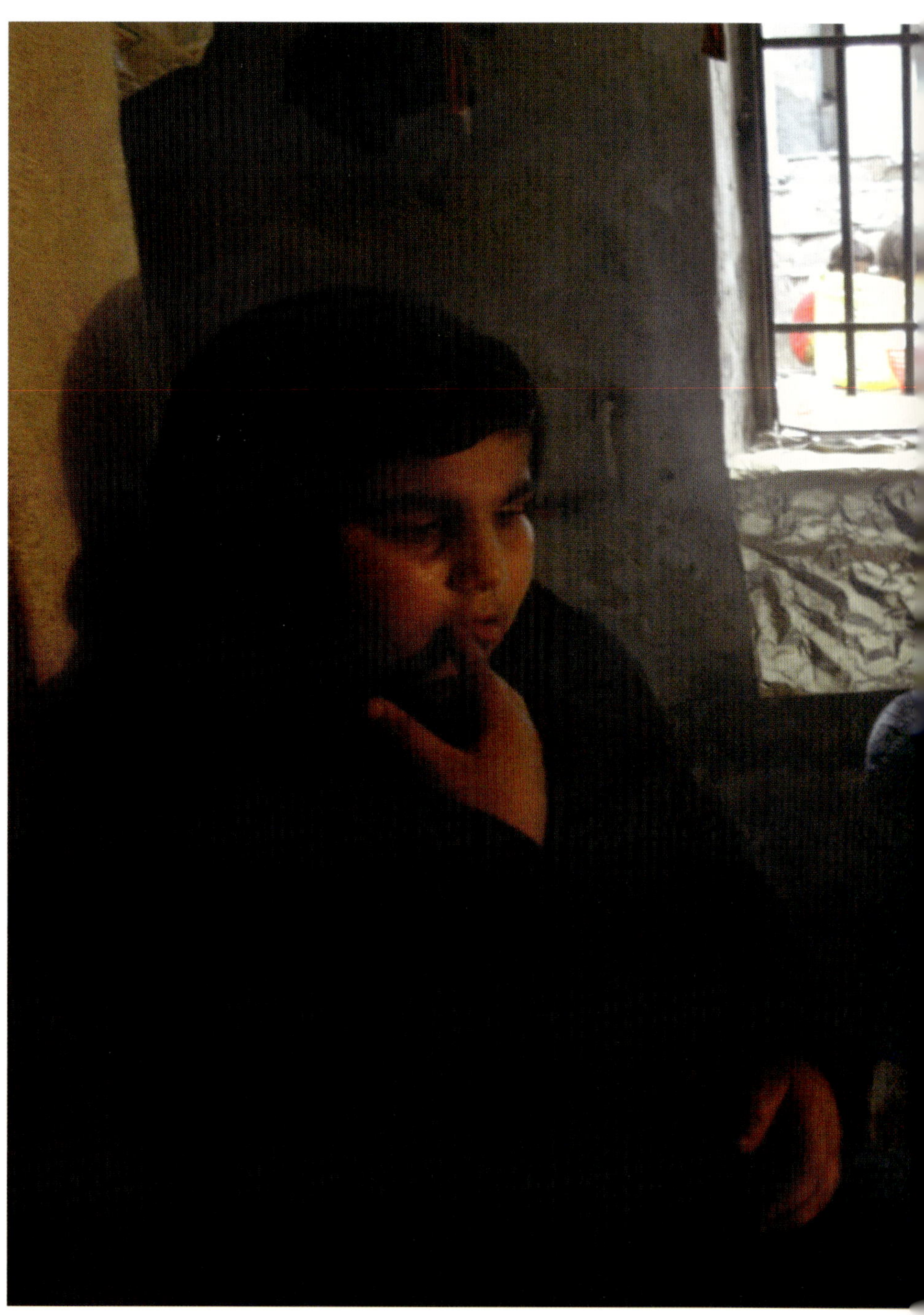

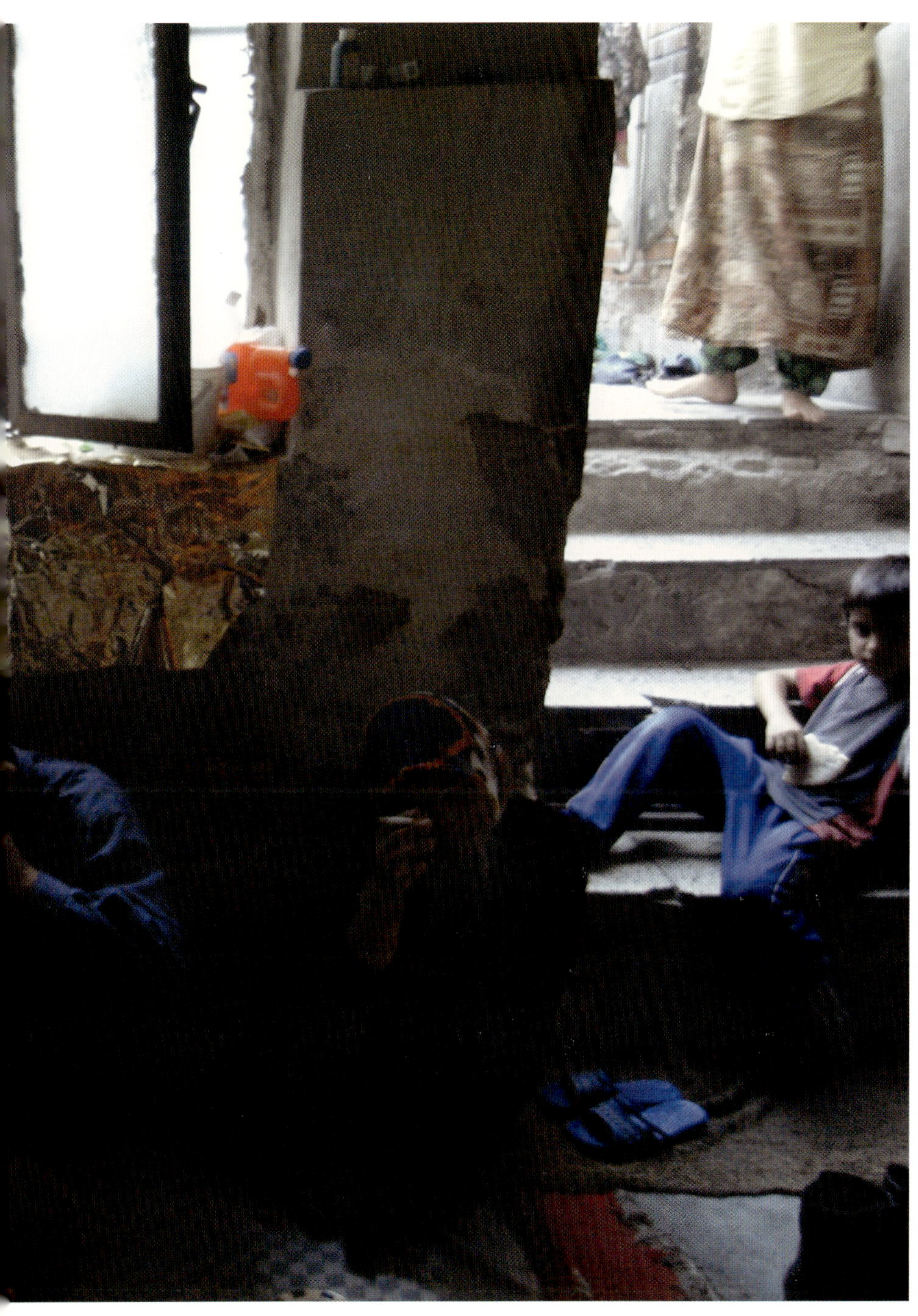

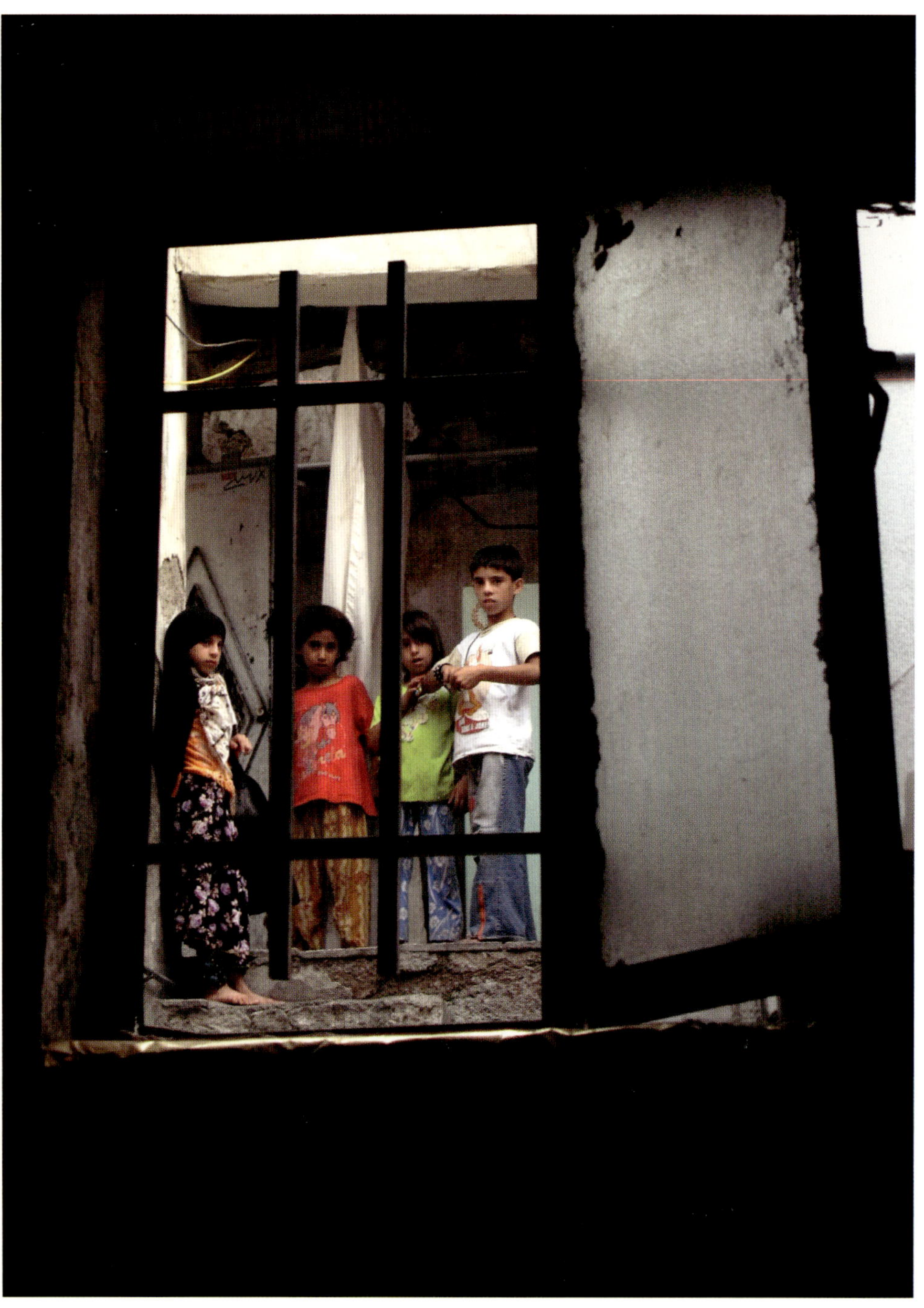

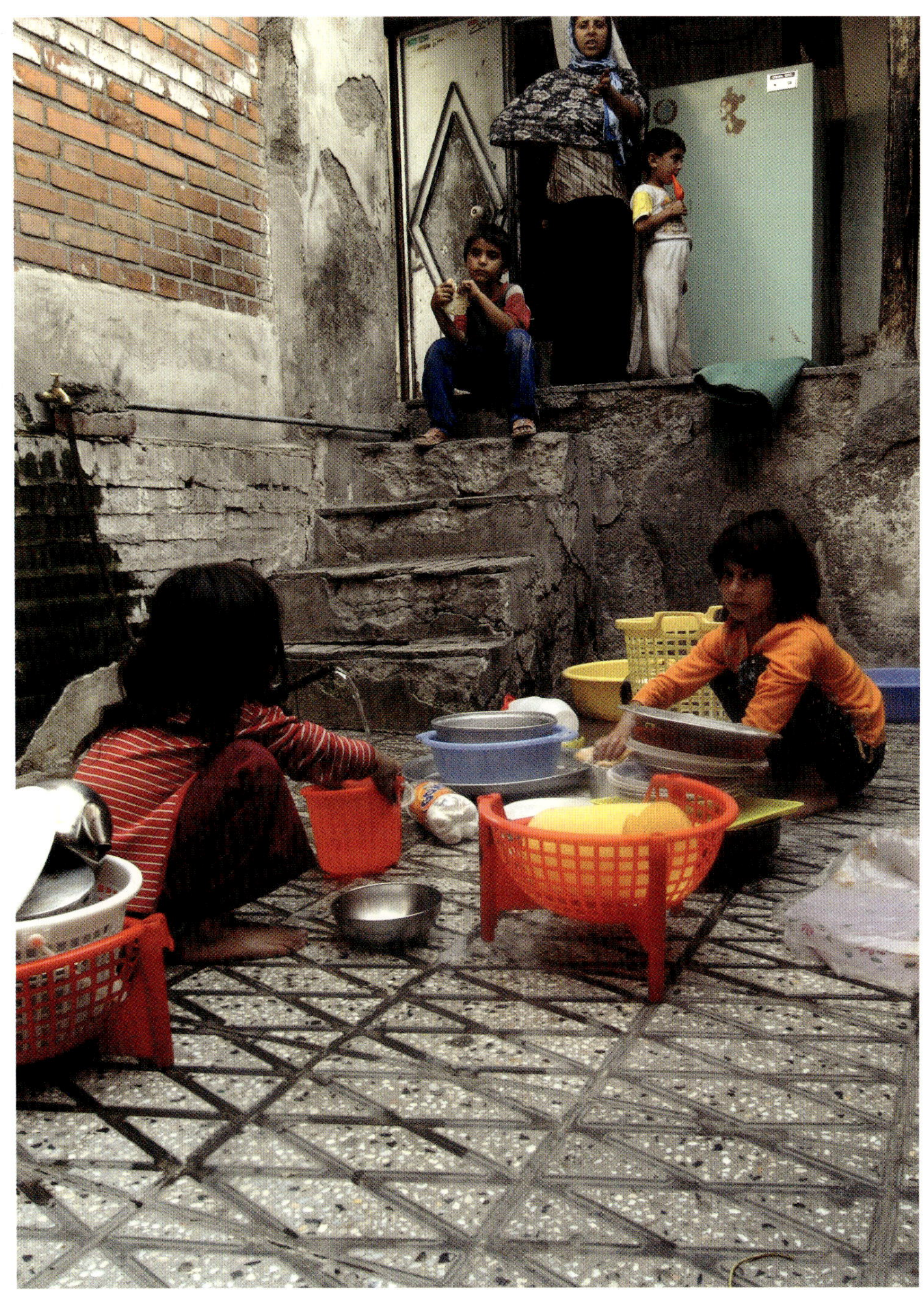

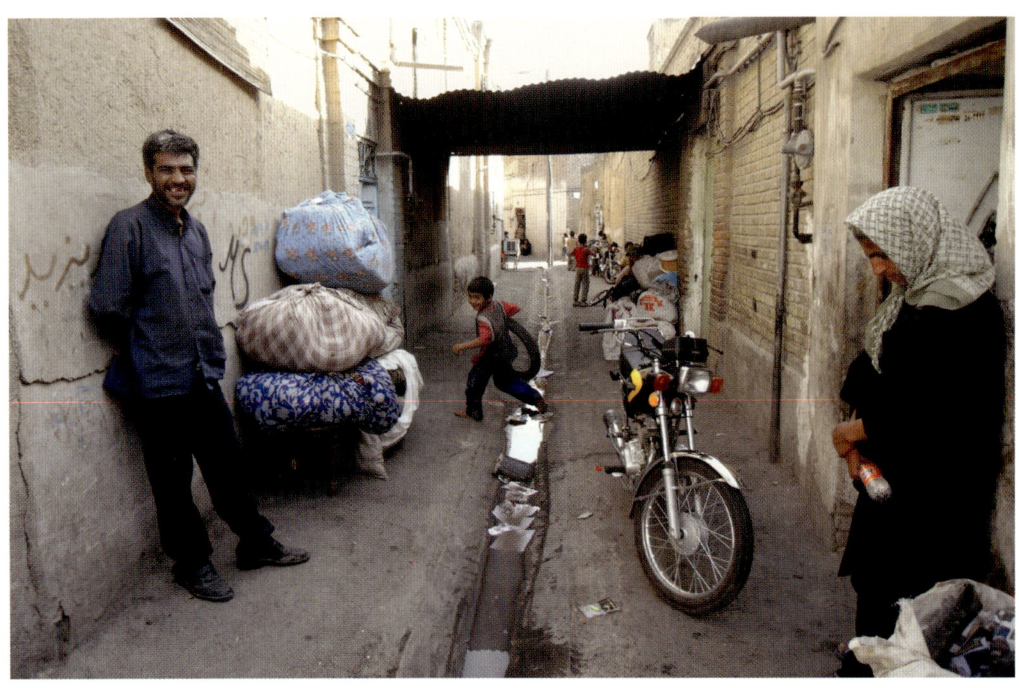

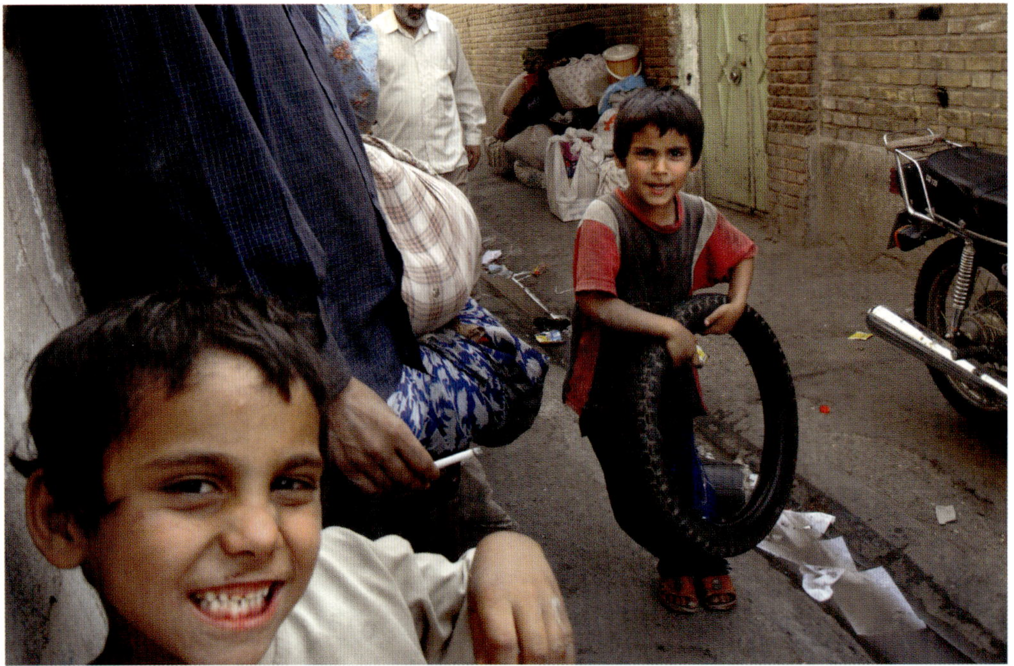

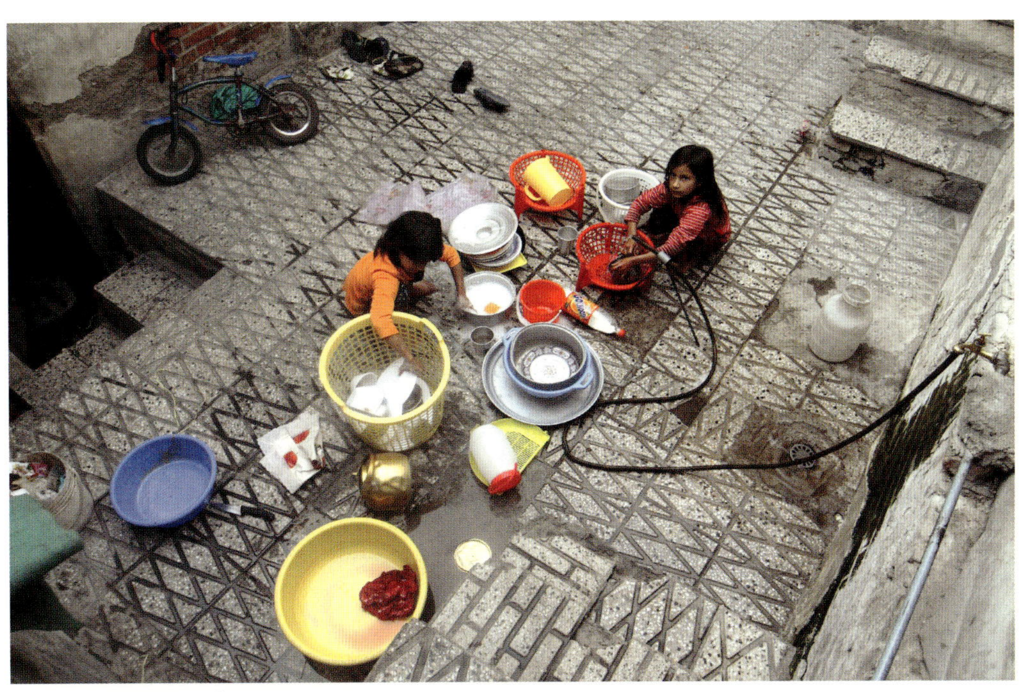

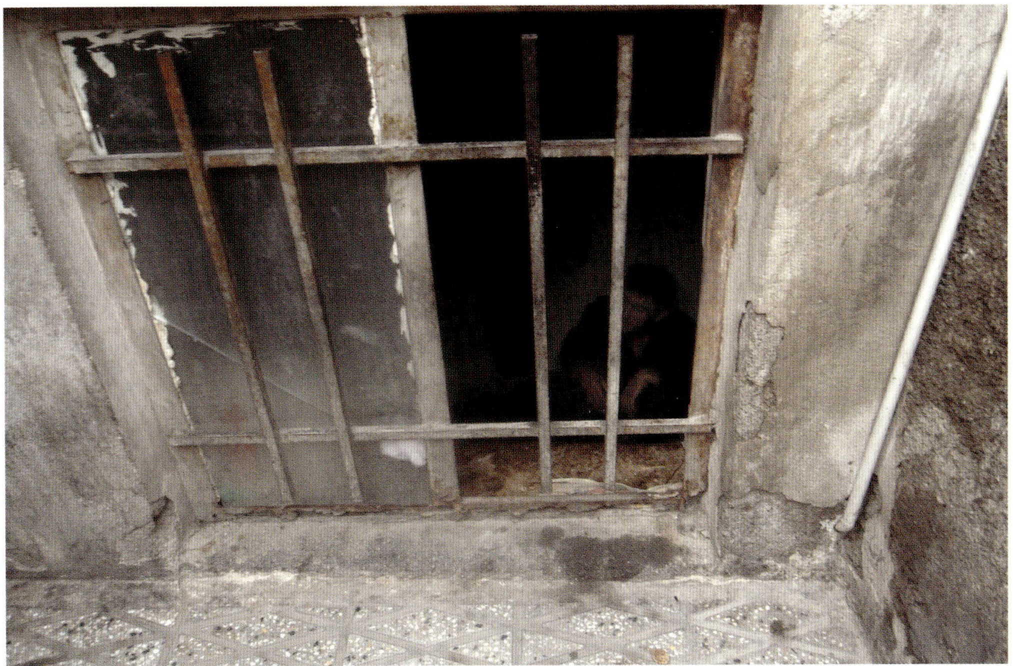

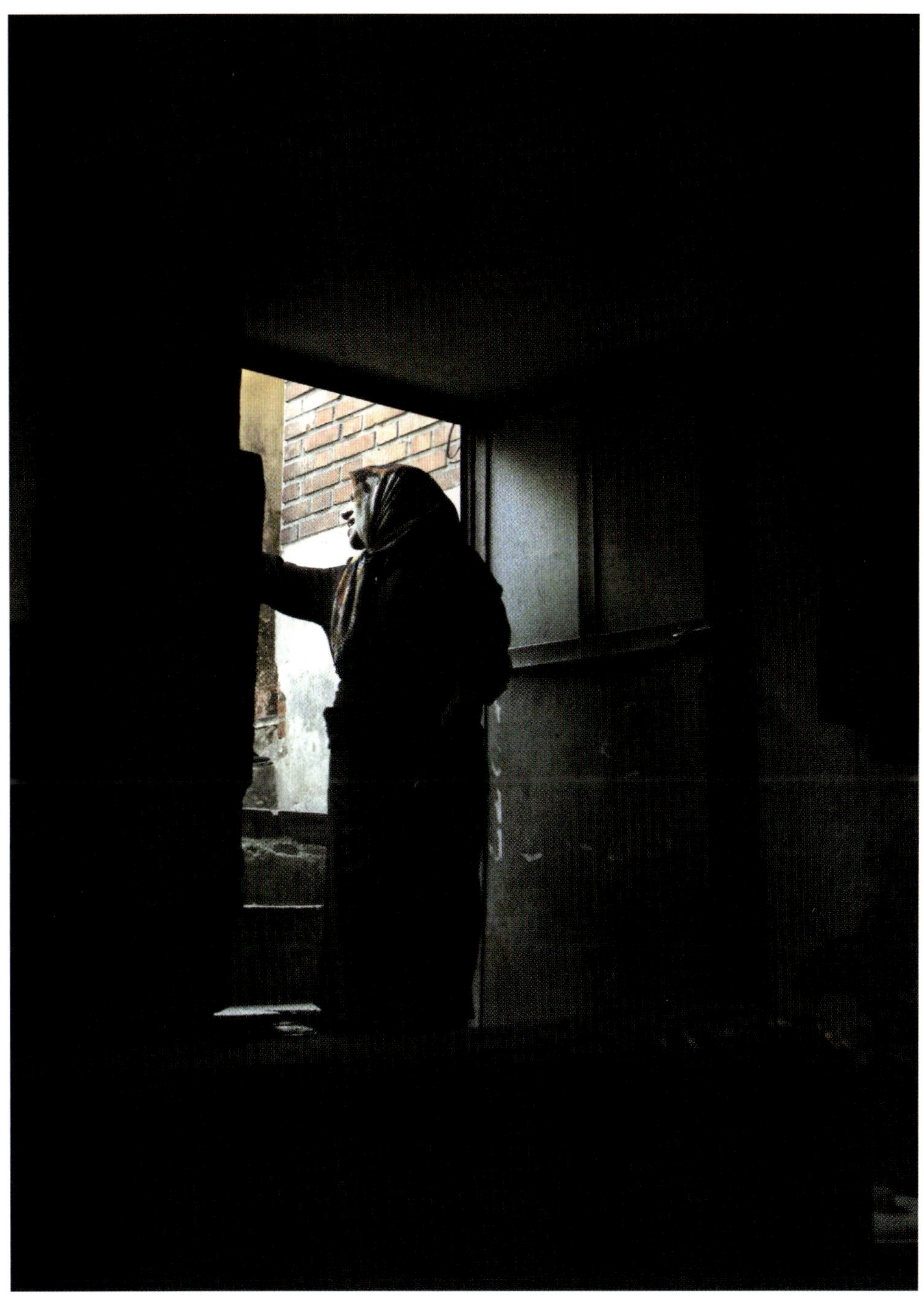

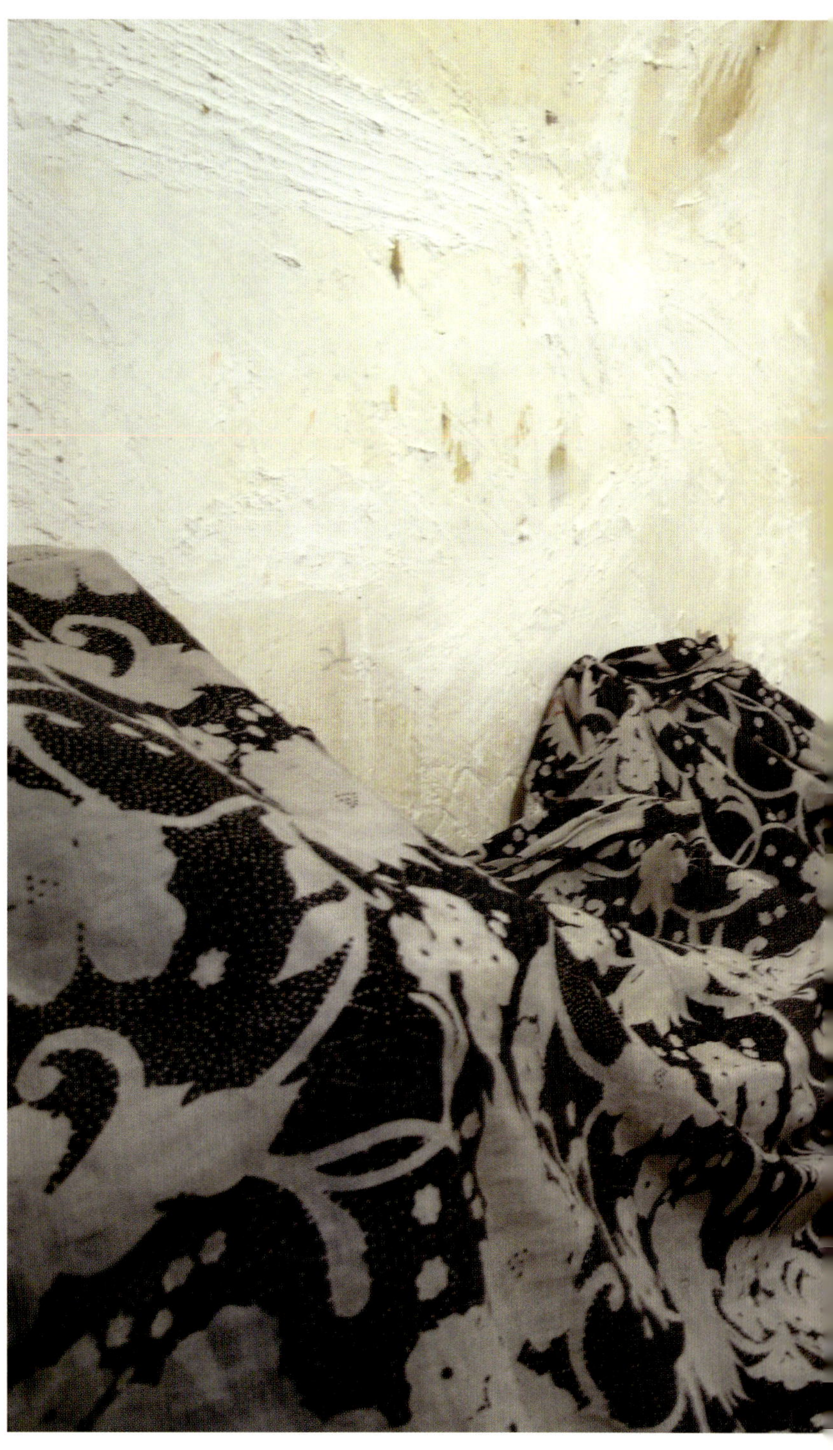

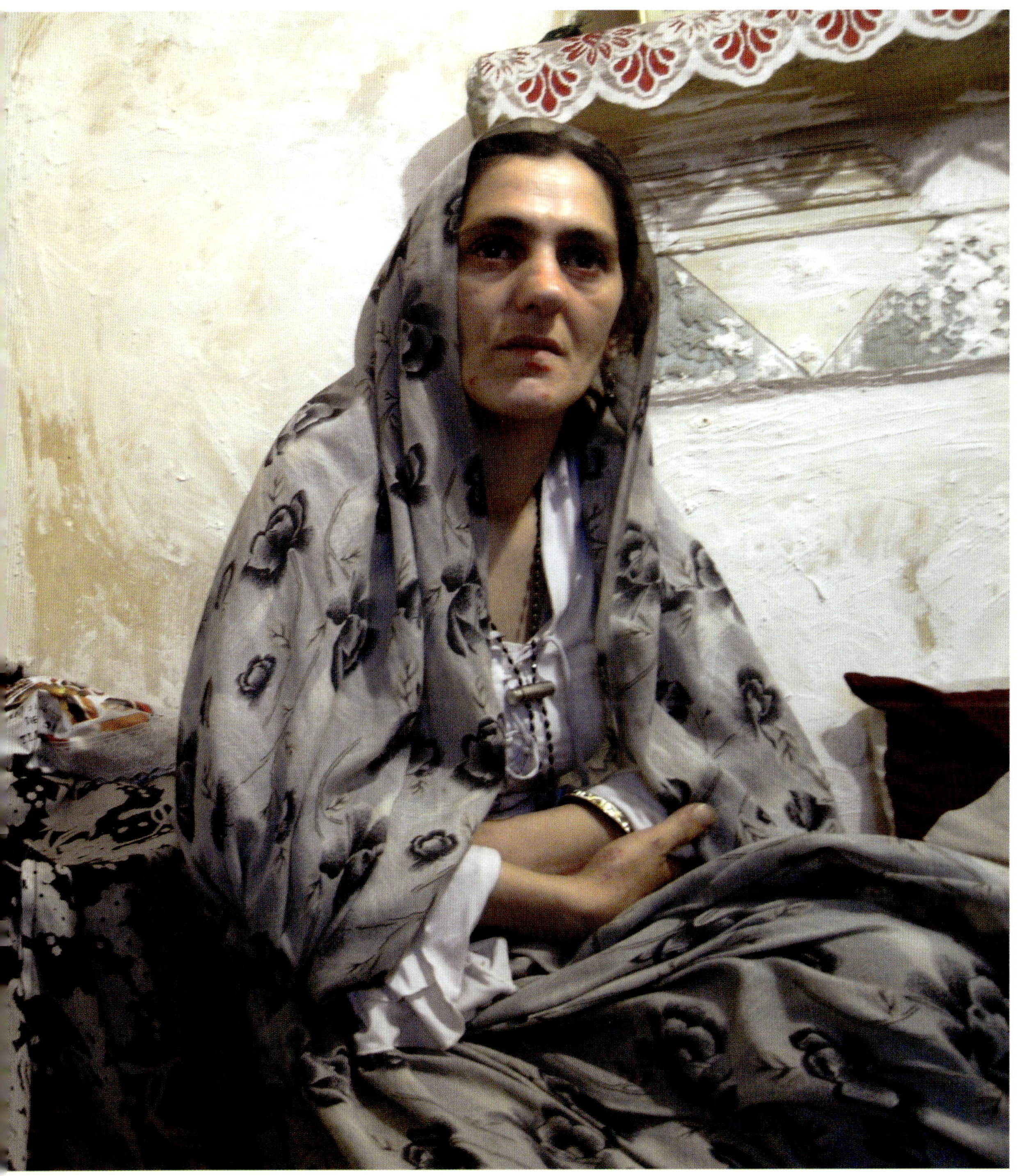

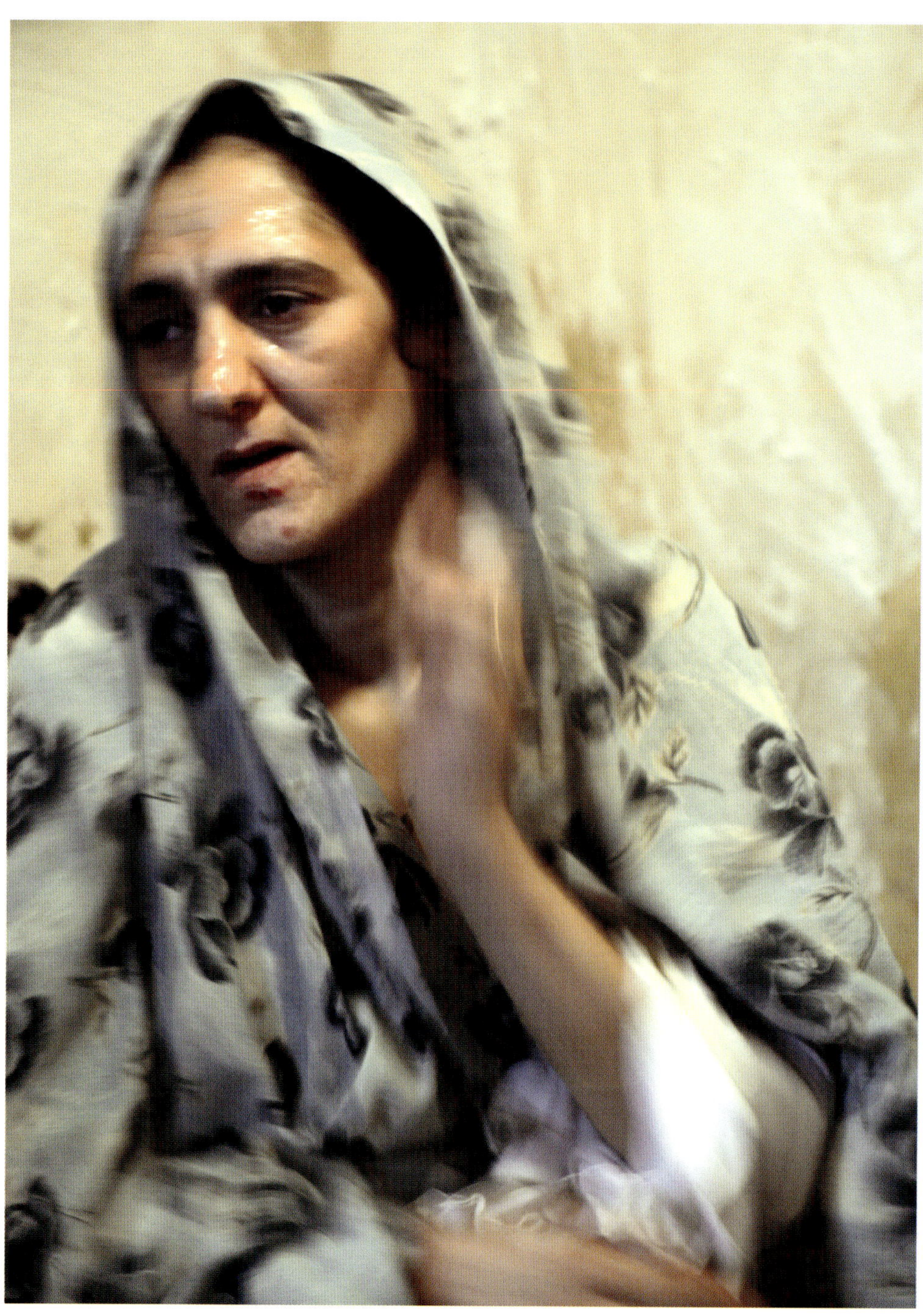

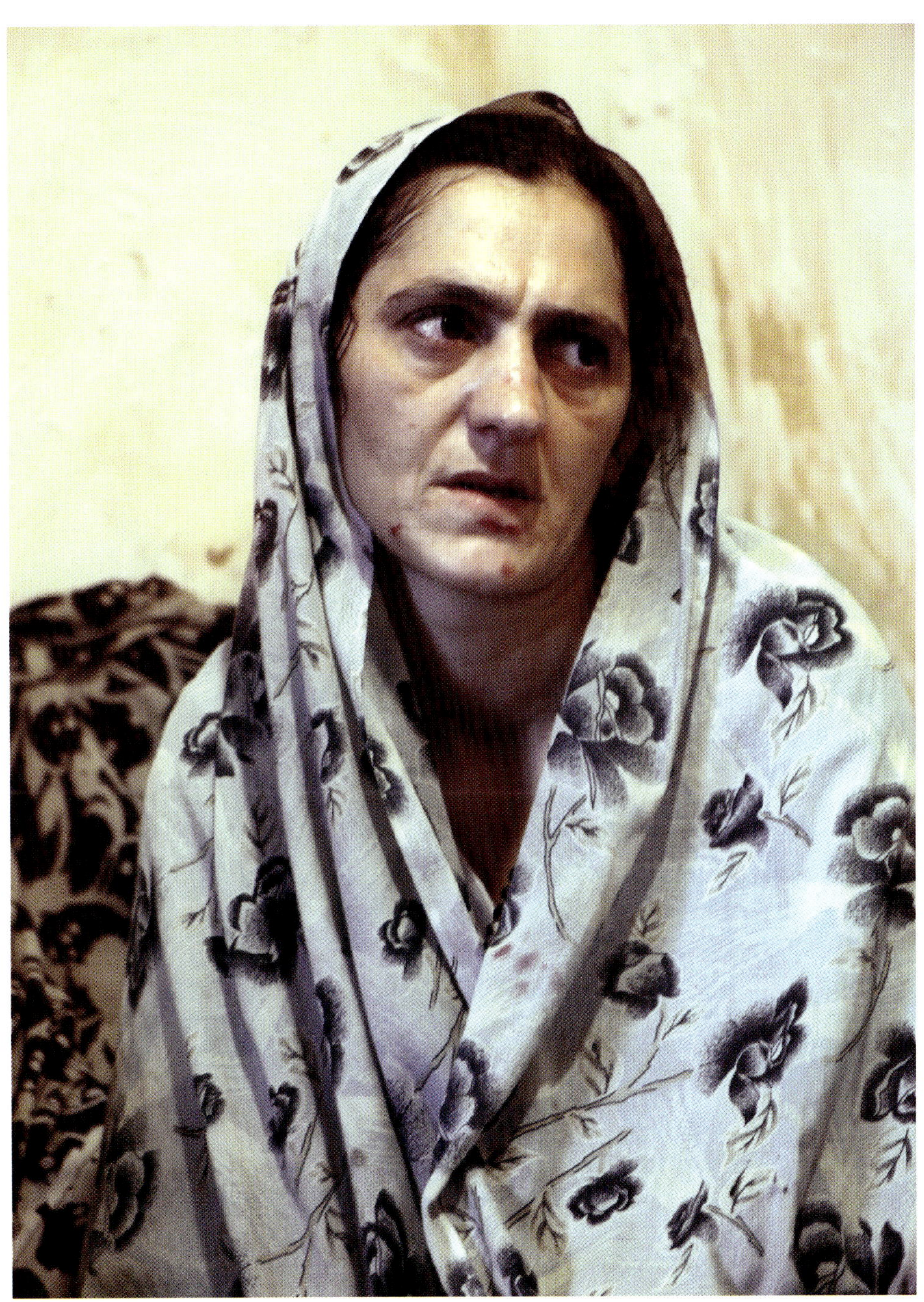

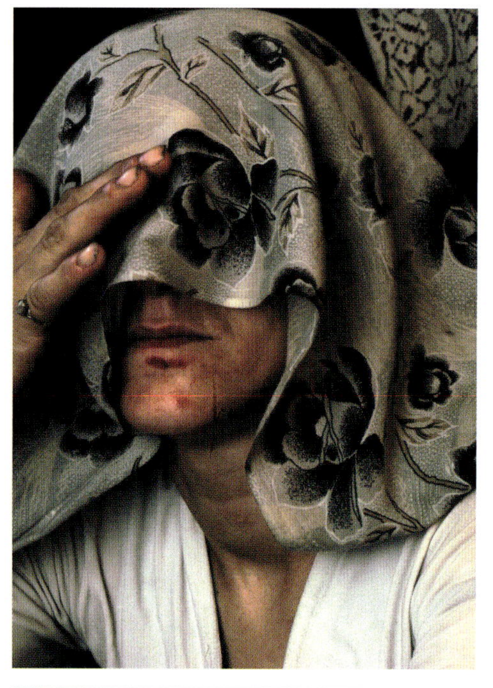
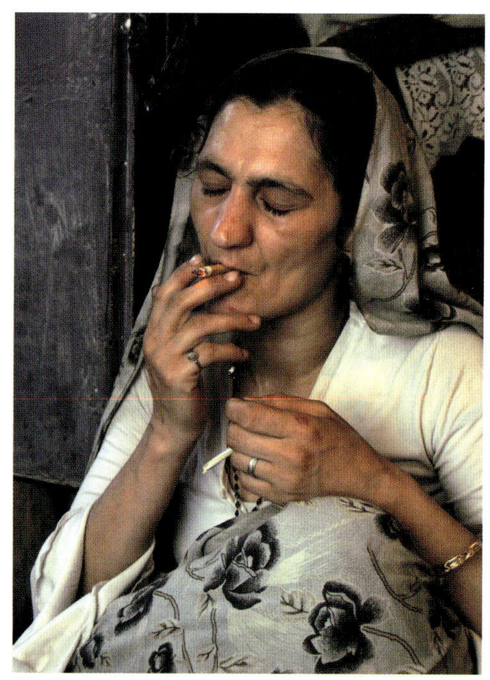
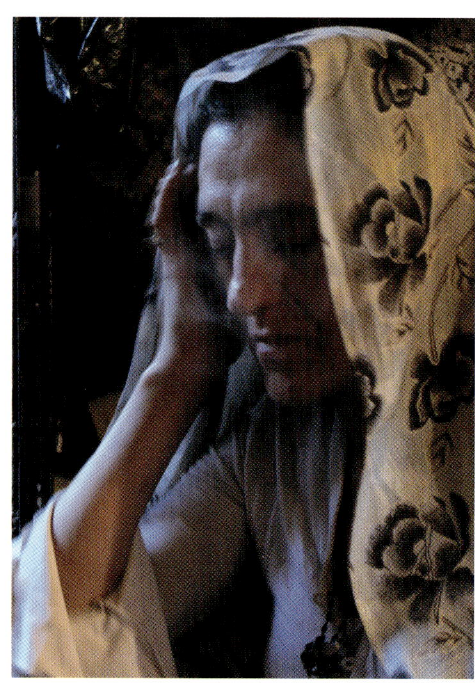
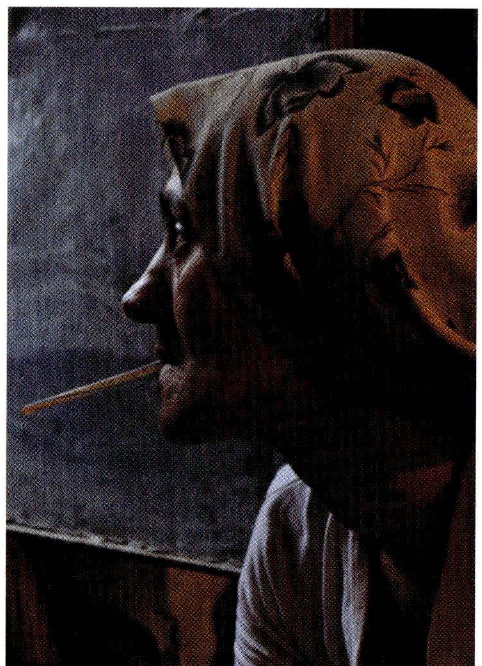

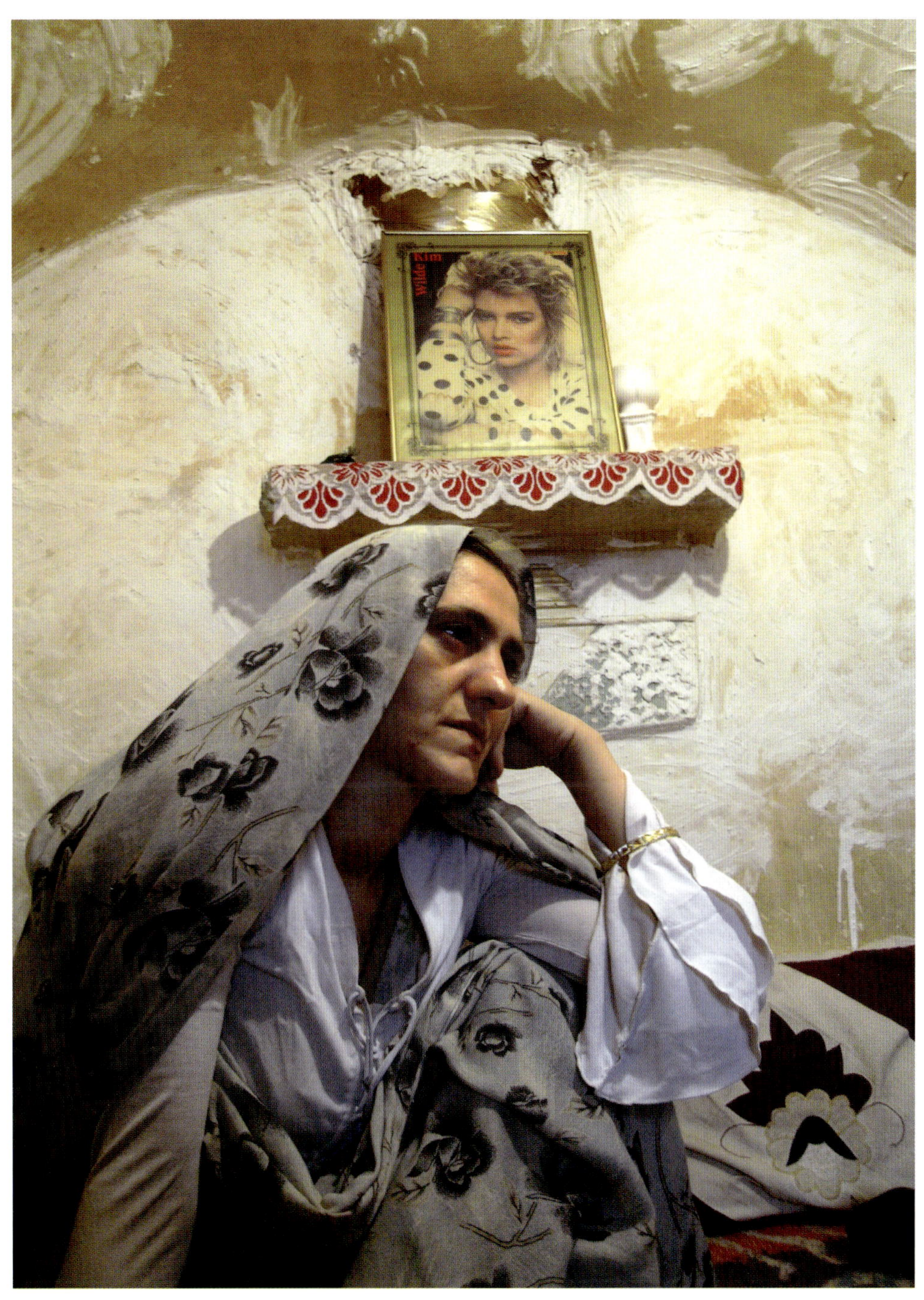
Kim
Wilde

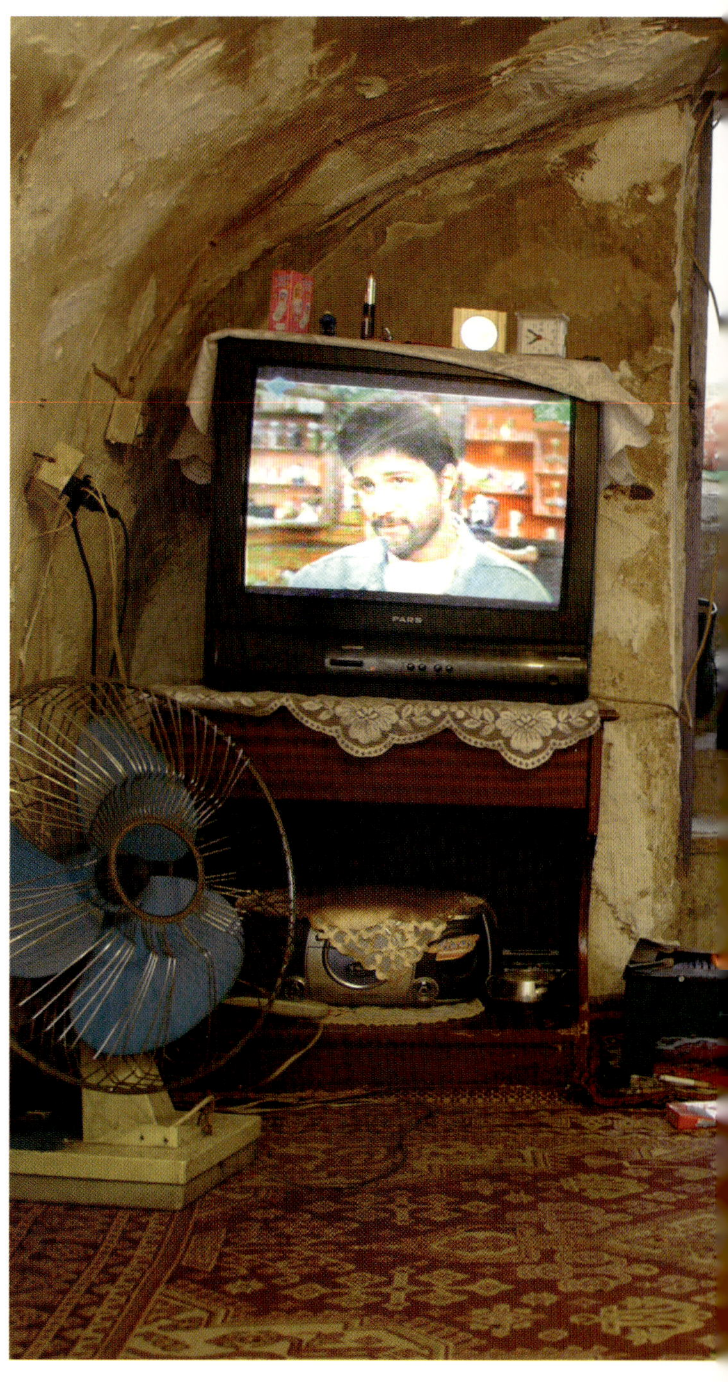
PARS

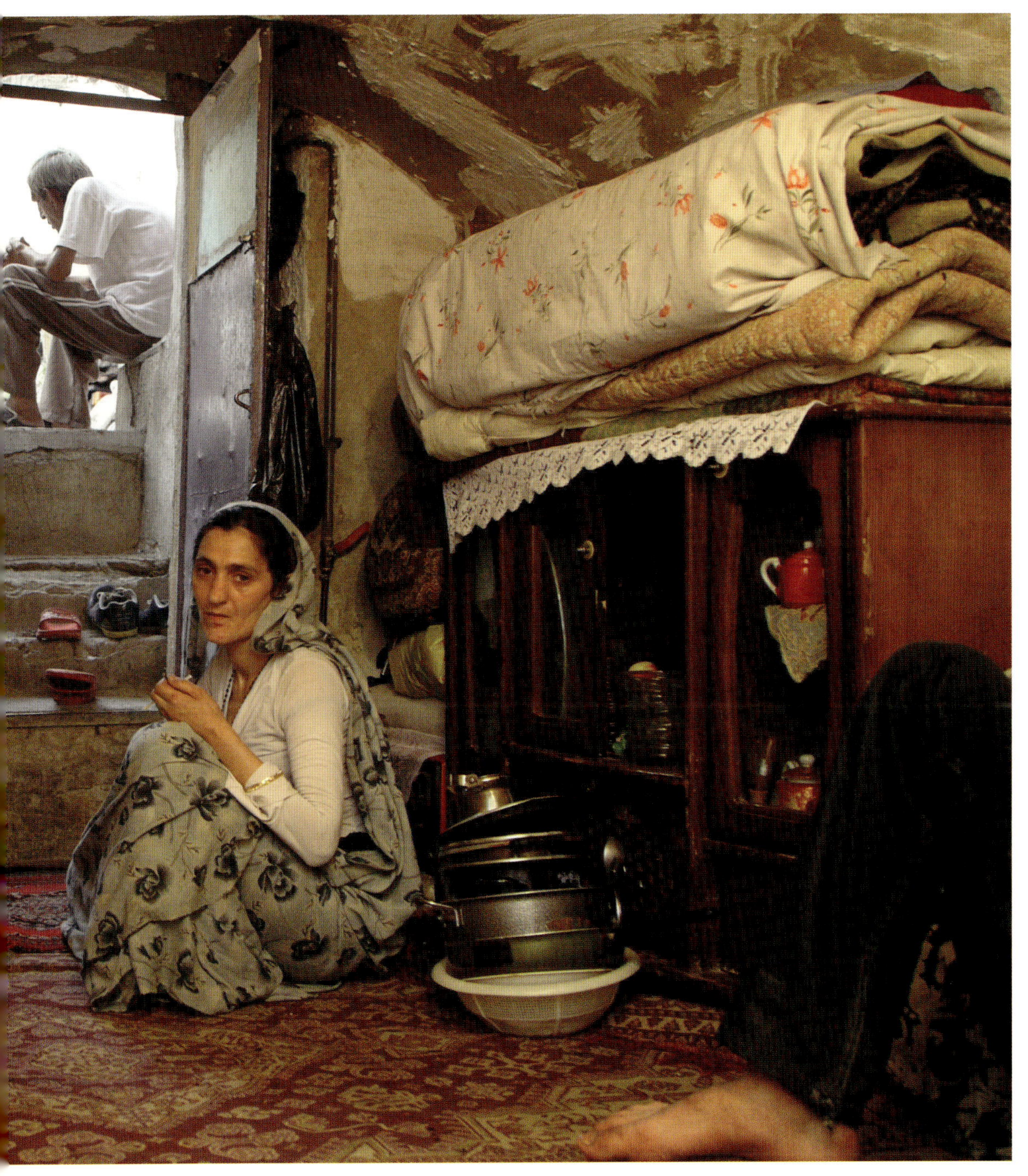

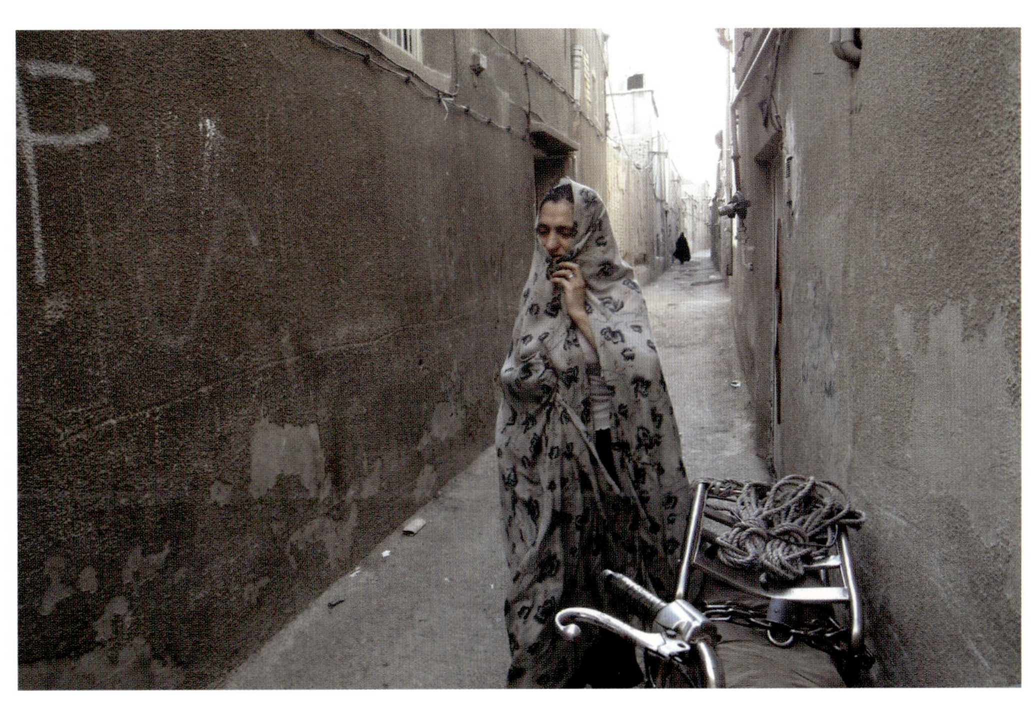

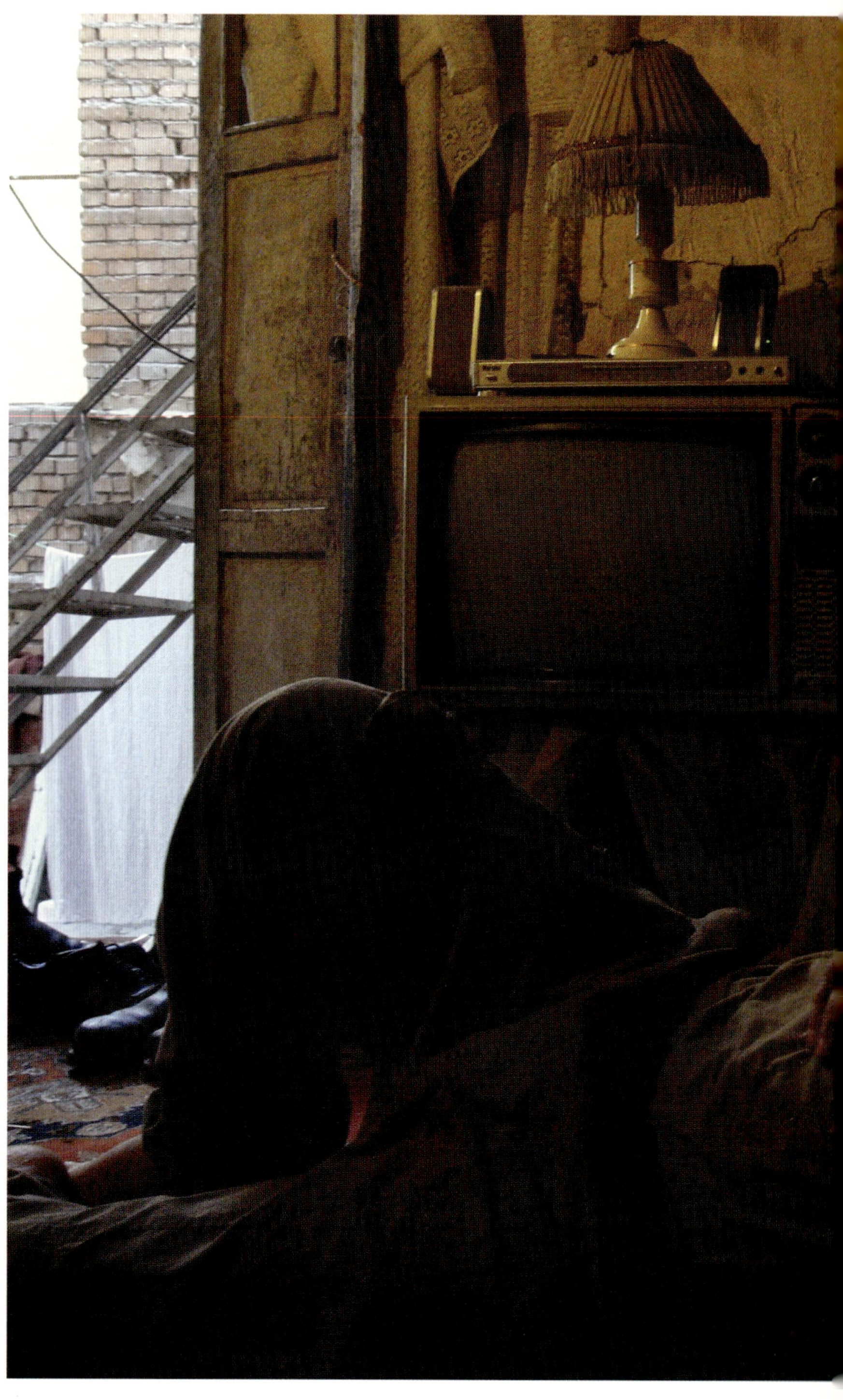

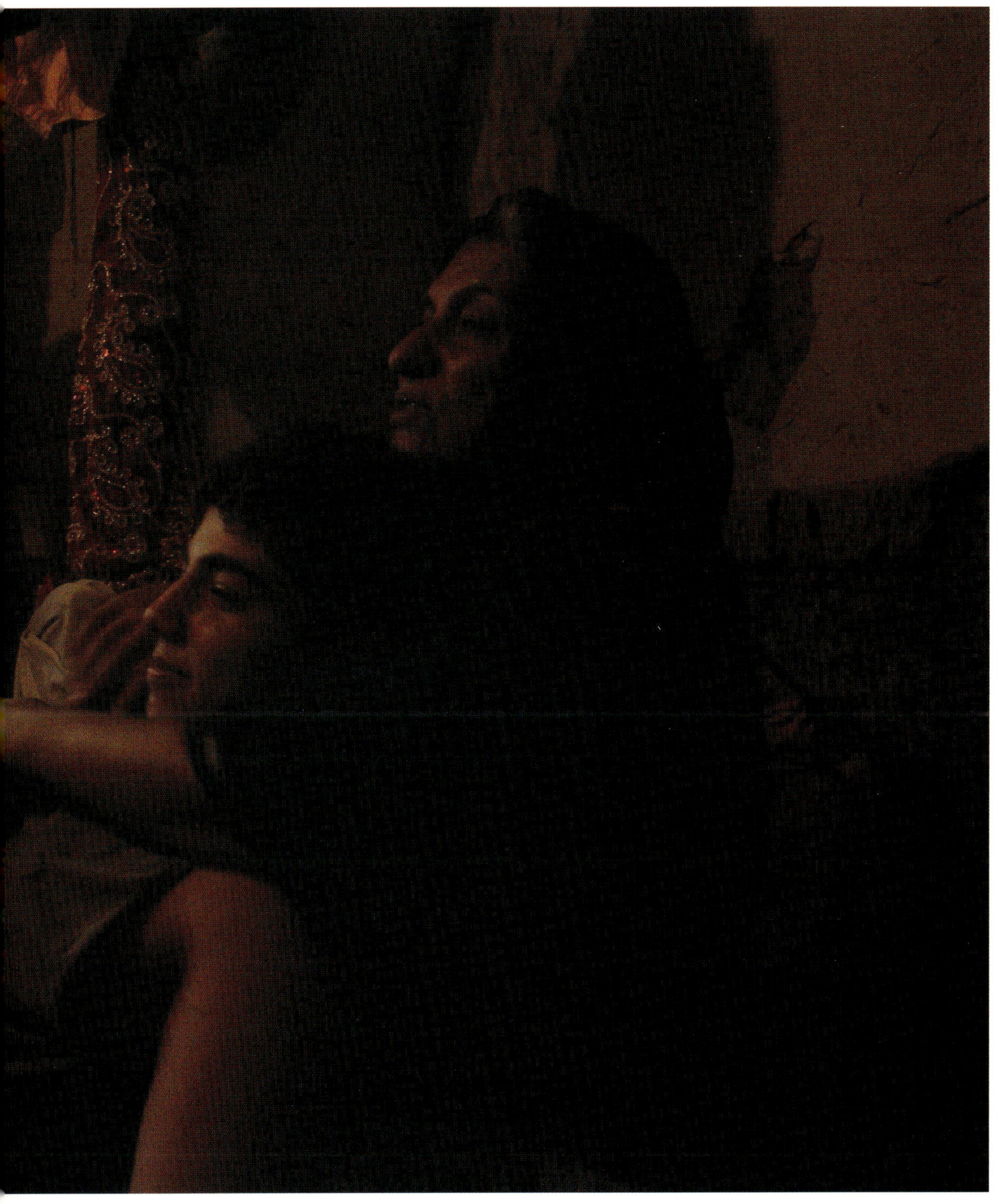

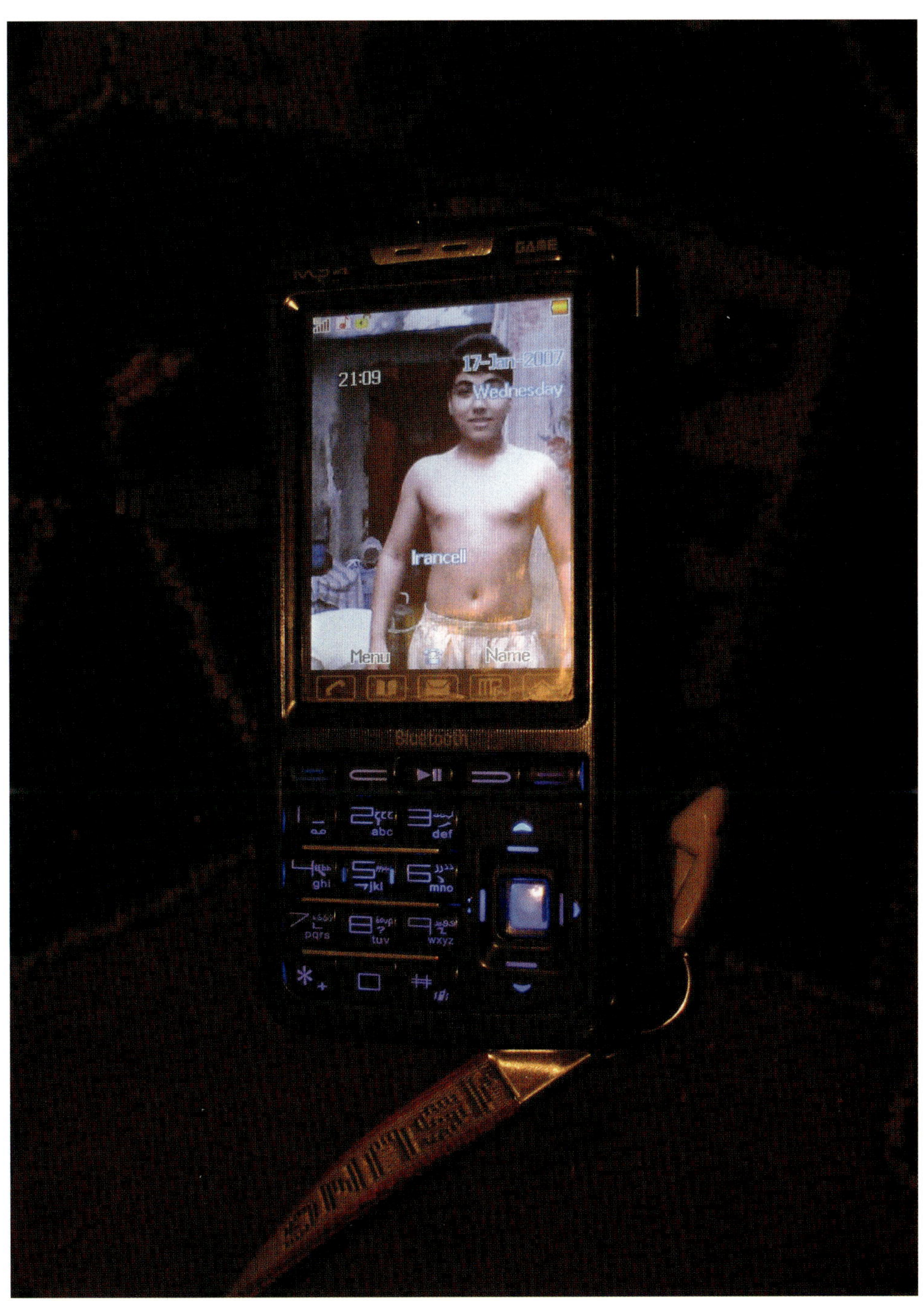
17-Jan-2007
21:09
Wednesday
Irancell
Menu
Name
Bluetooth
abc
def
ghi
jkl
mno
pqrs
tuv
wxyz

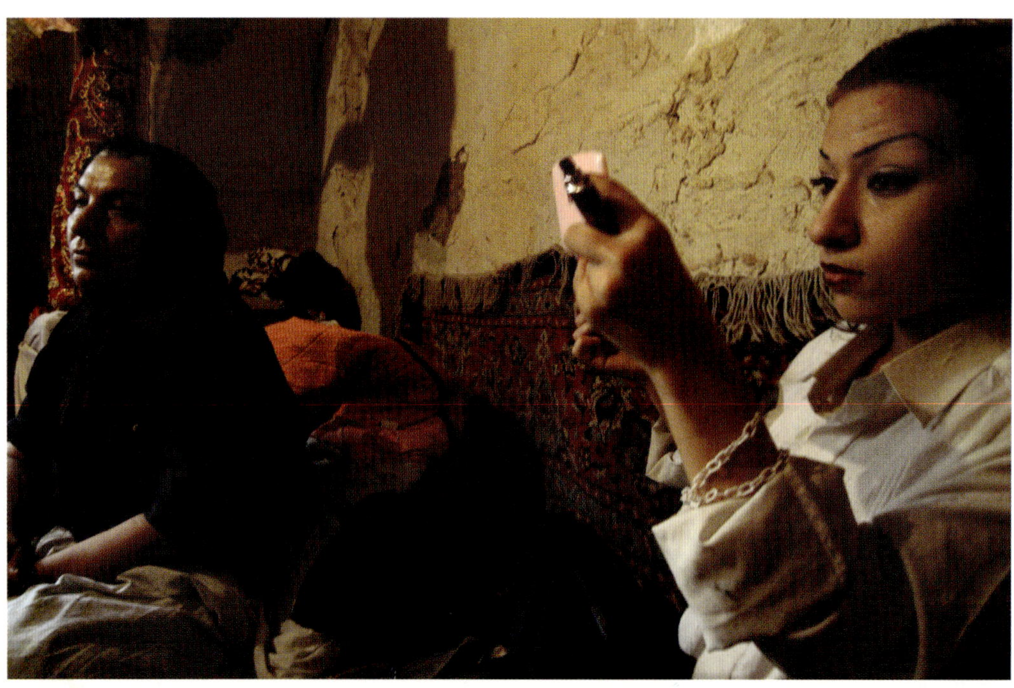

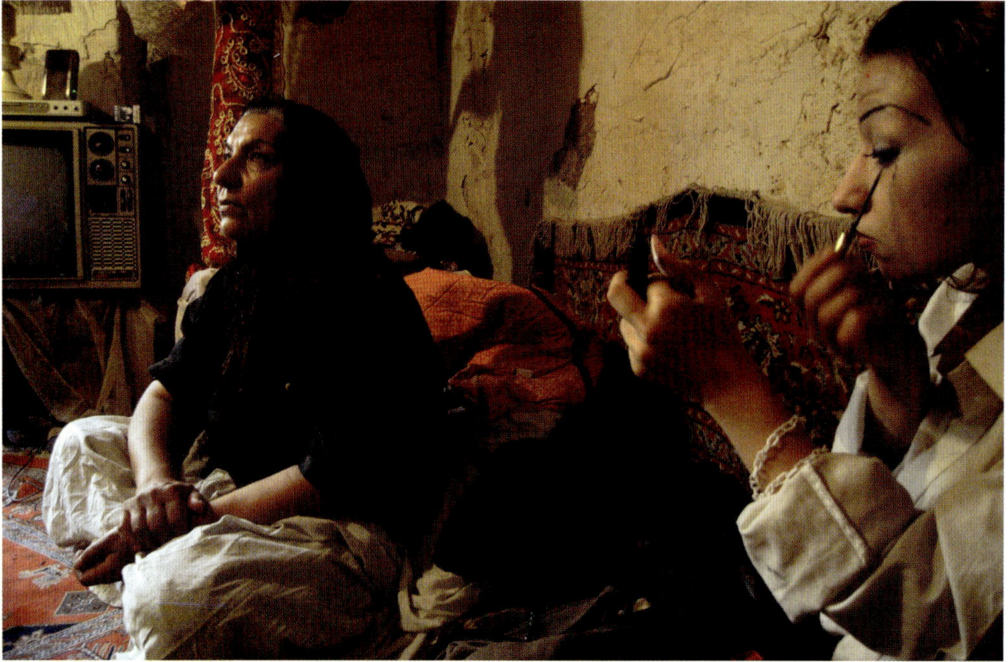

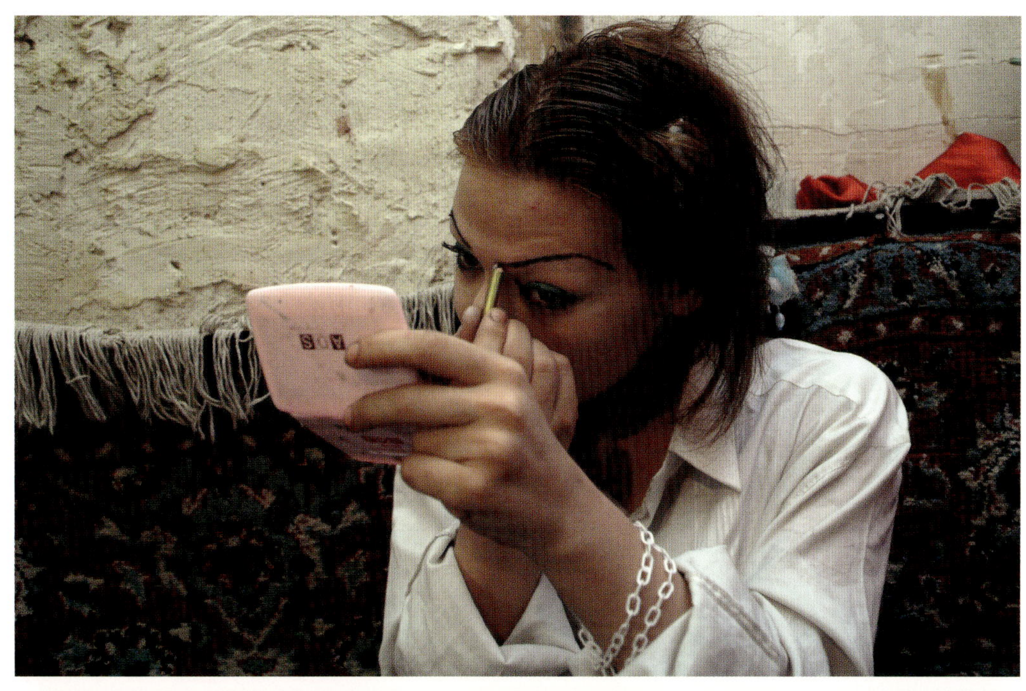

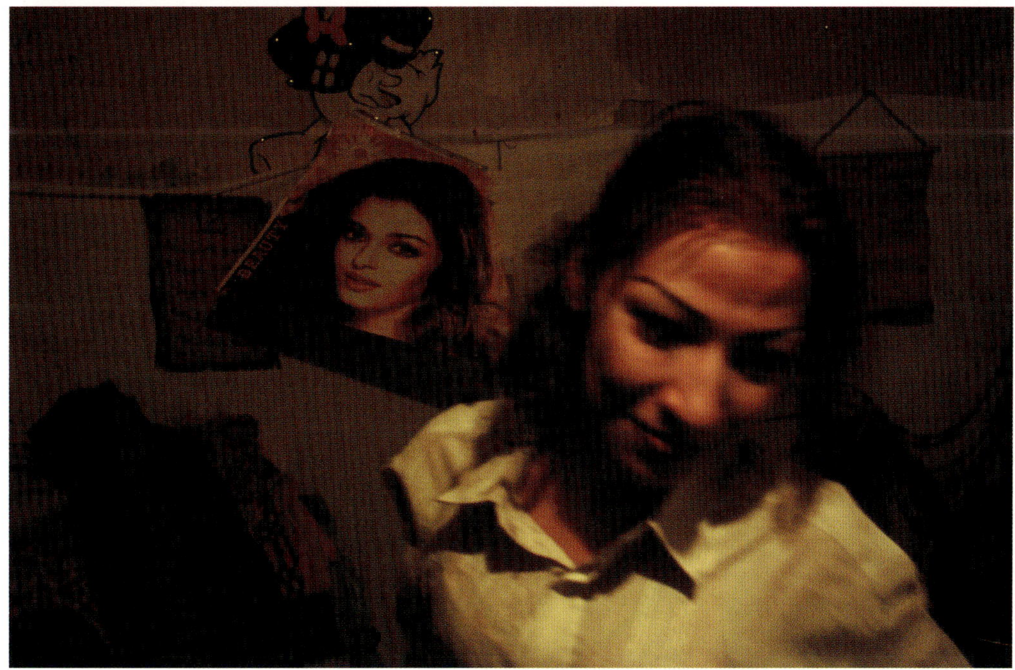

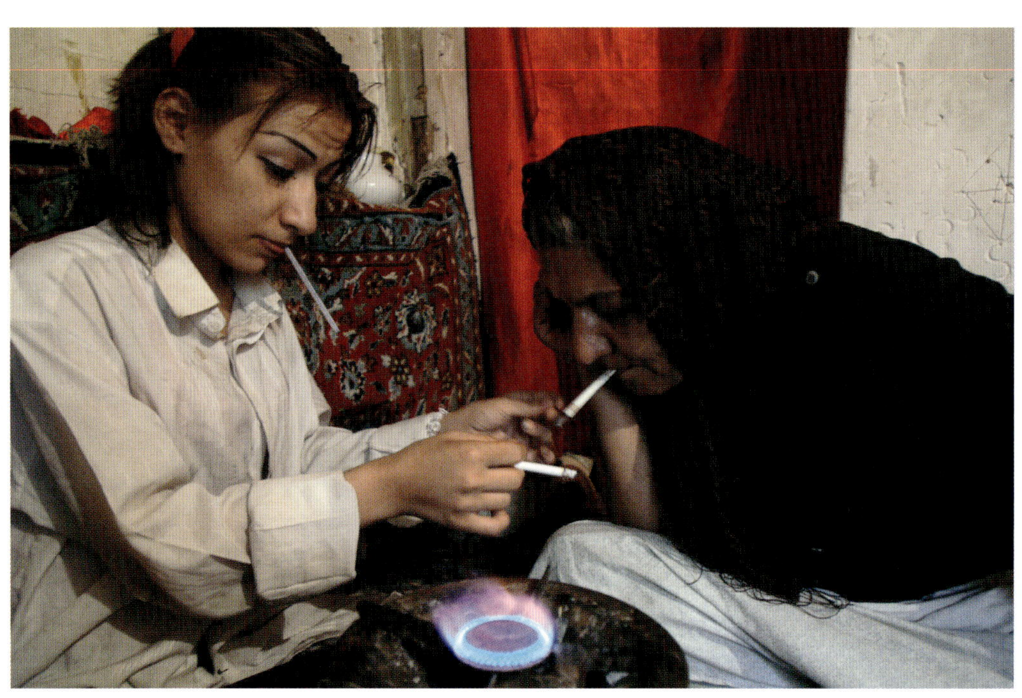

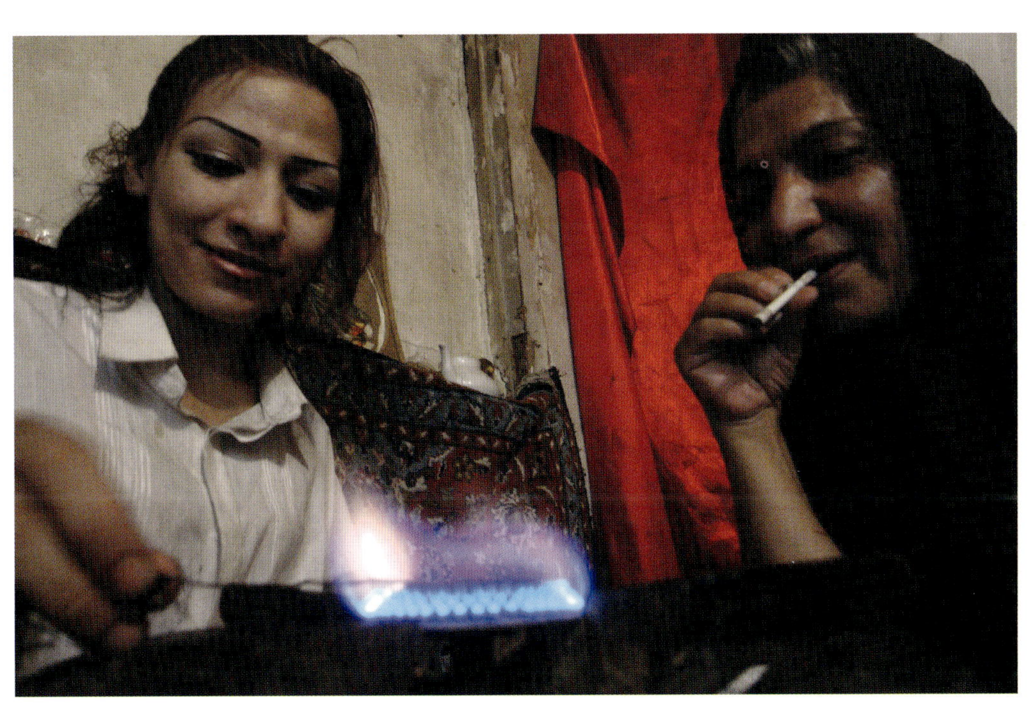

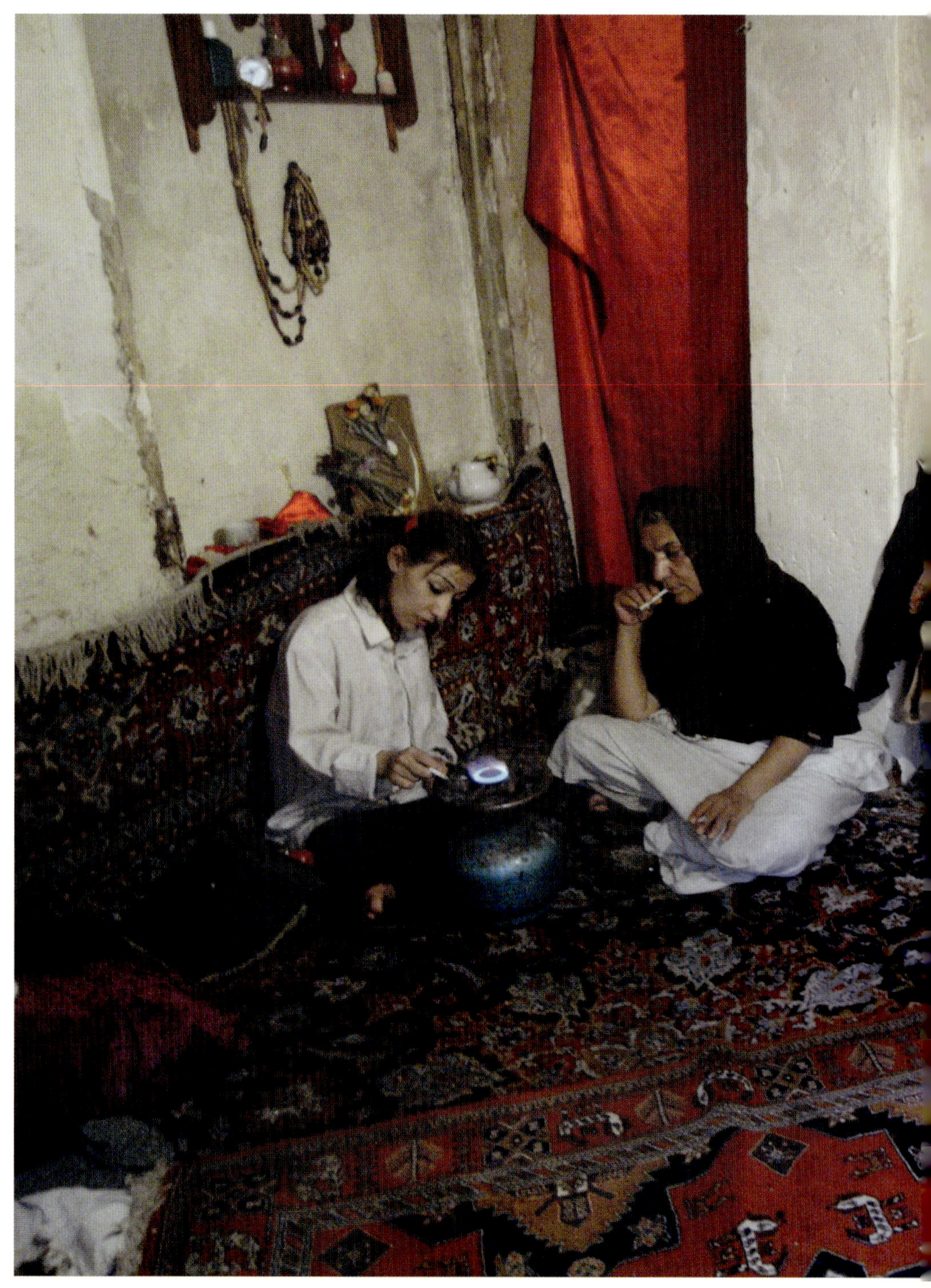

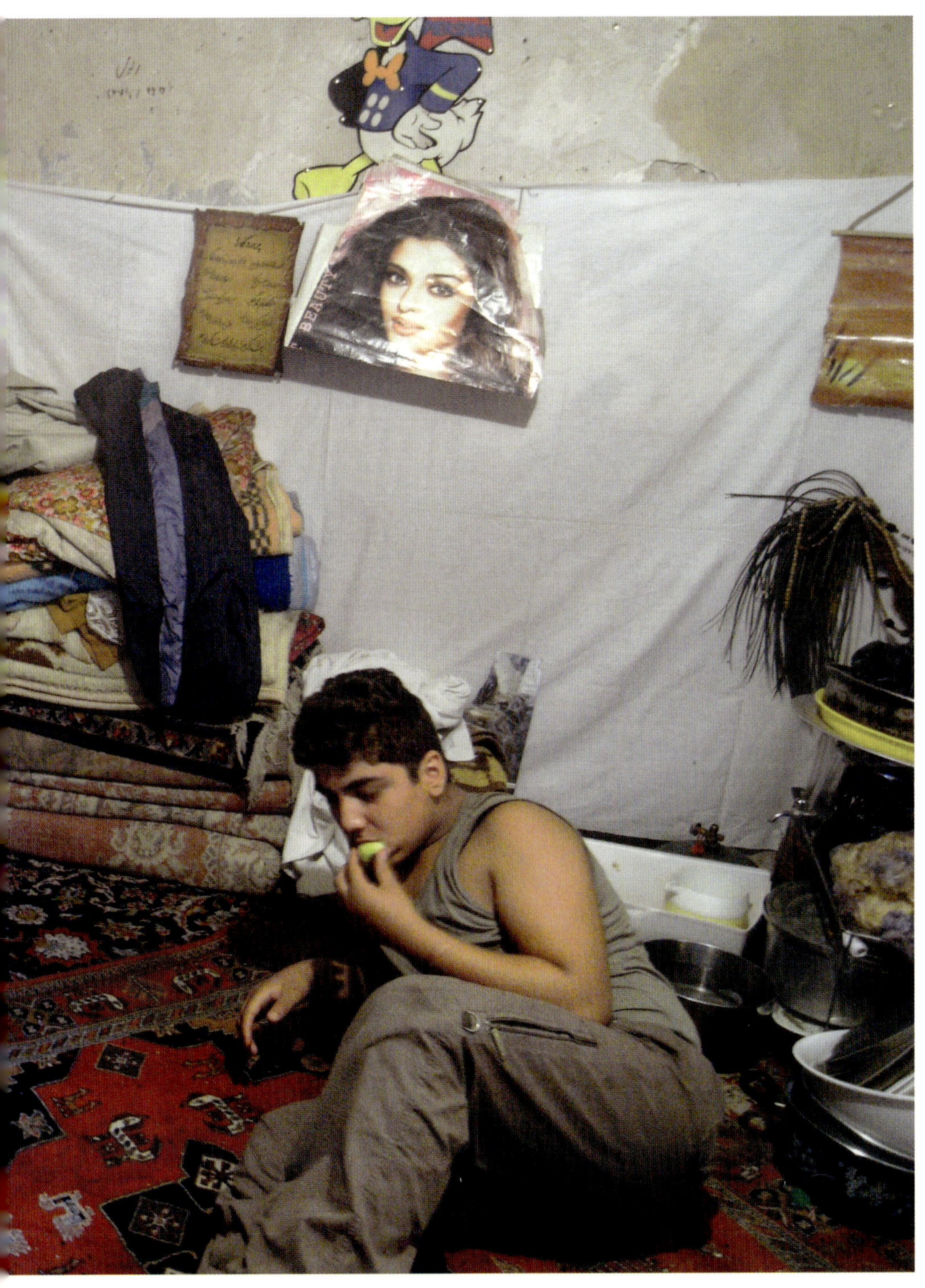
BEAUTY

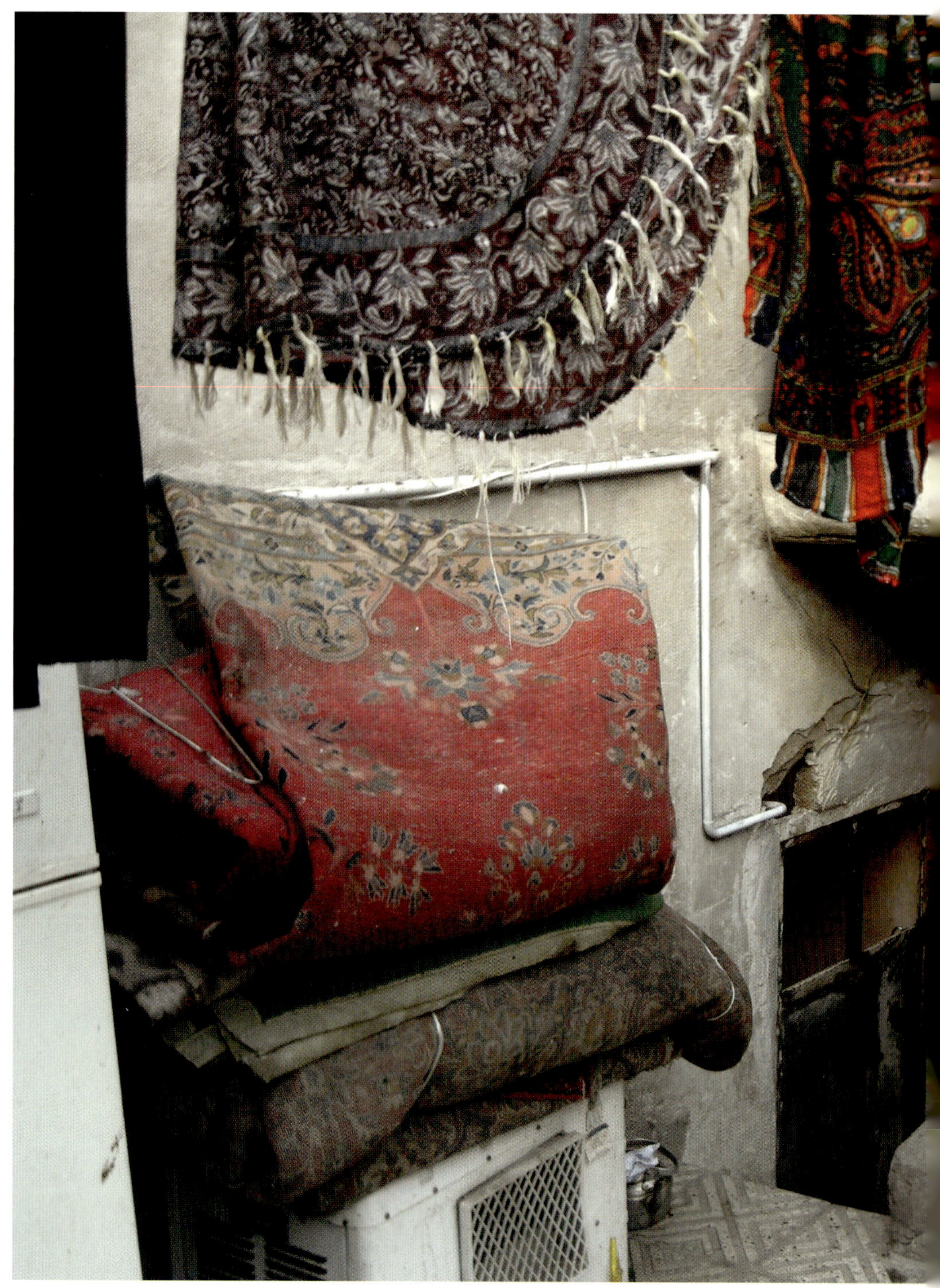

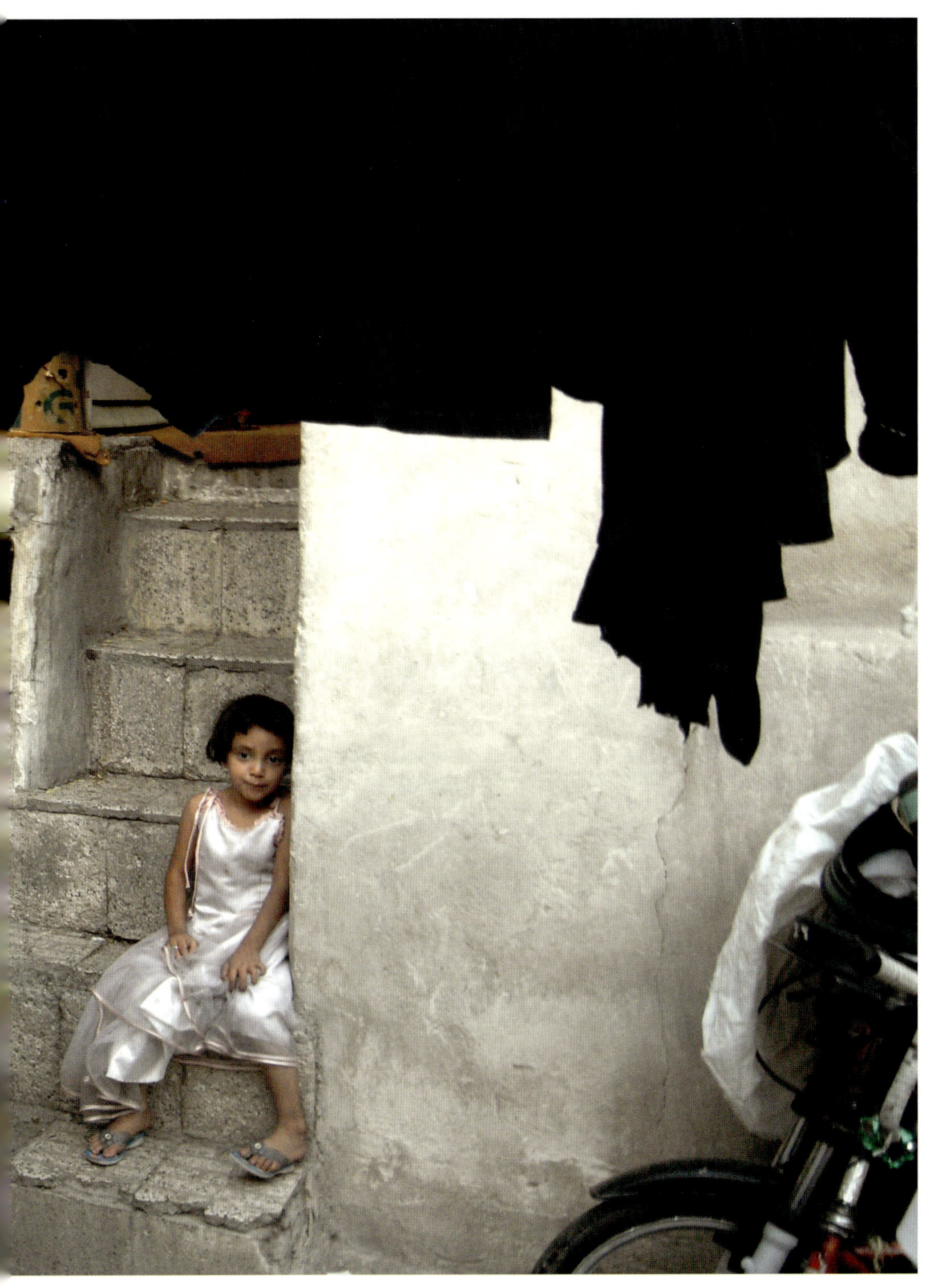

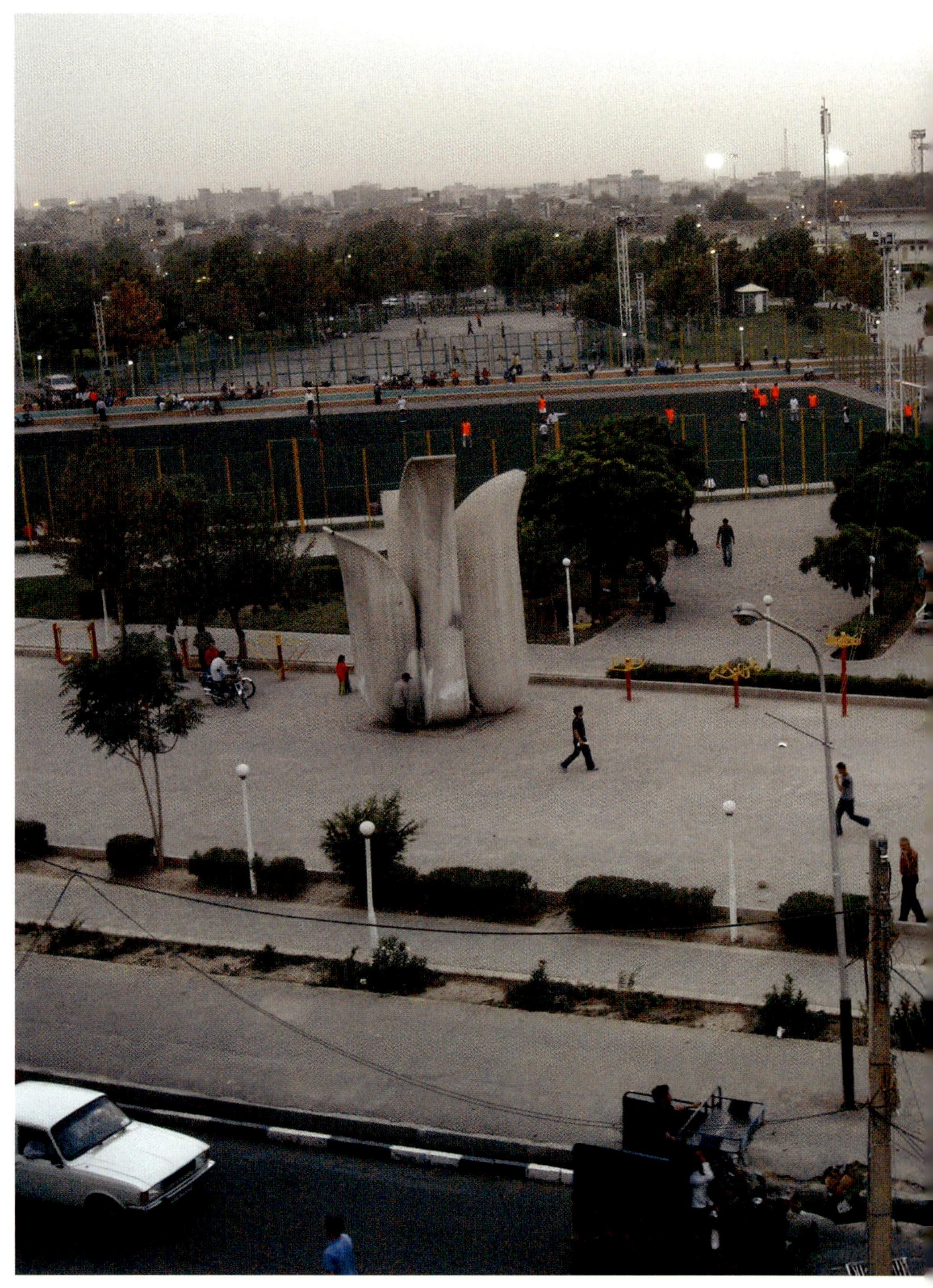

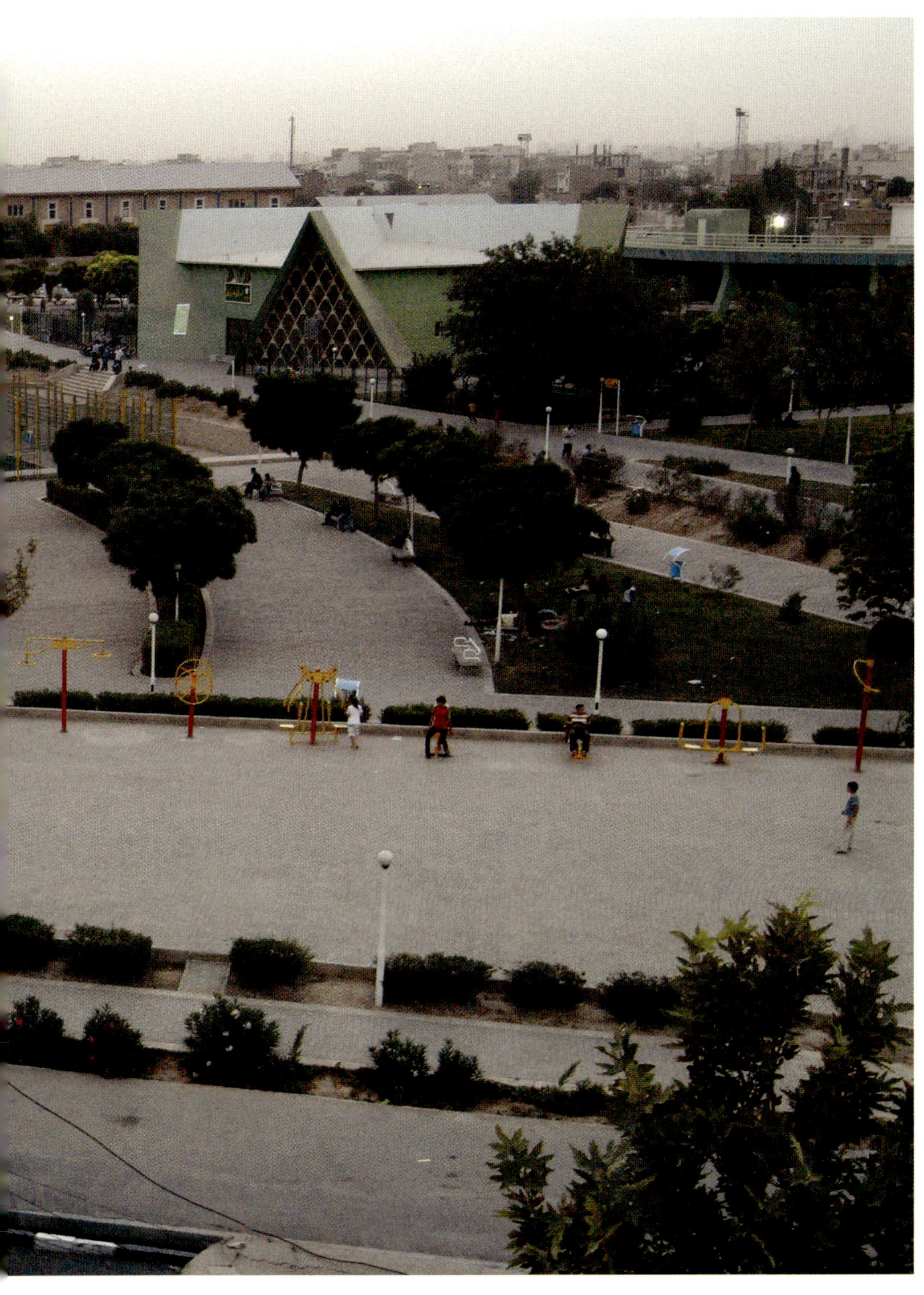

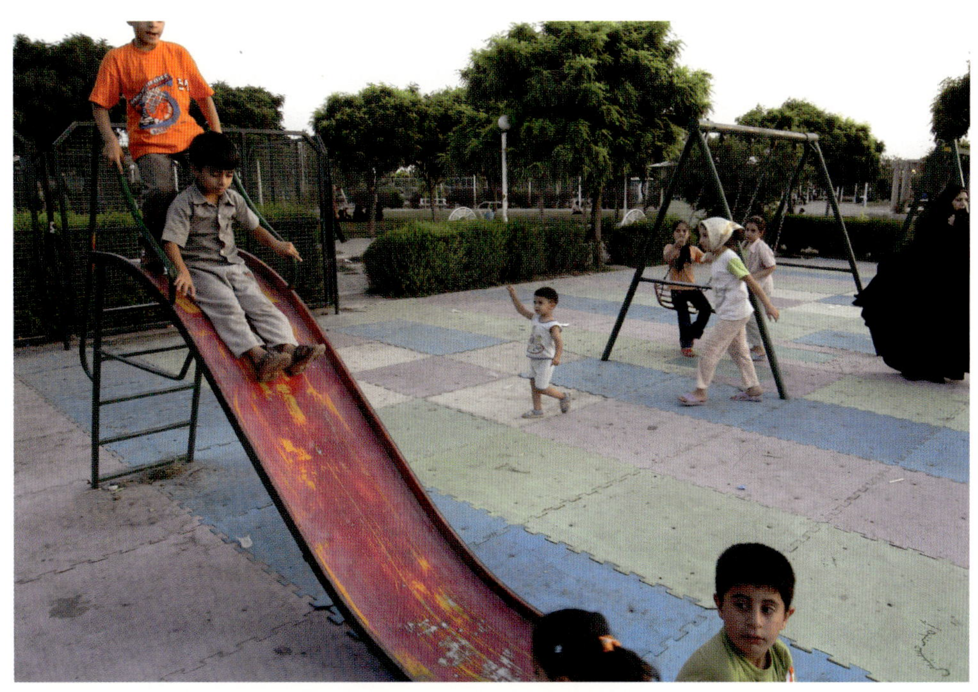

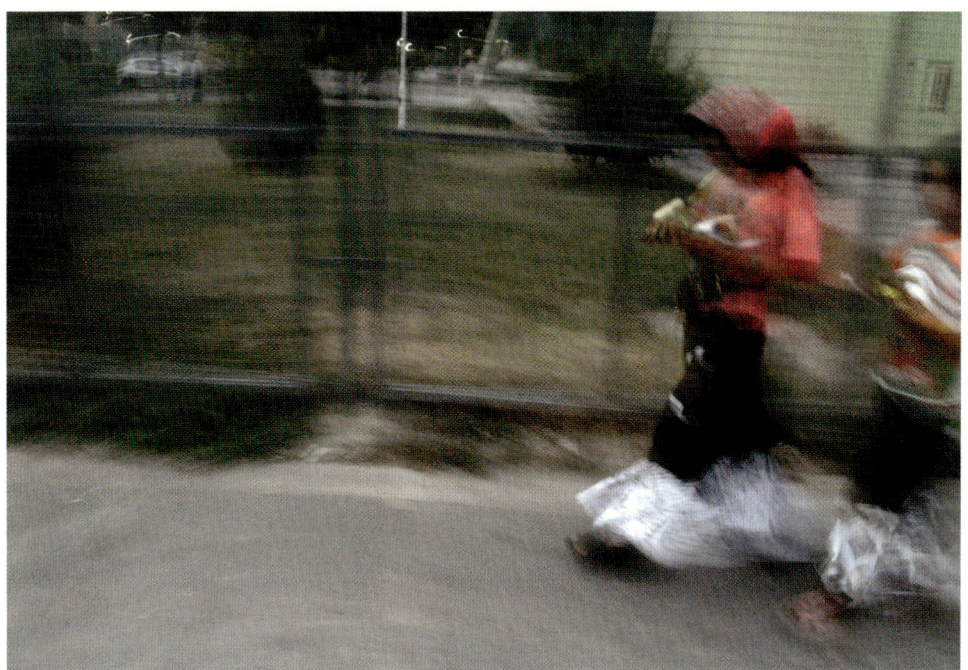

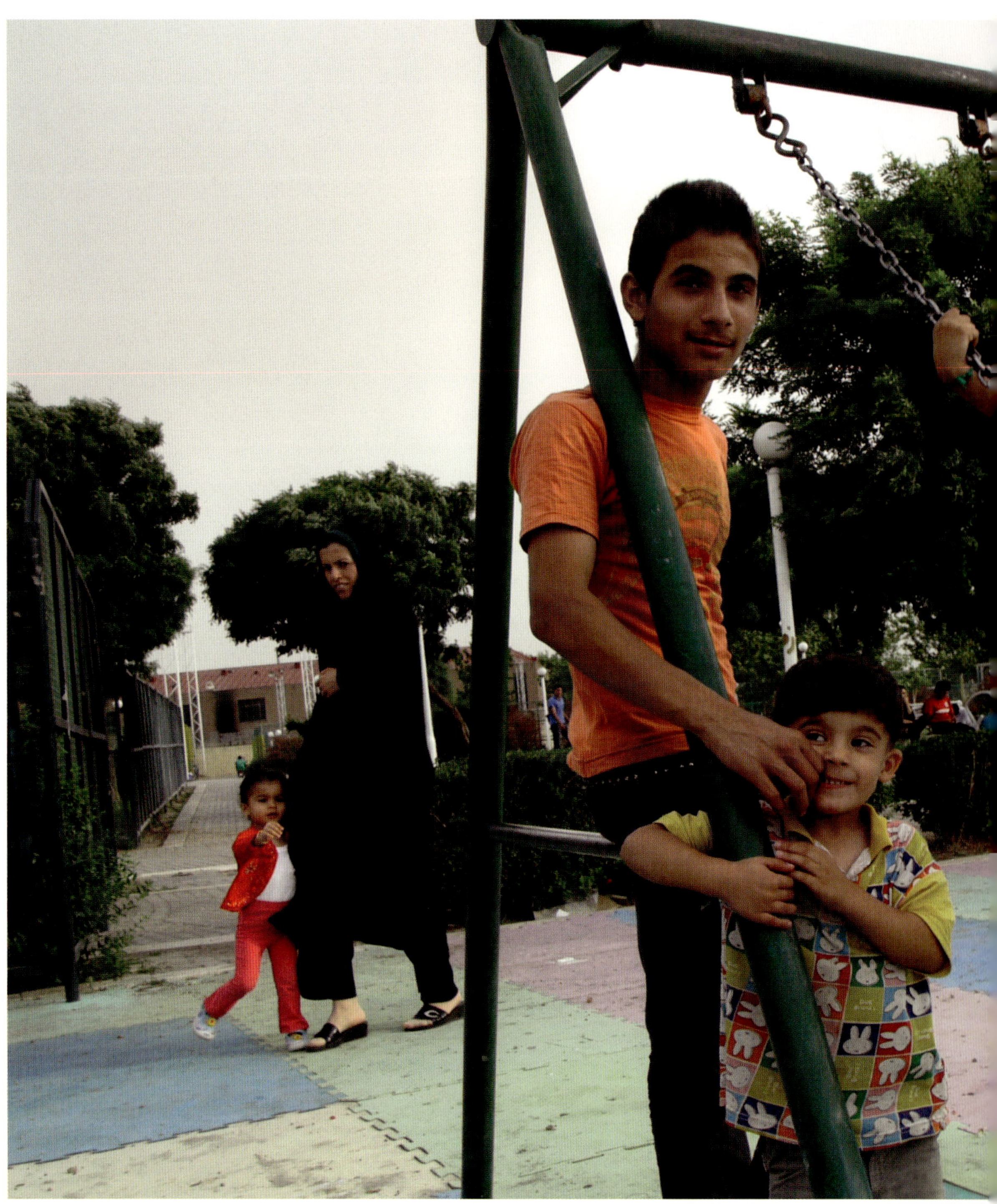

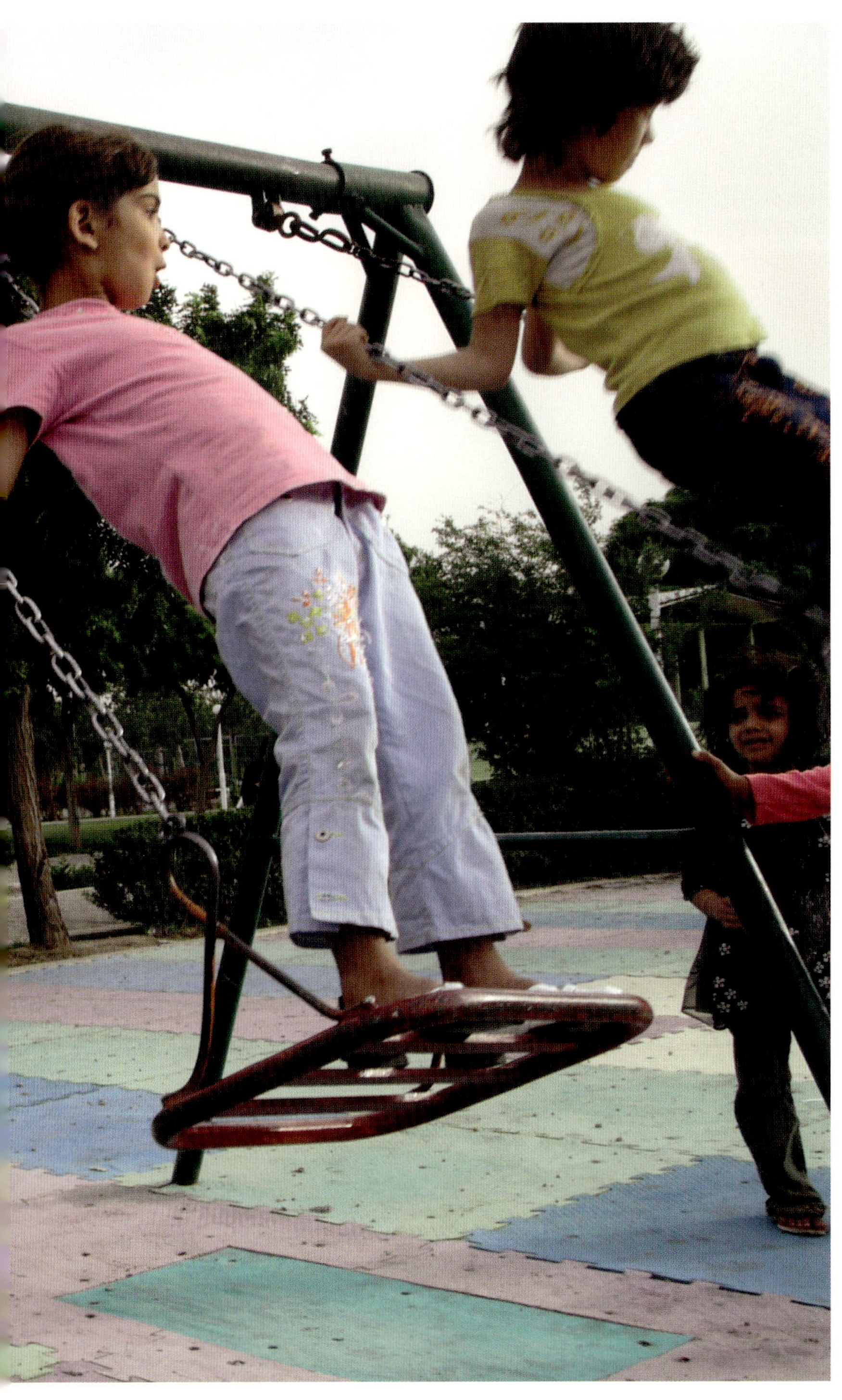

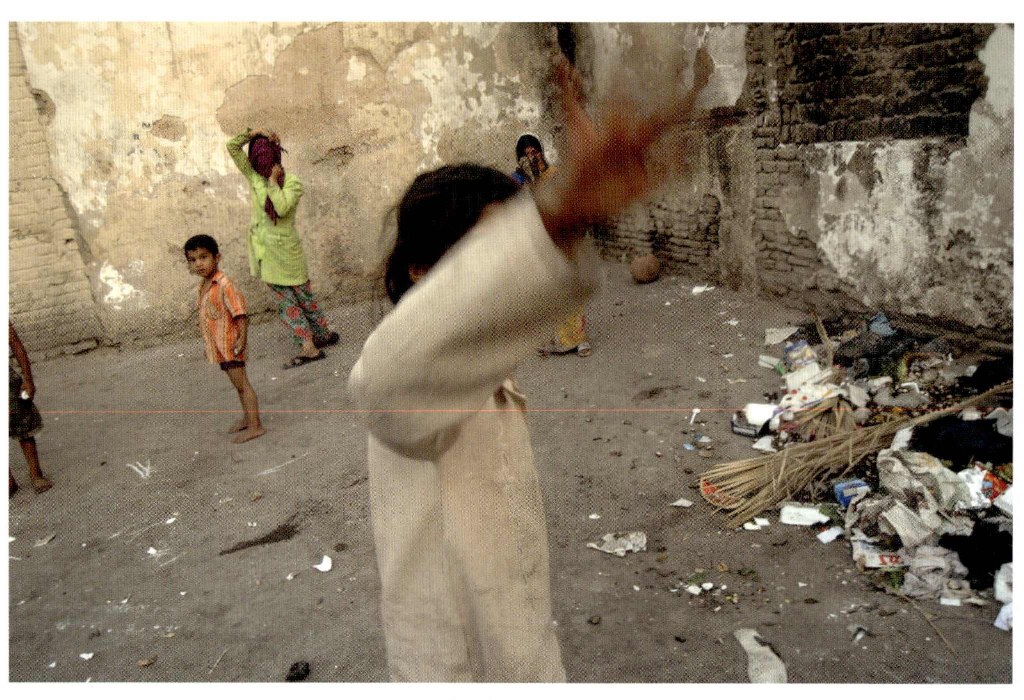

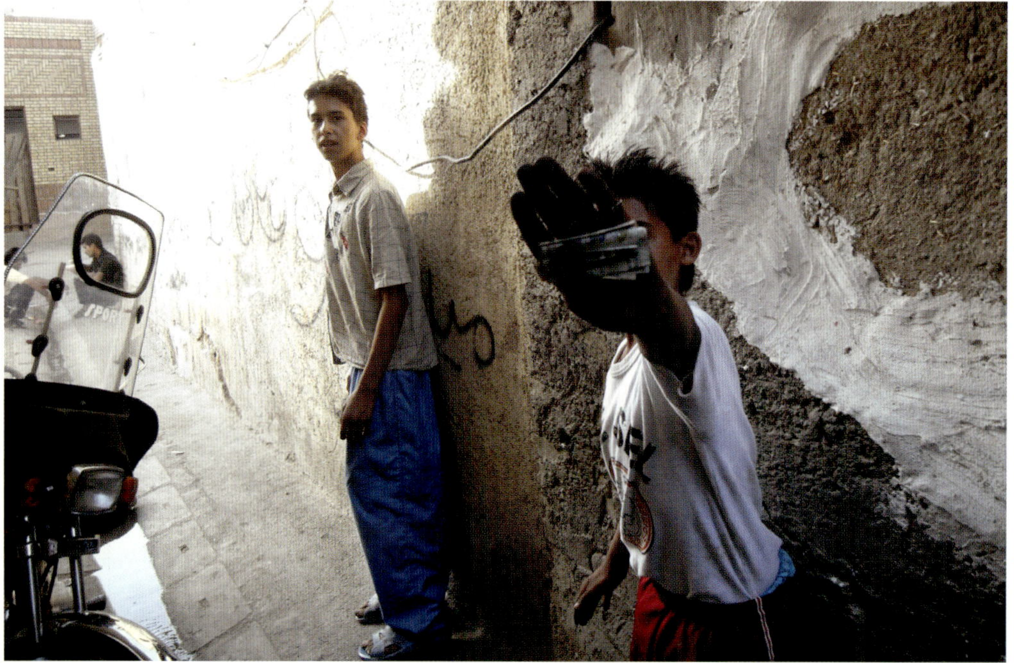

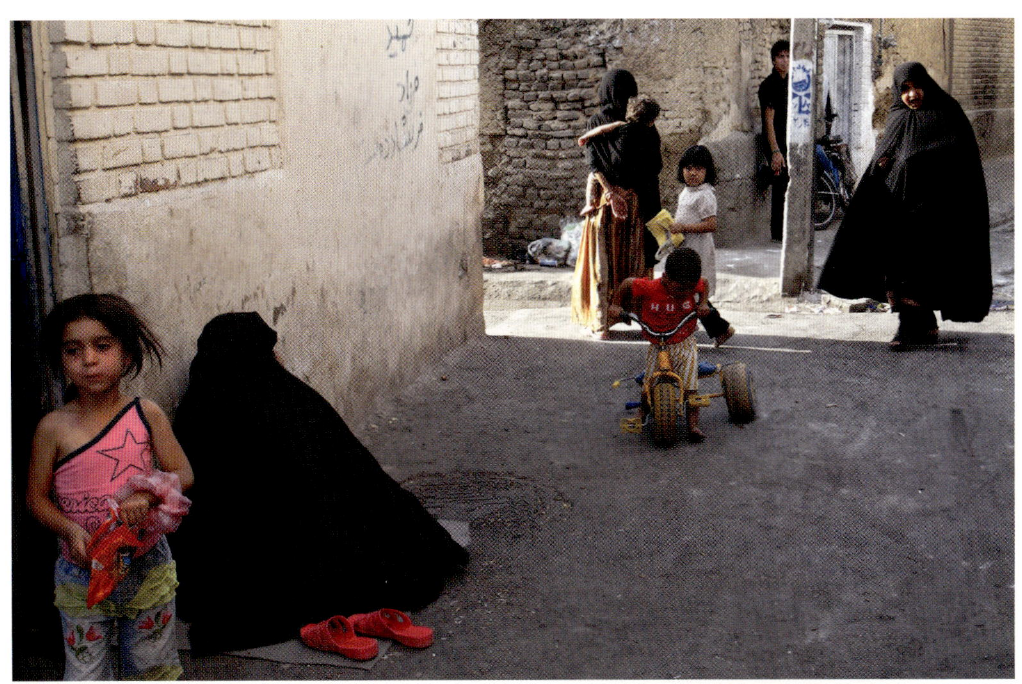

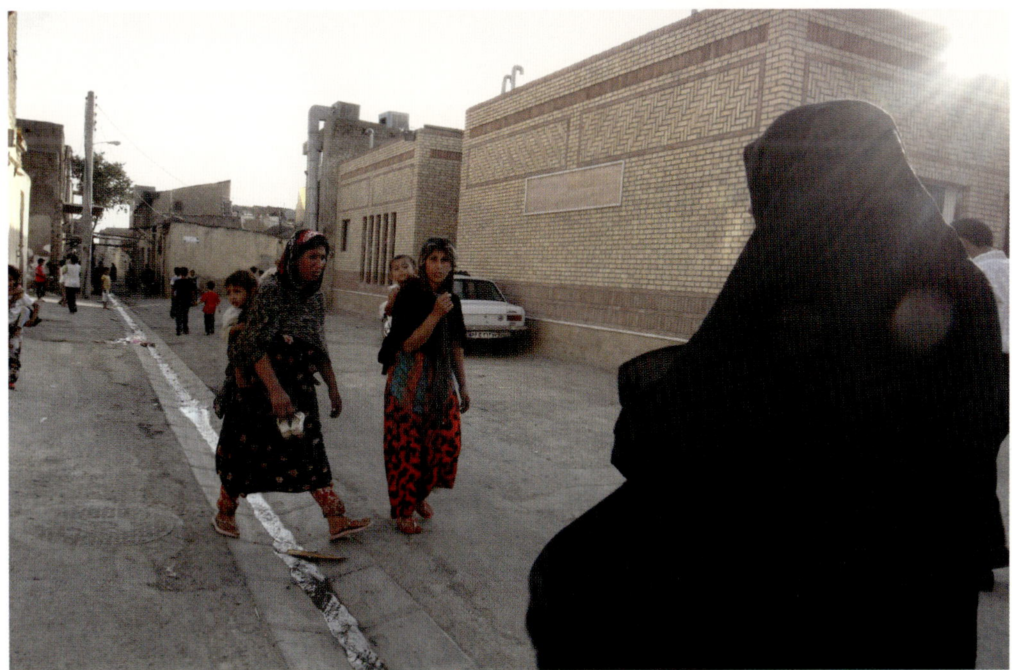

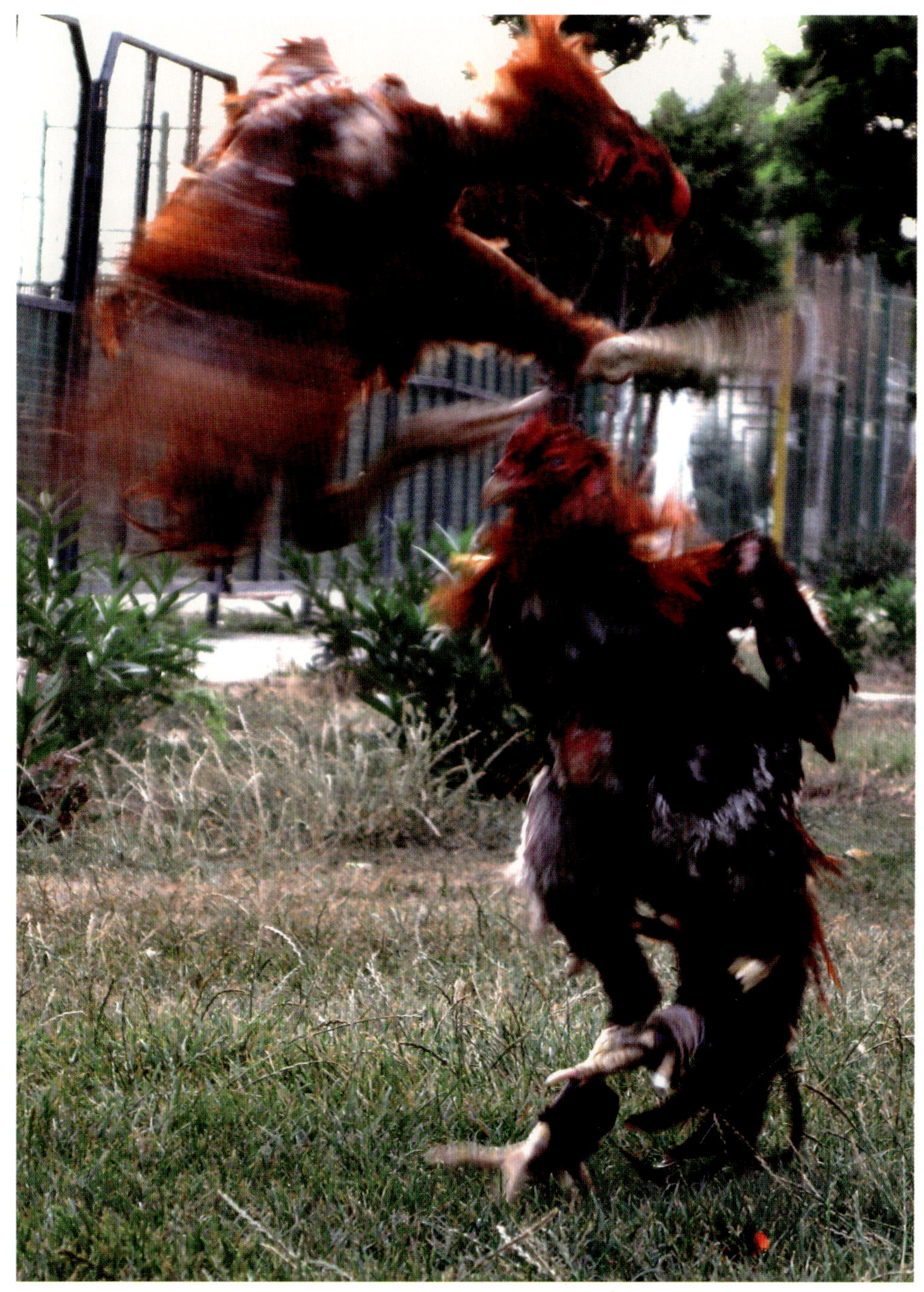

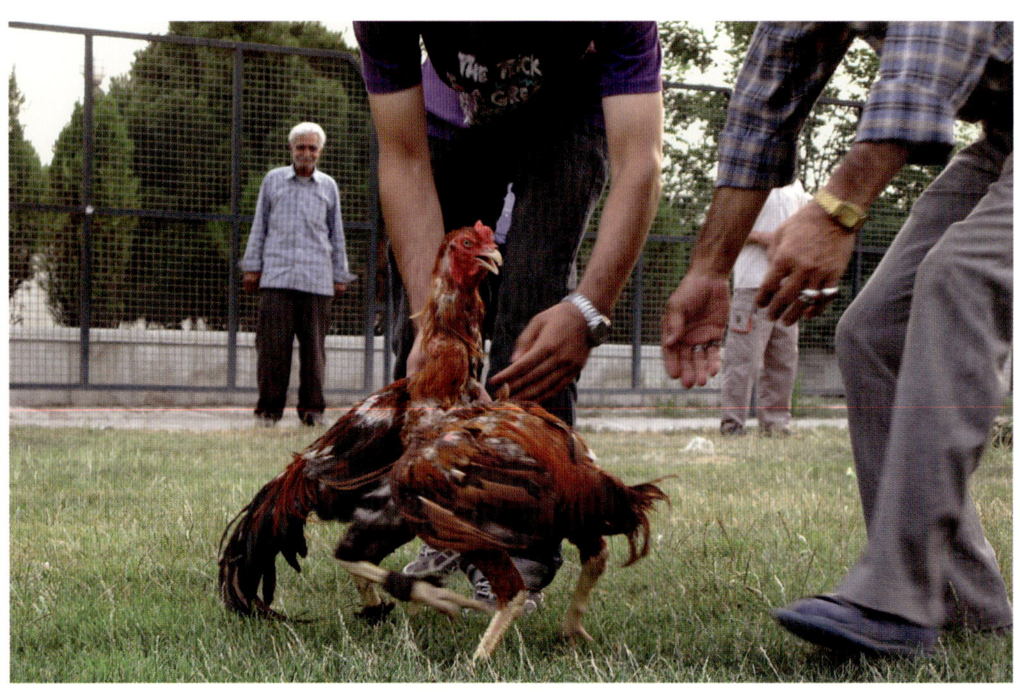

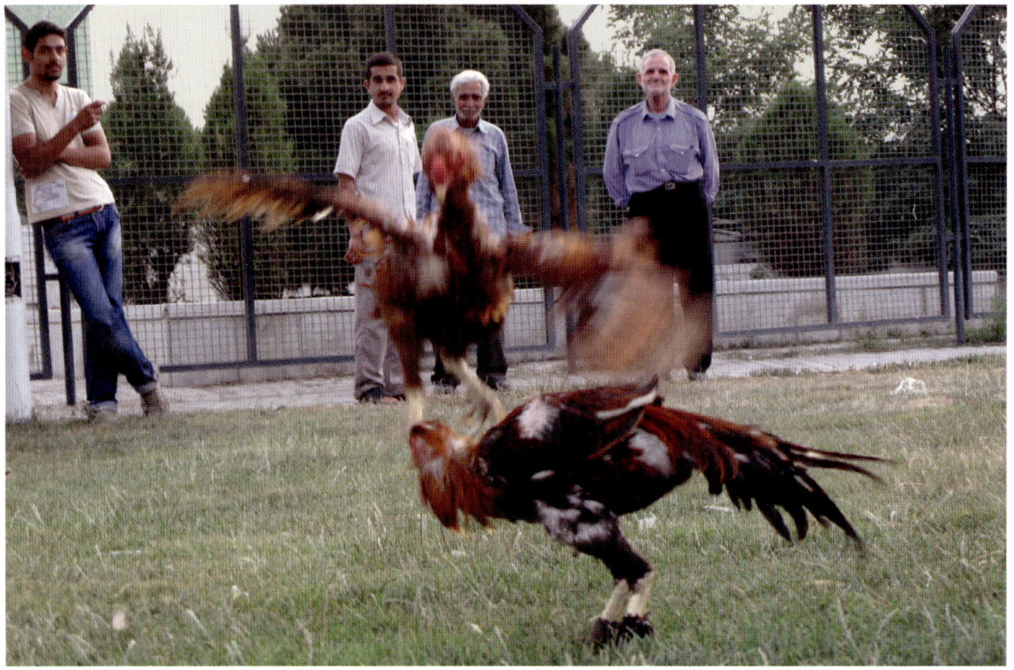

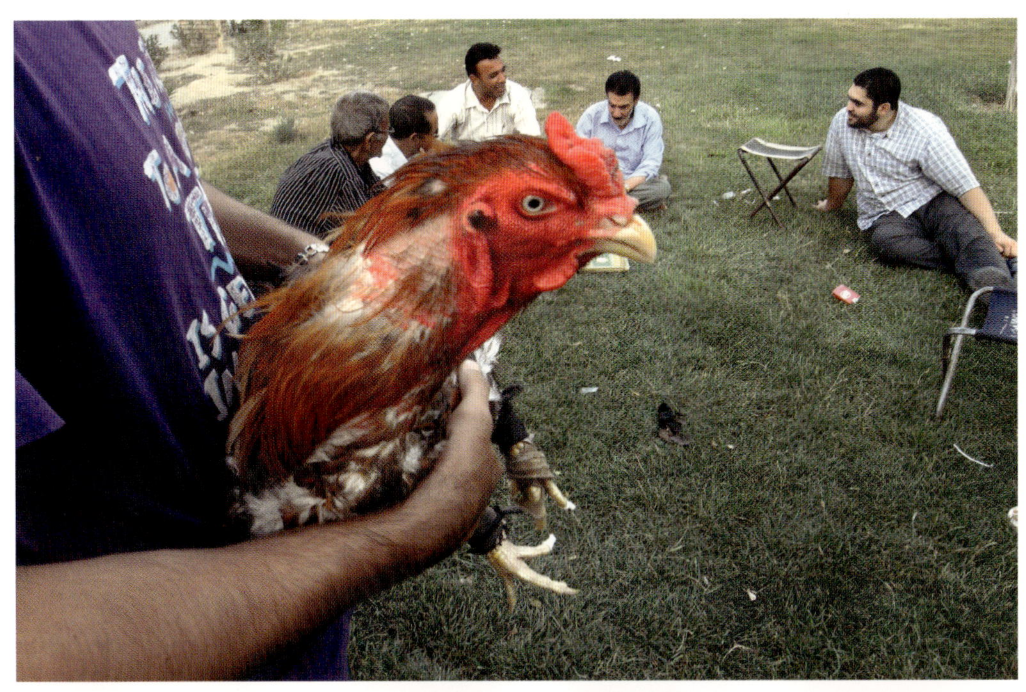

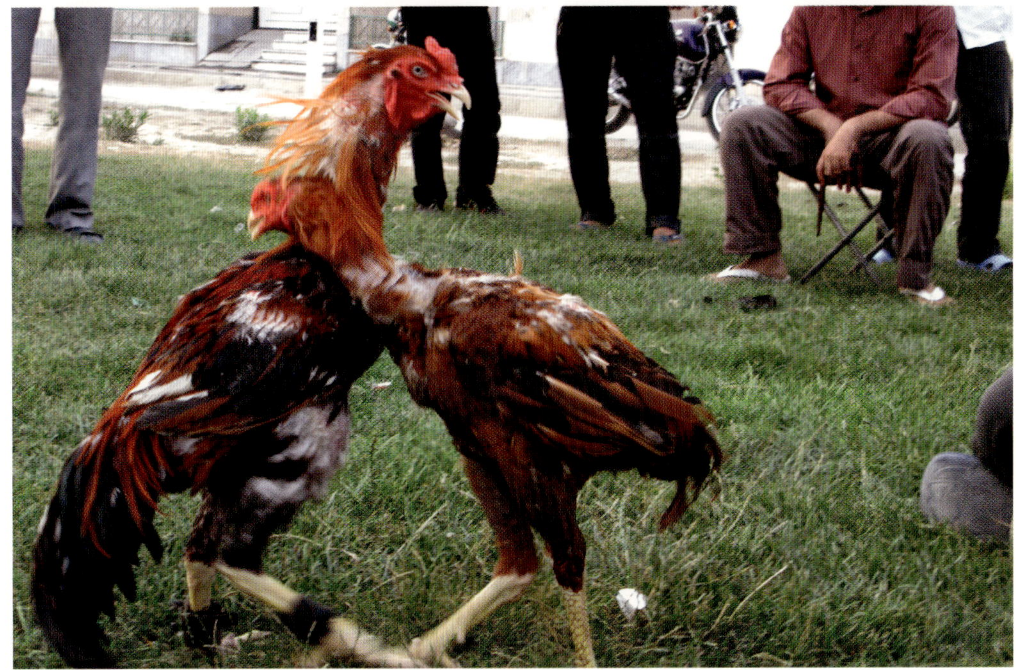

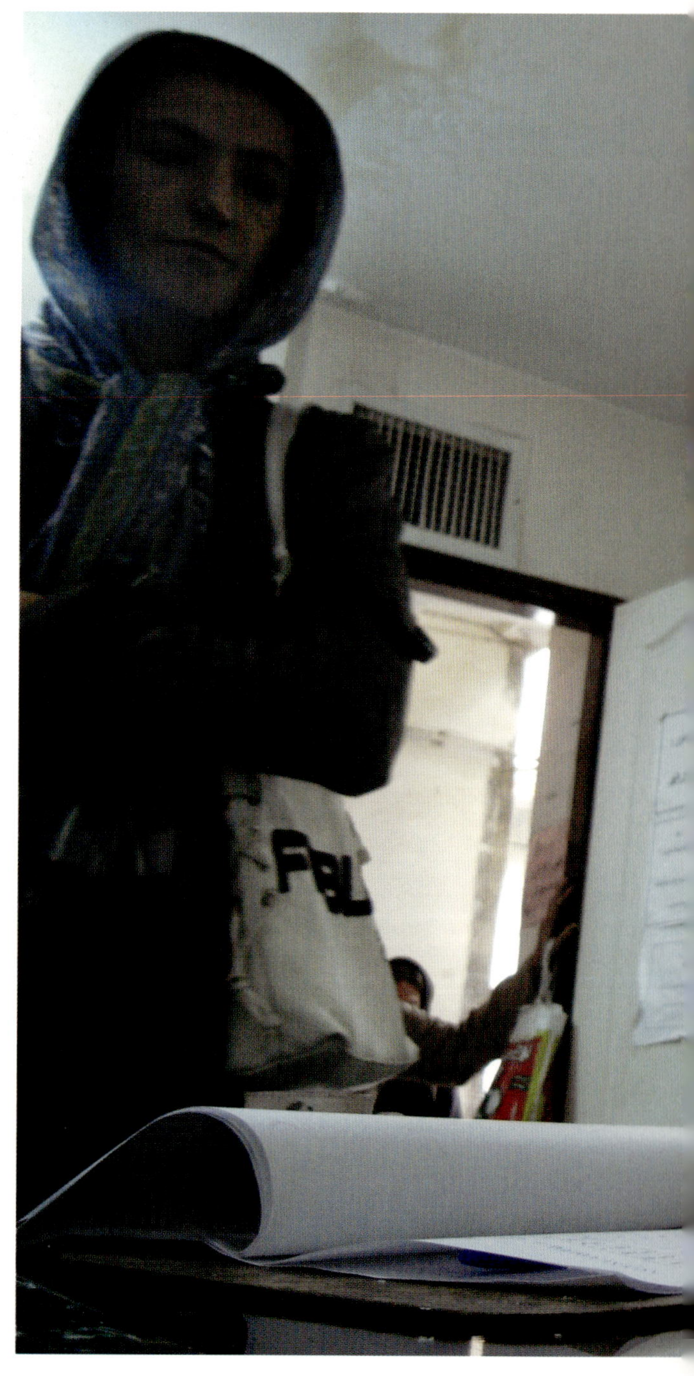

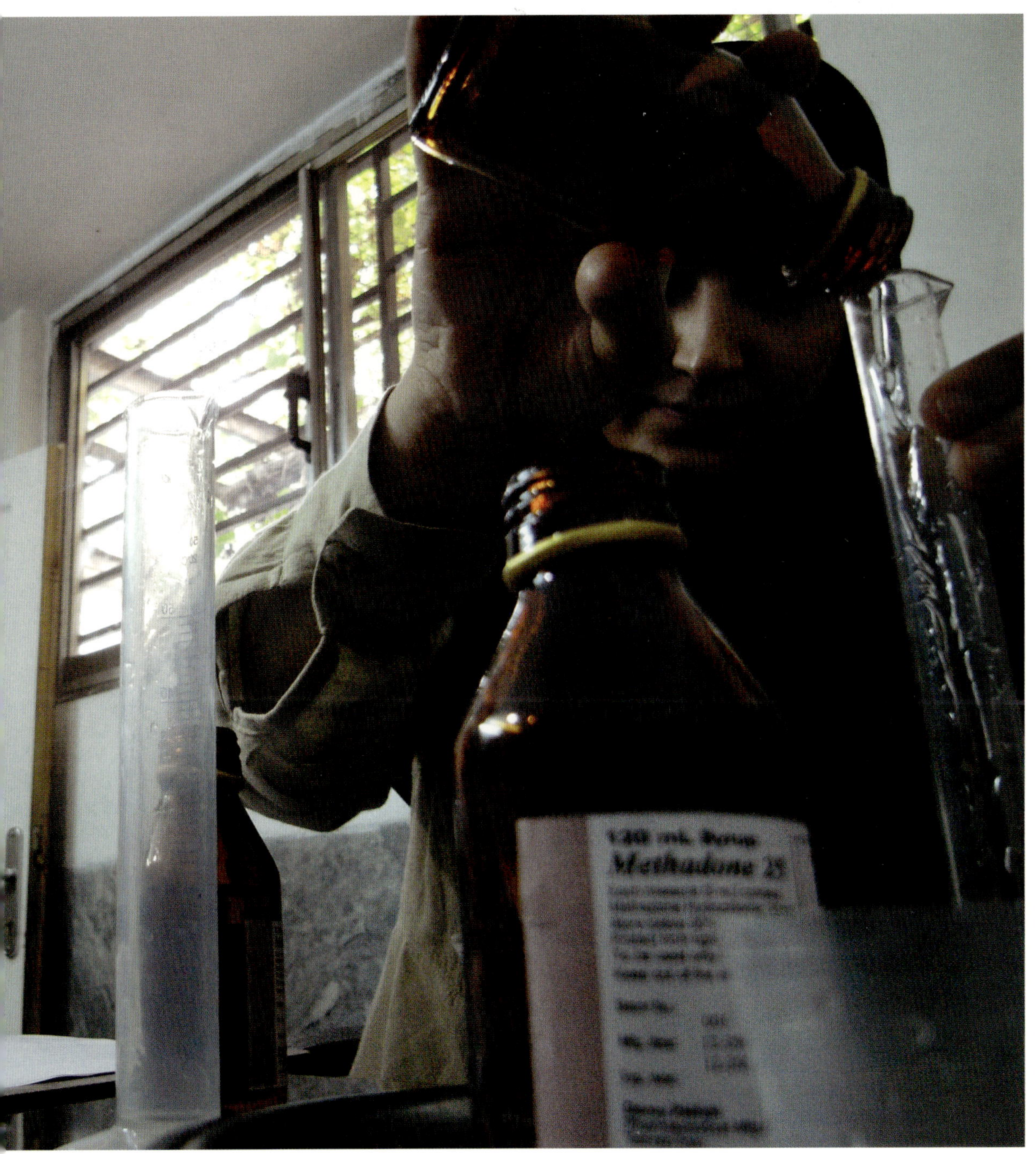
Methadone 25

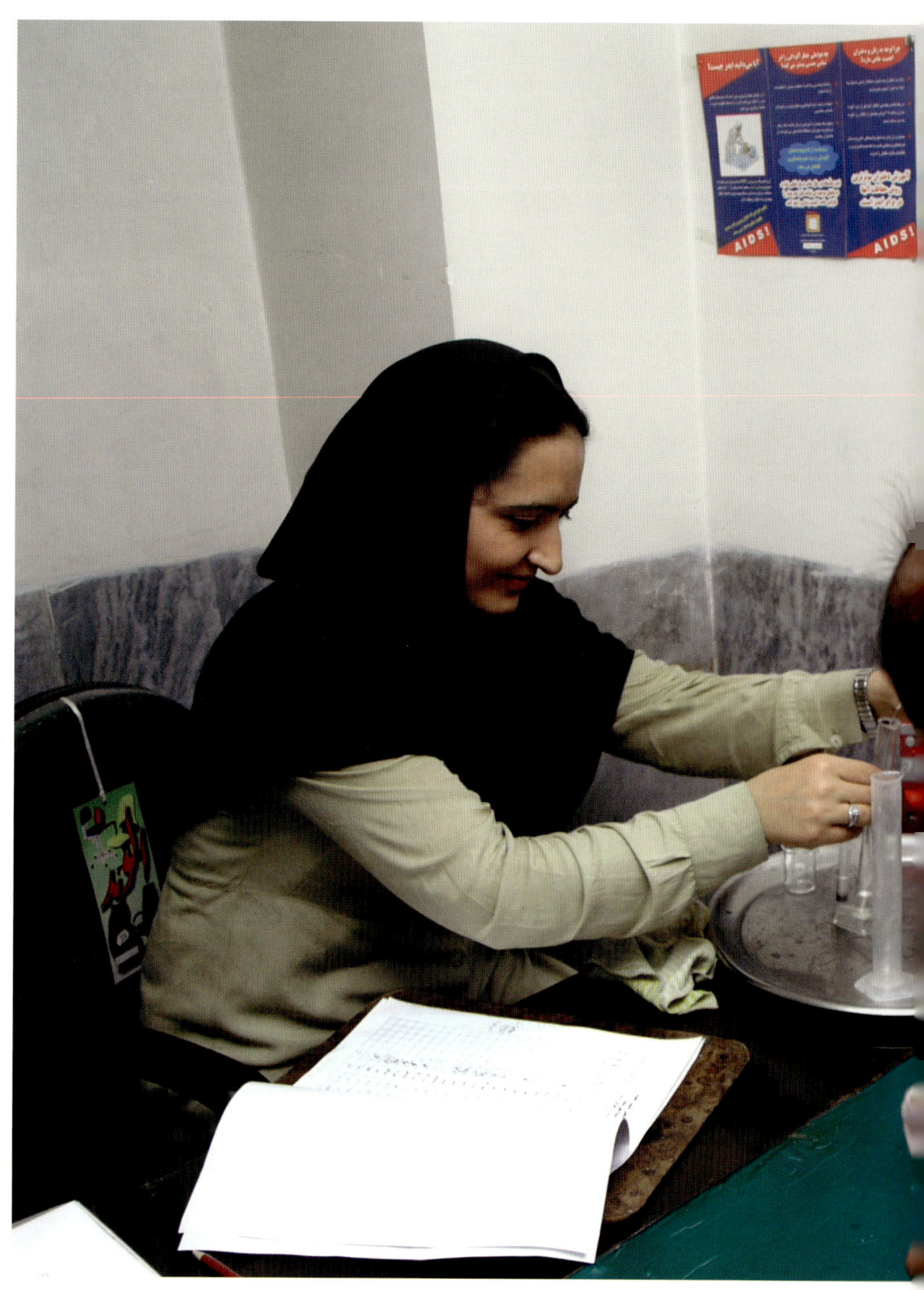
AIDS!
AIDS!

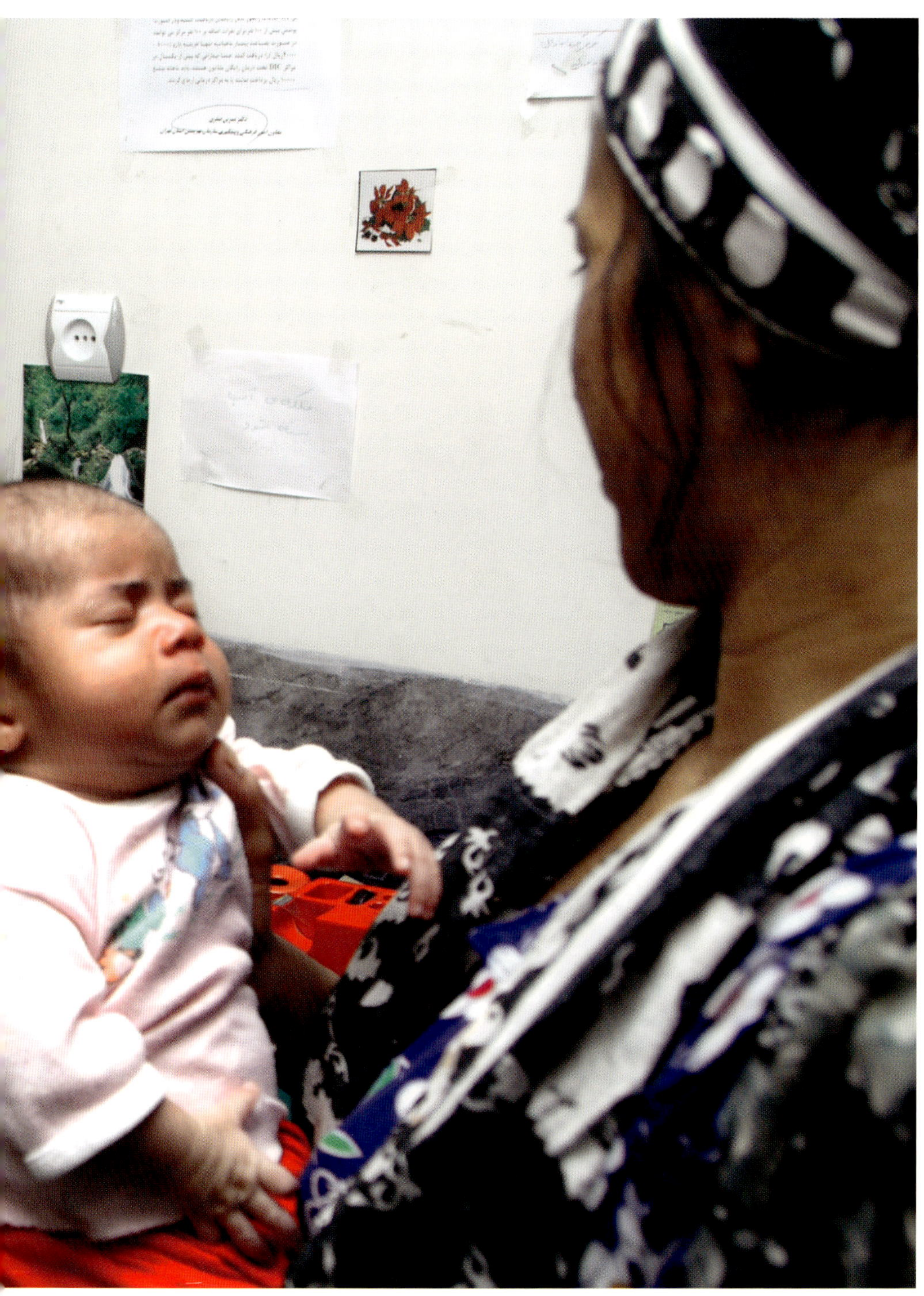

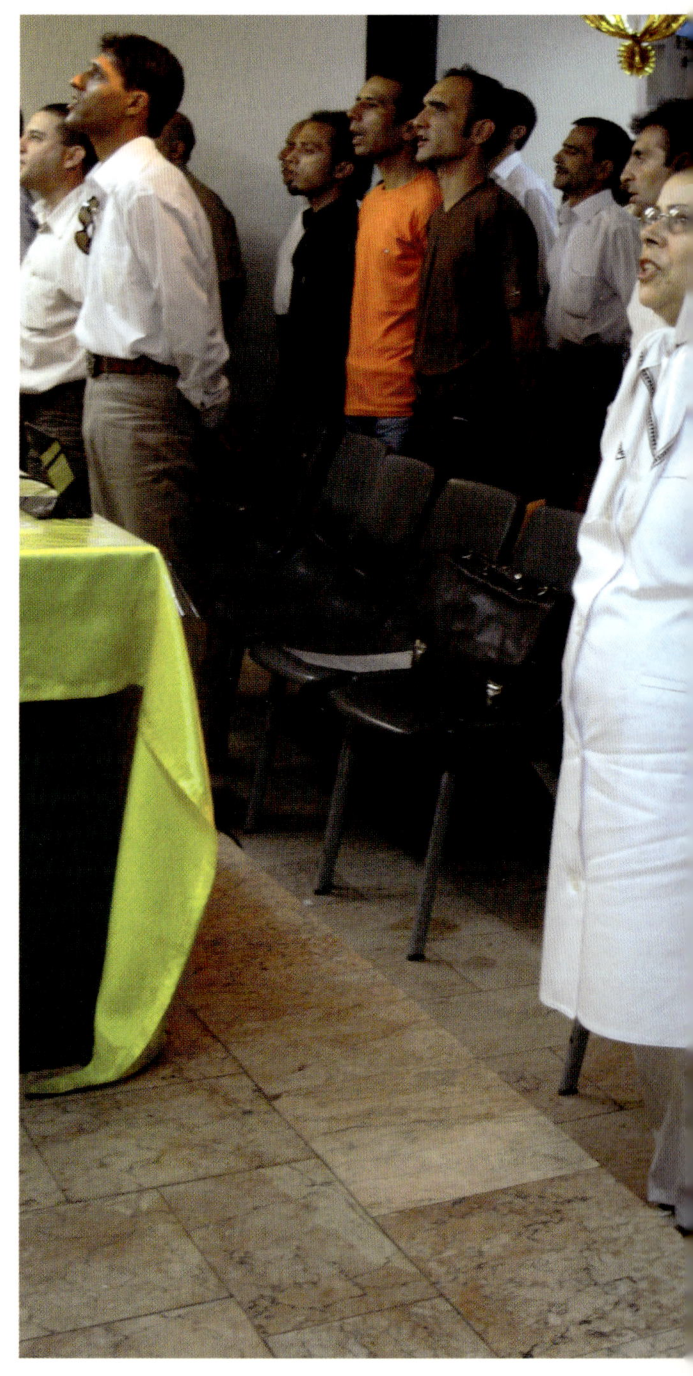

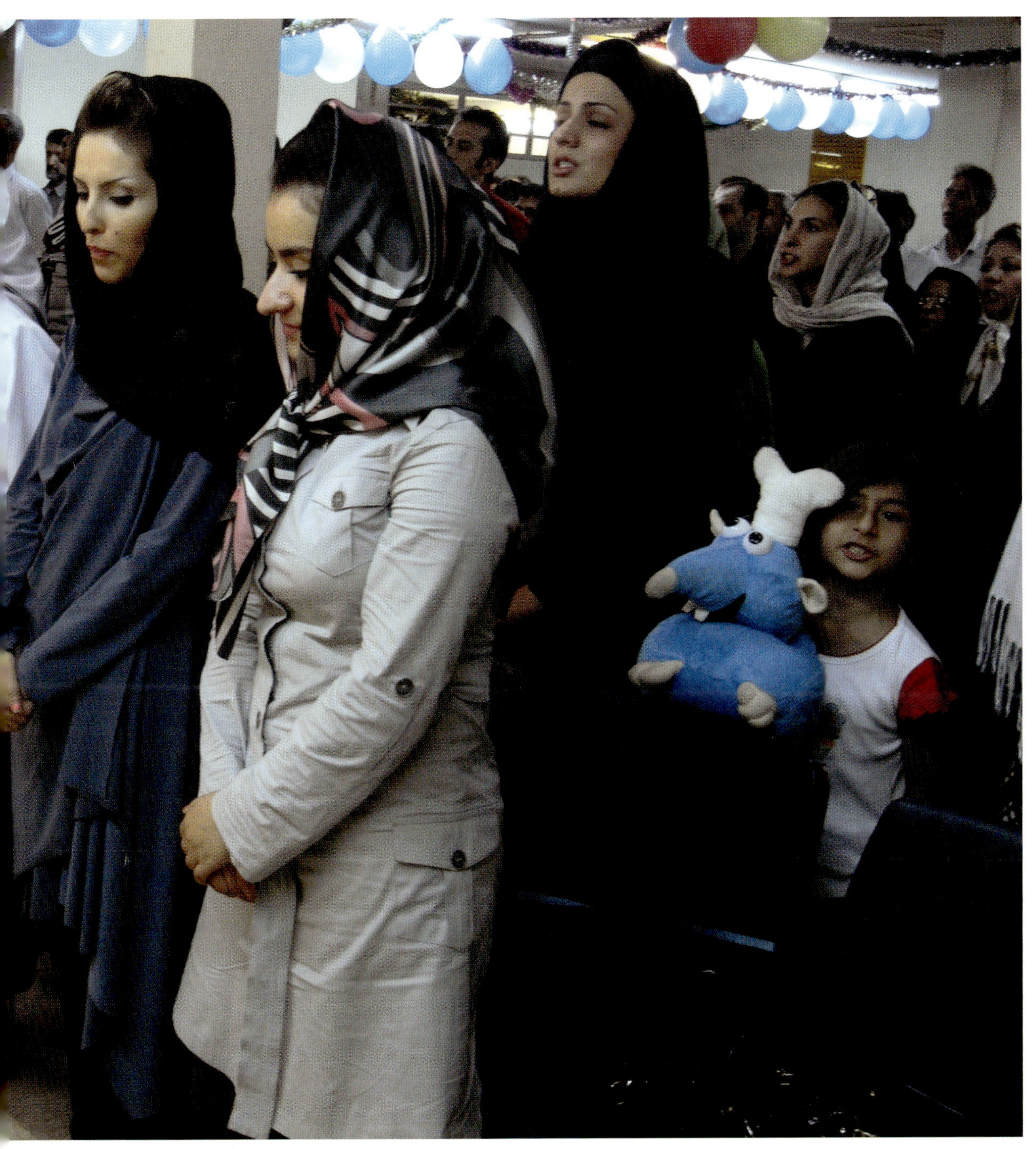

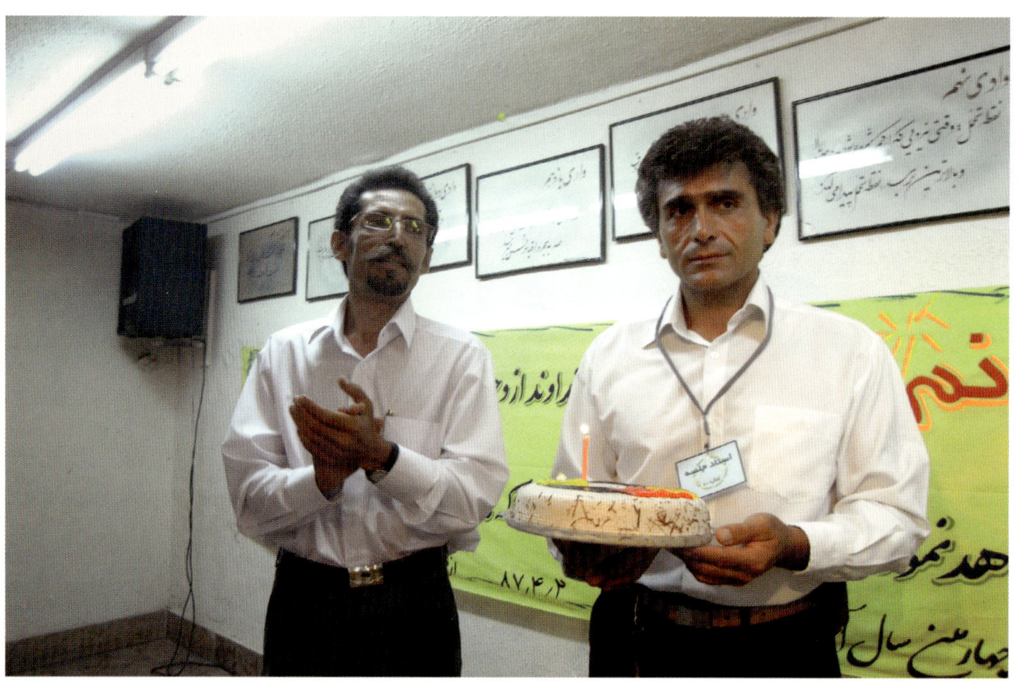

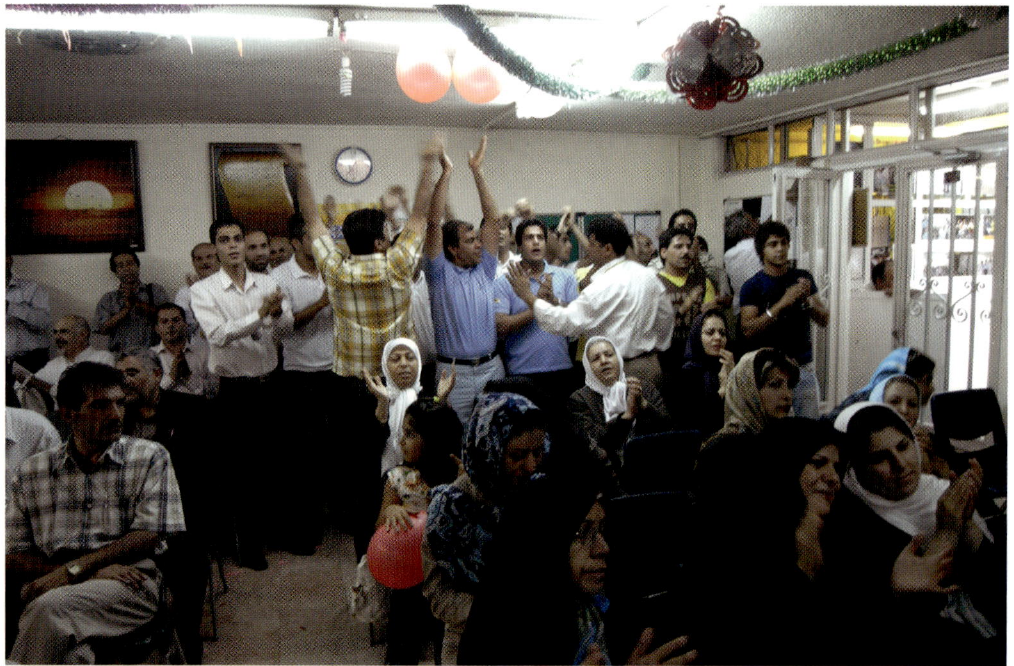

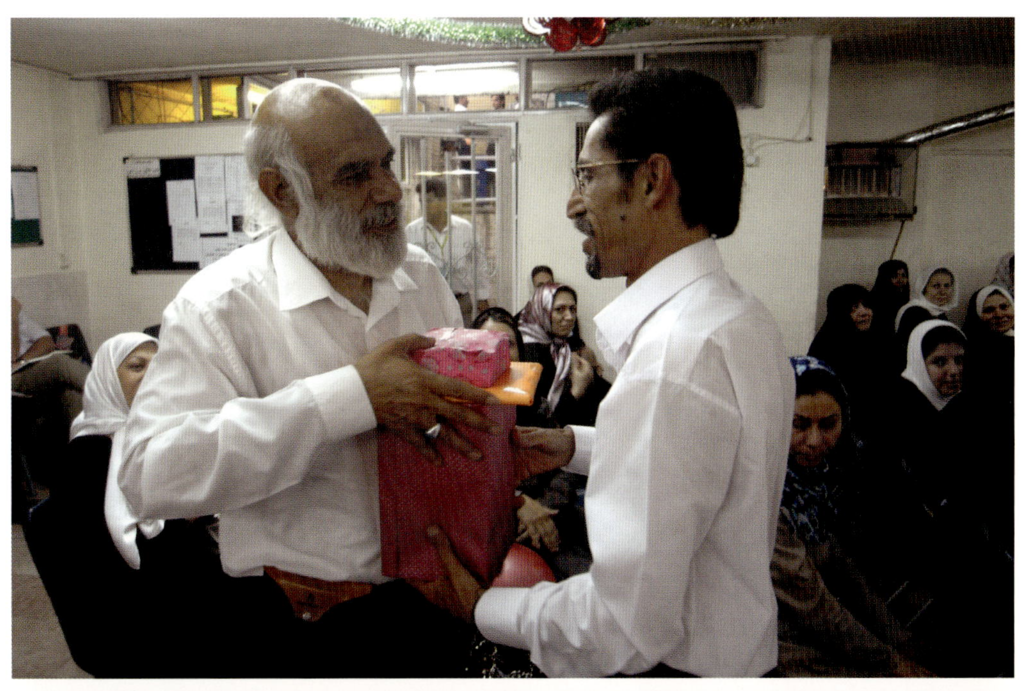

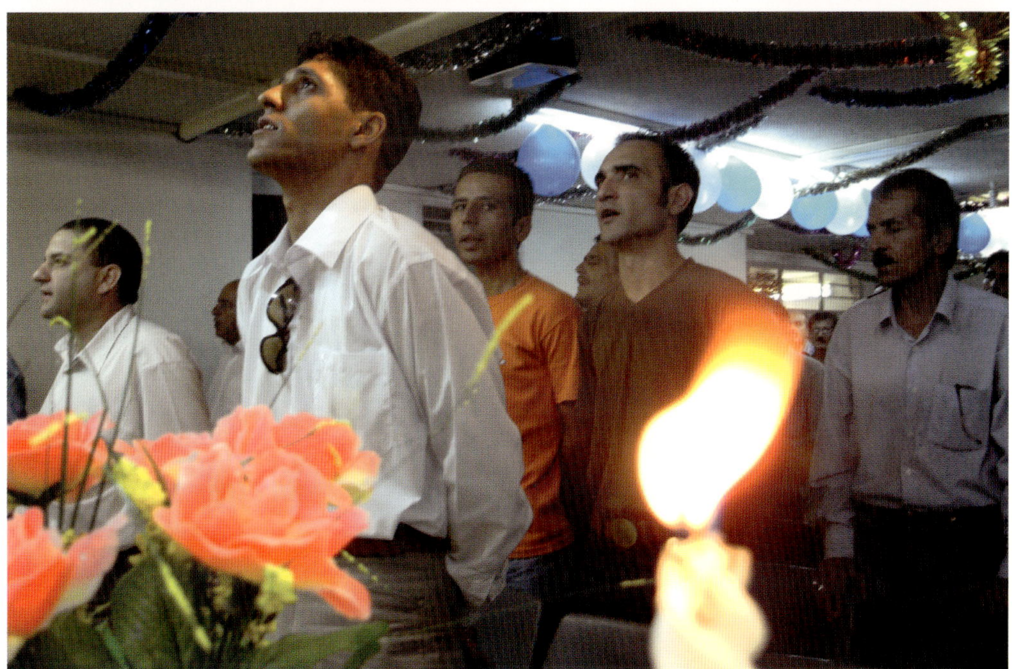

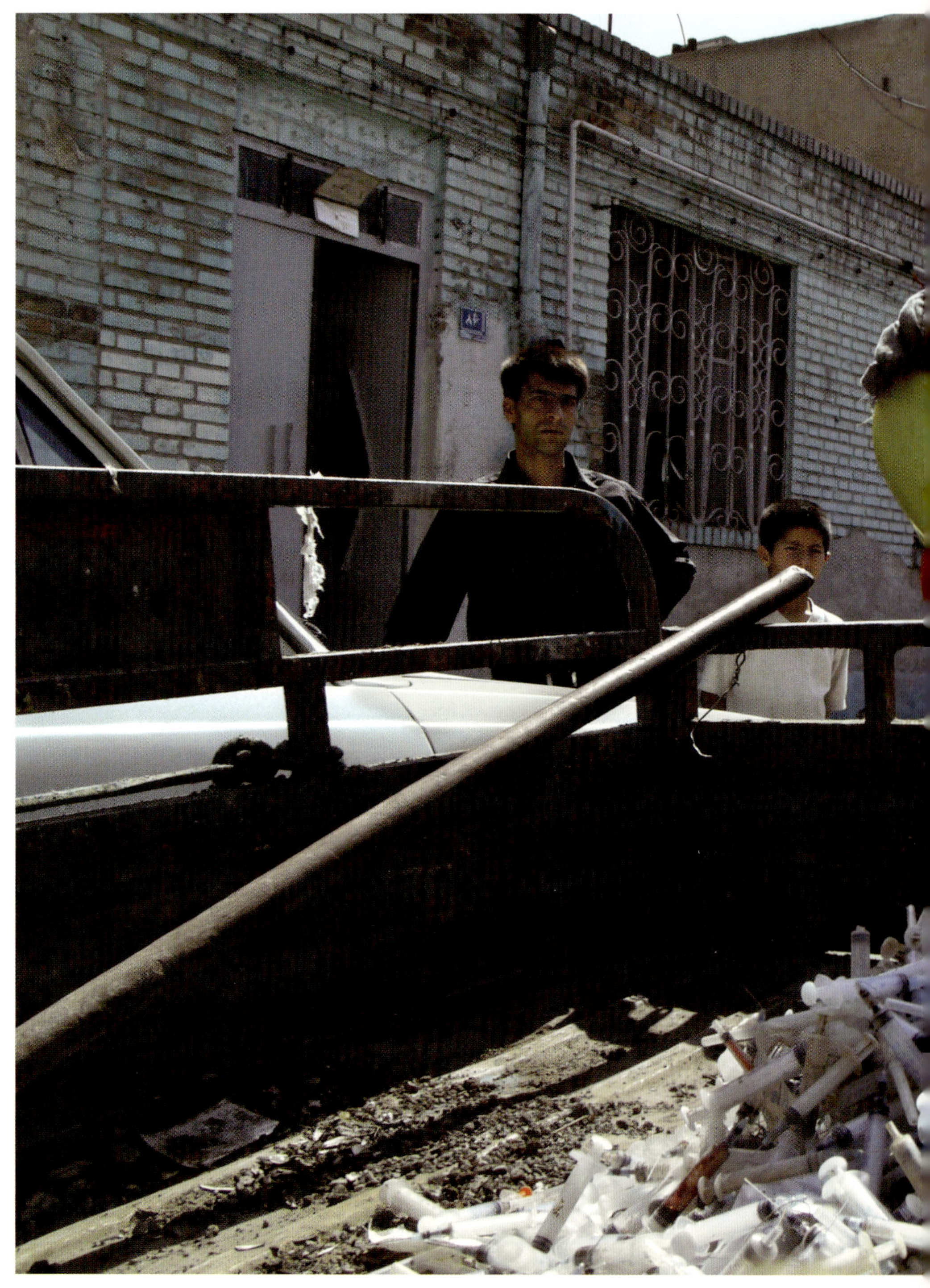

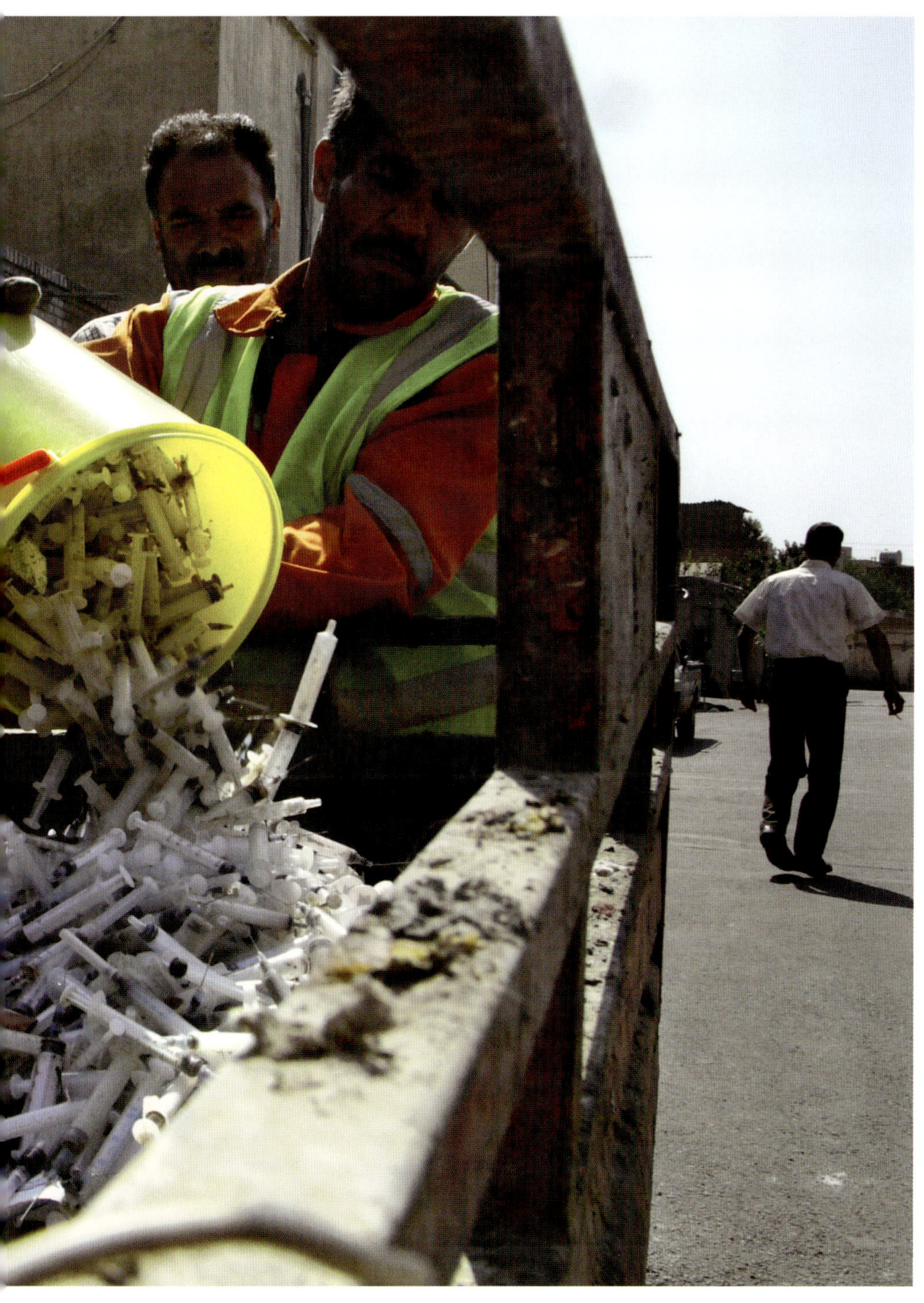

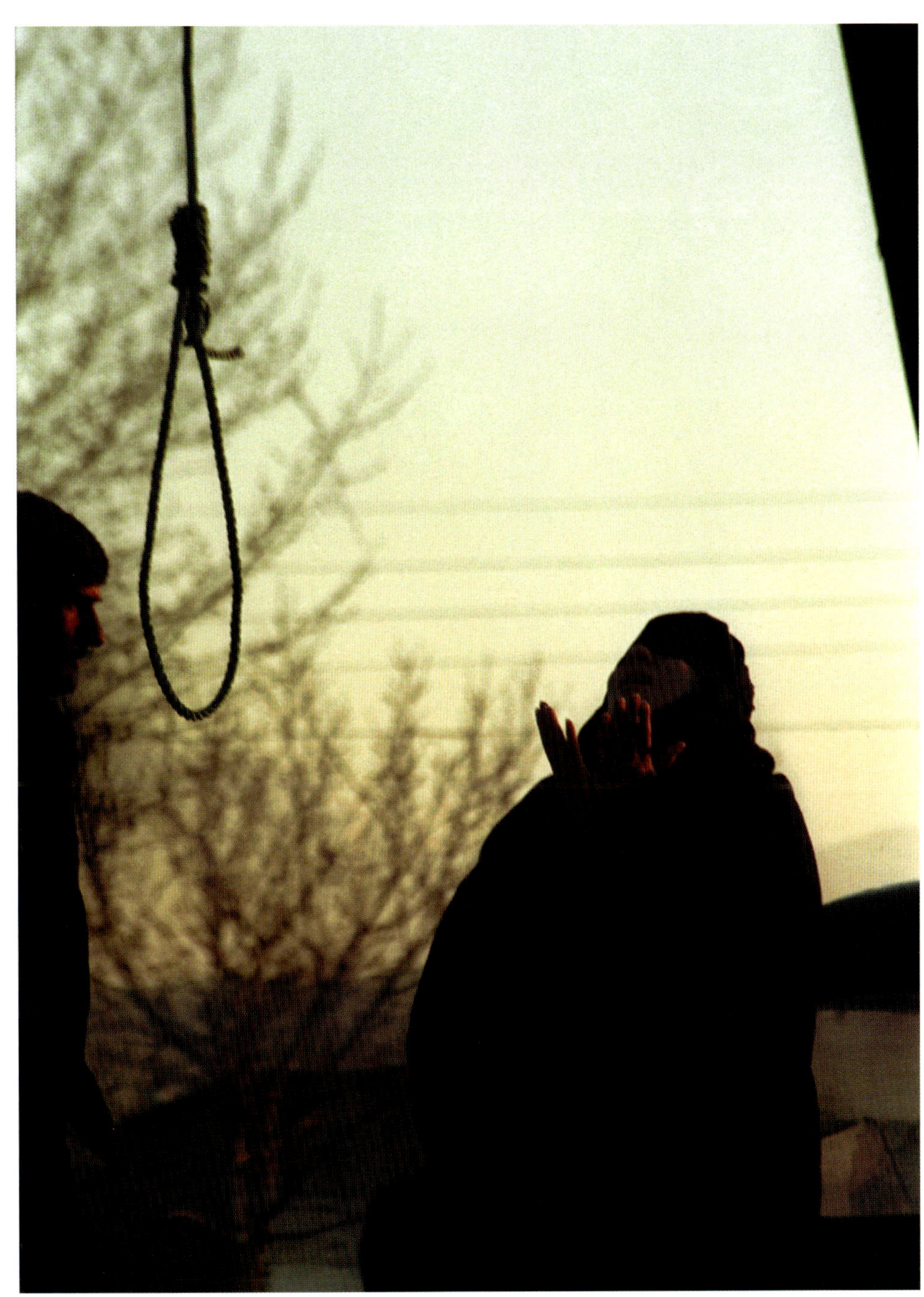

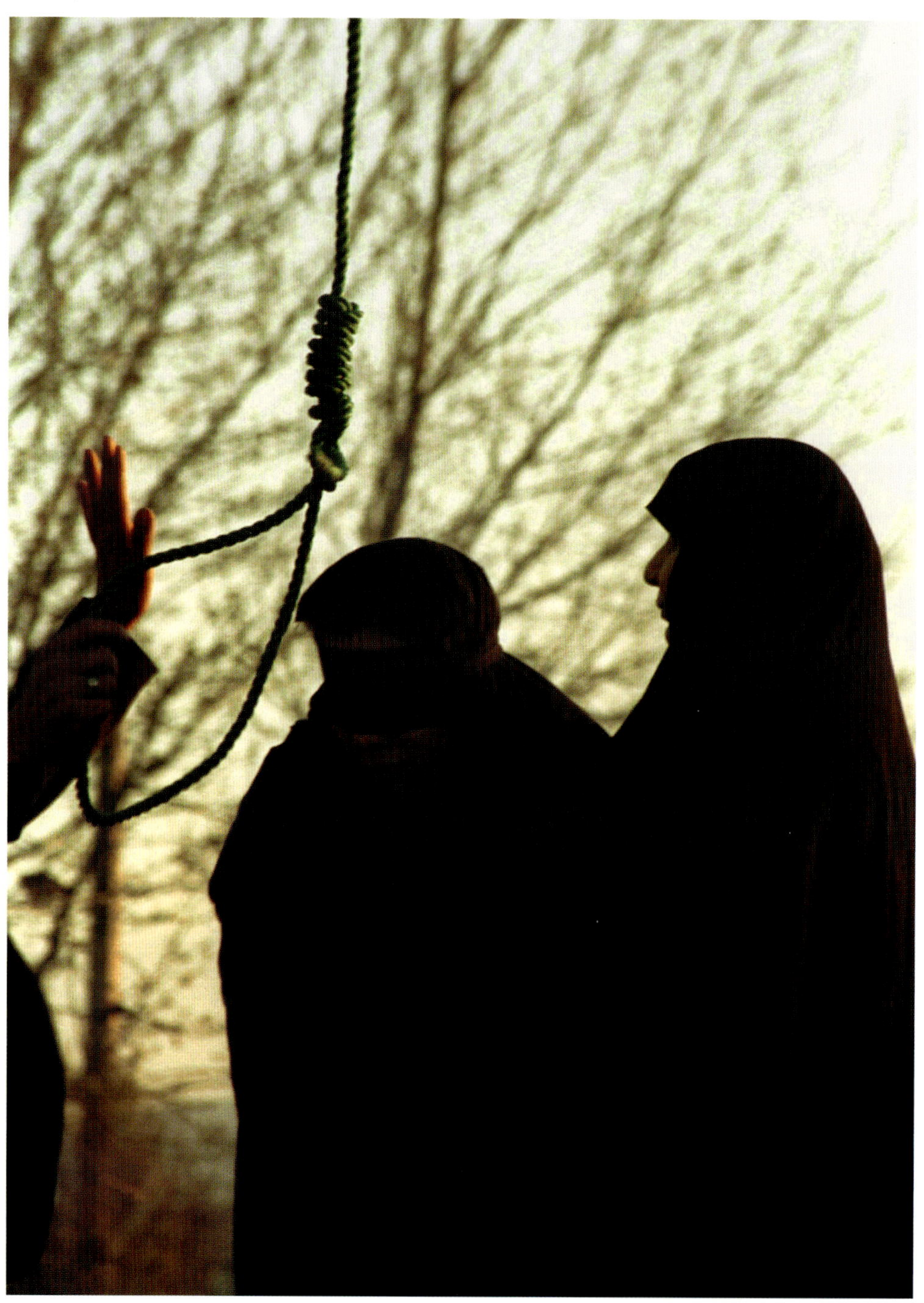

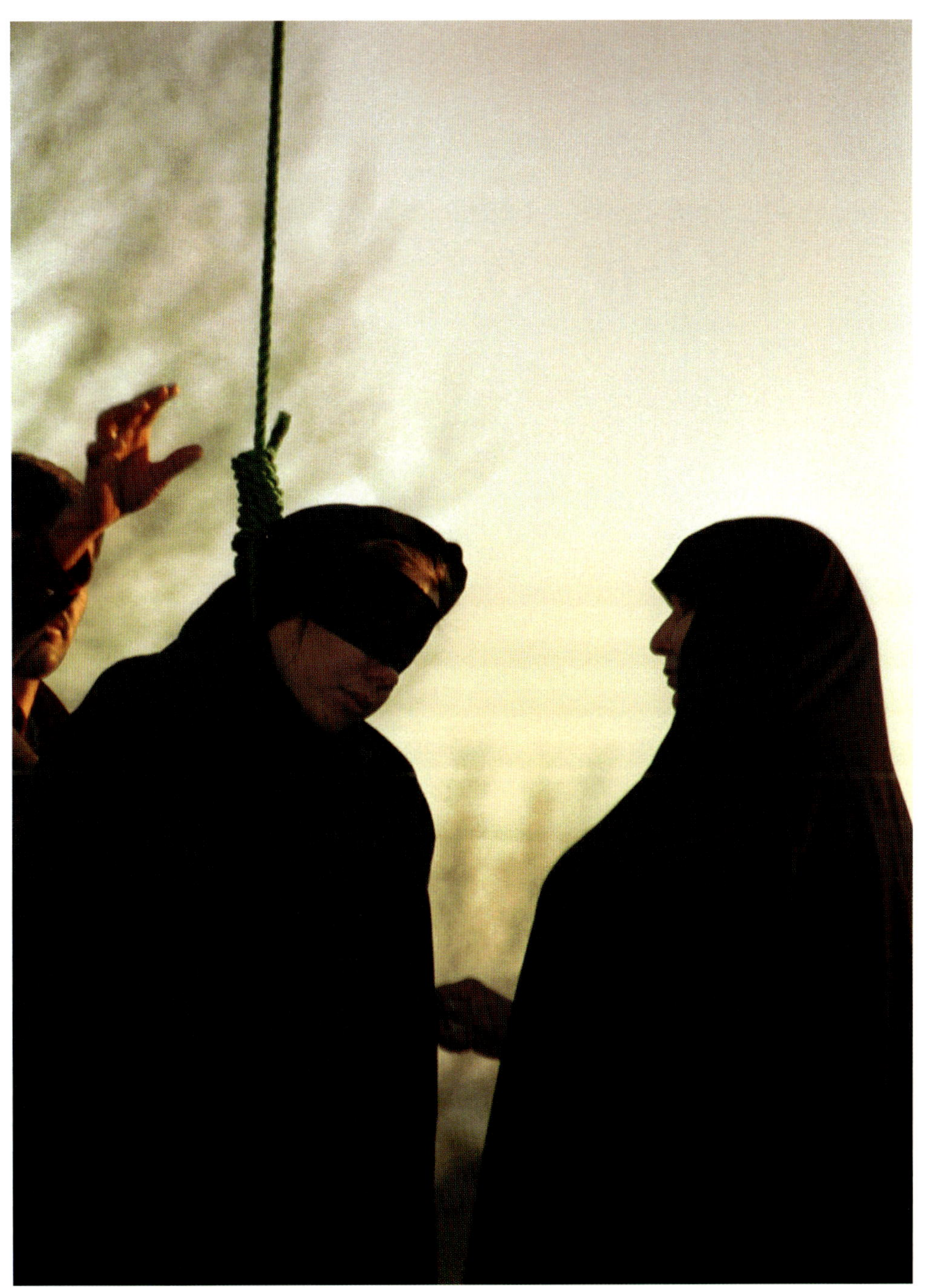

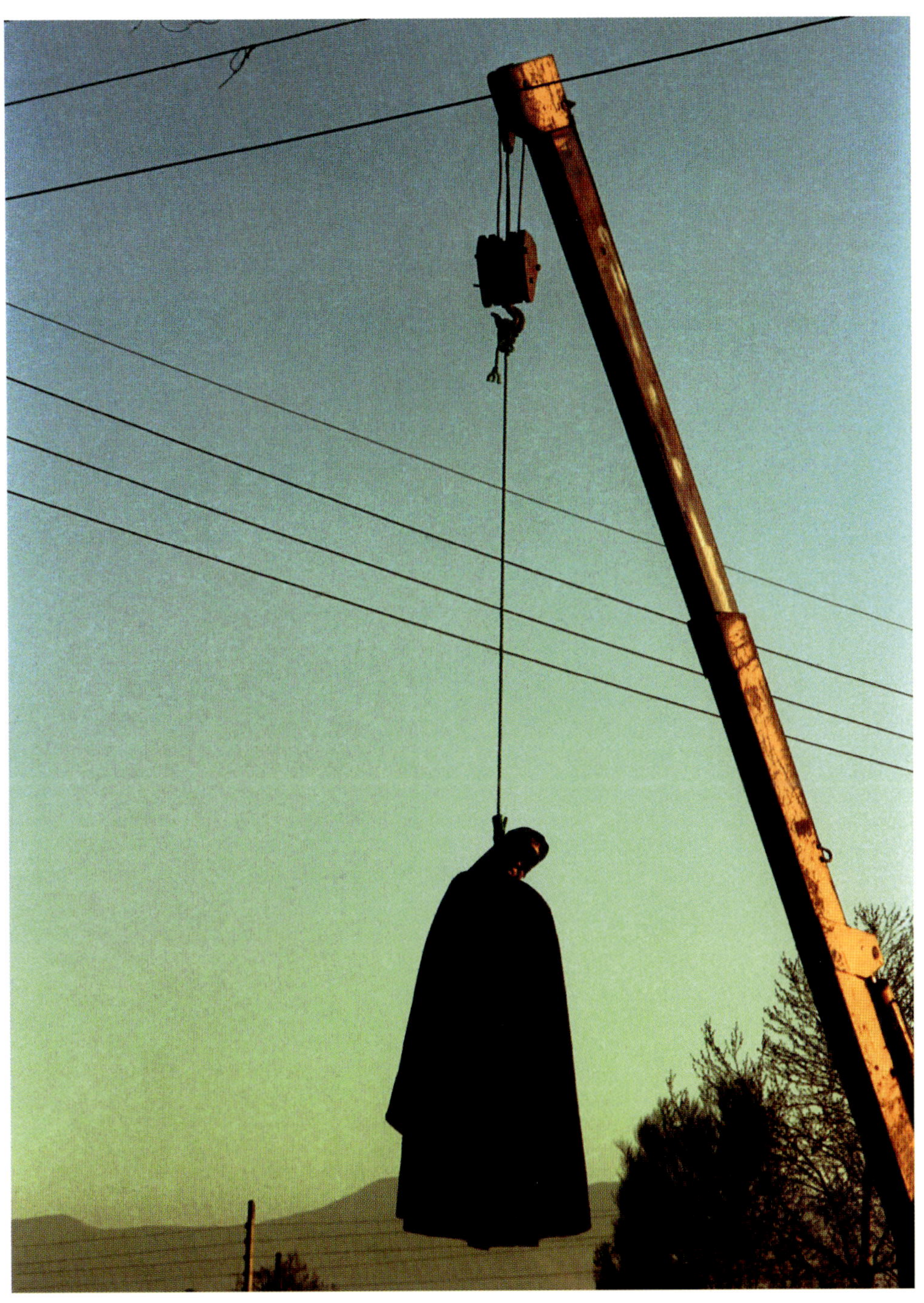

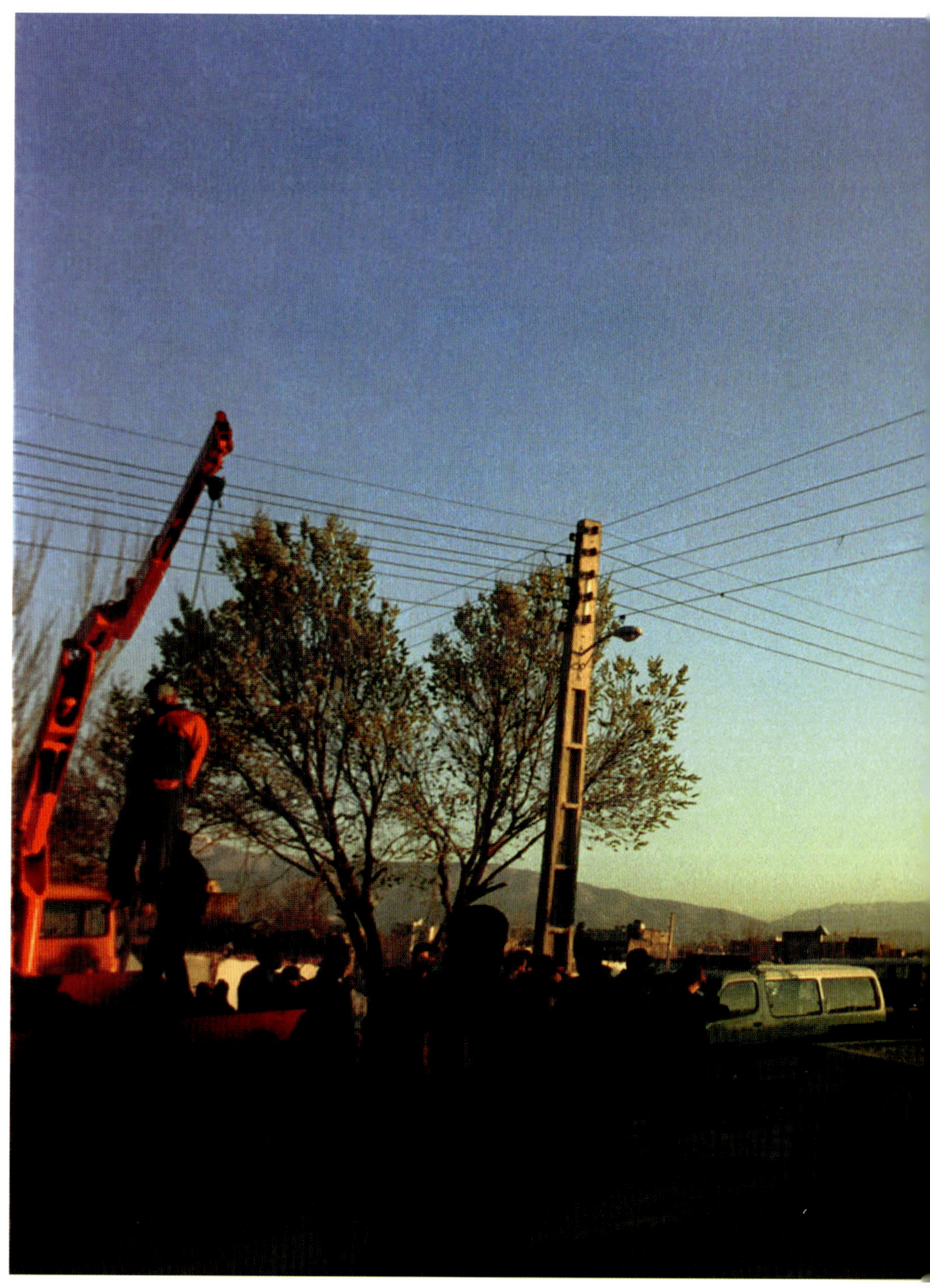

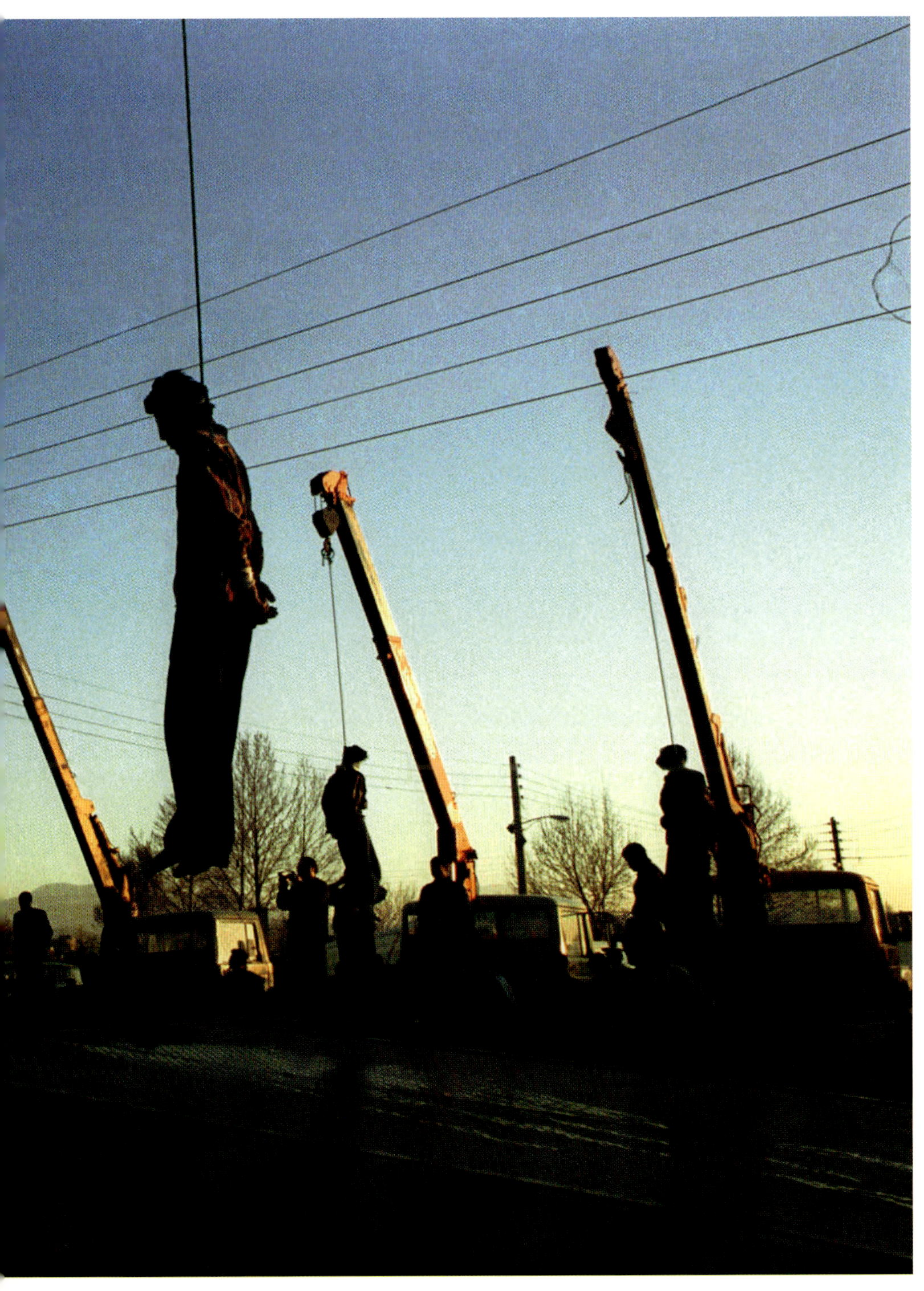

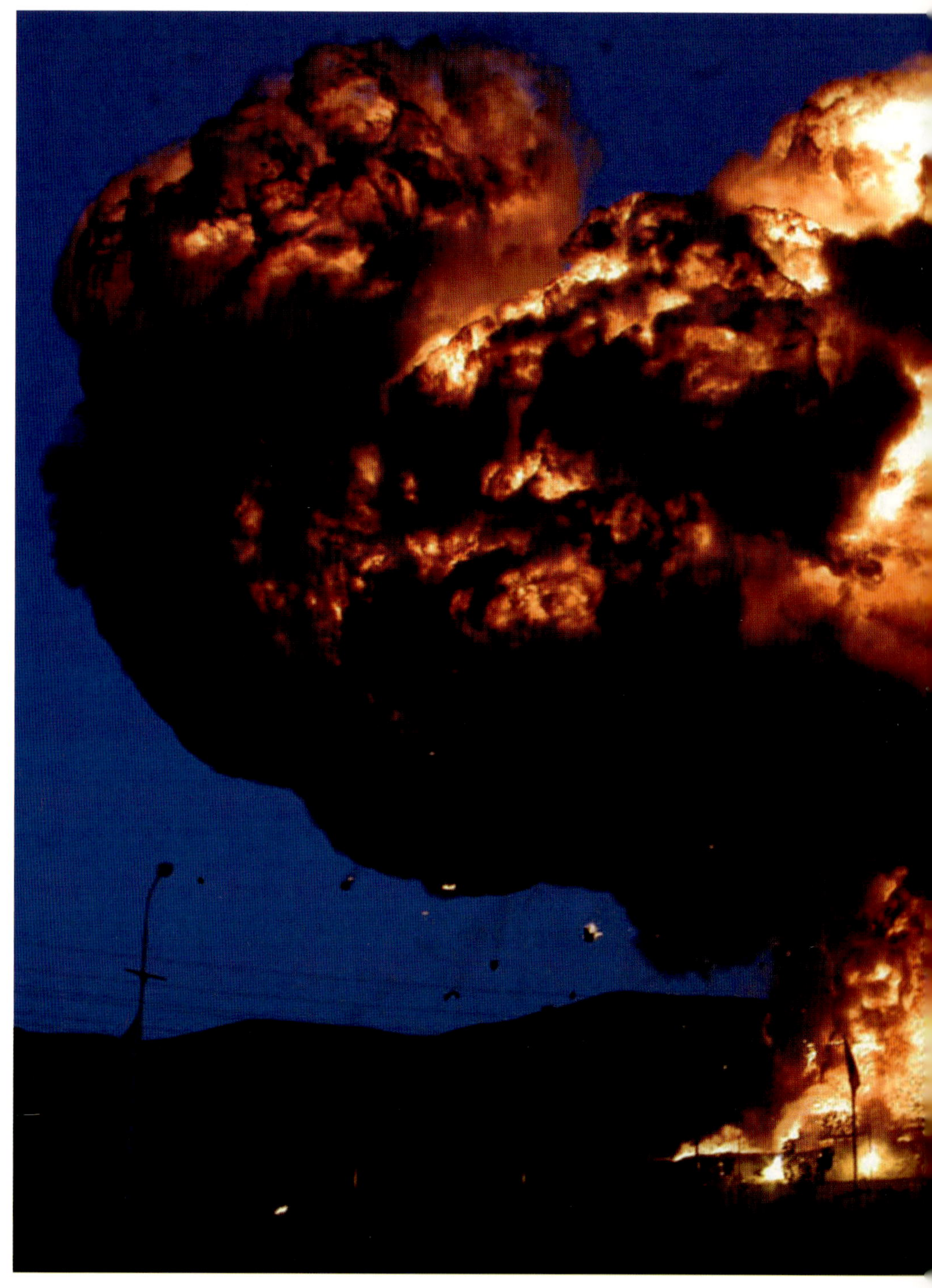

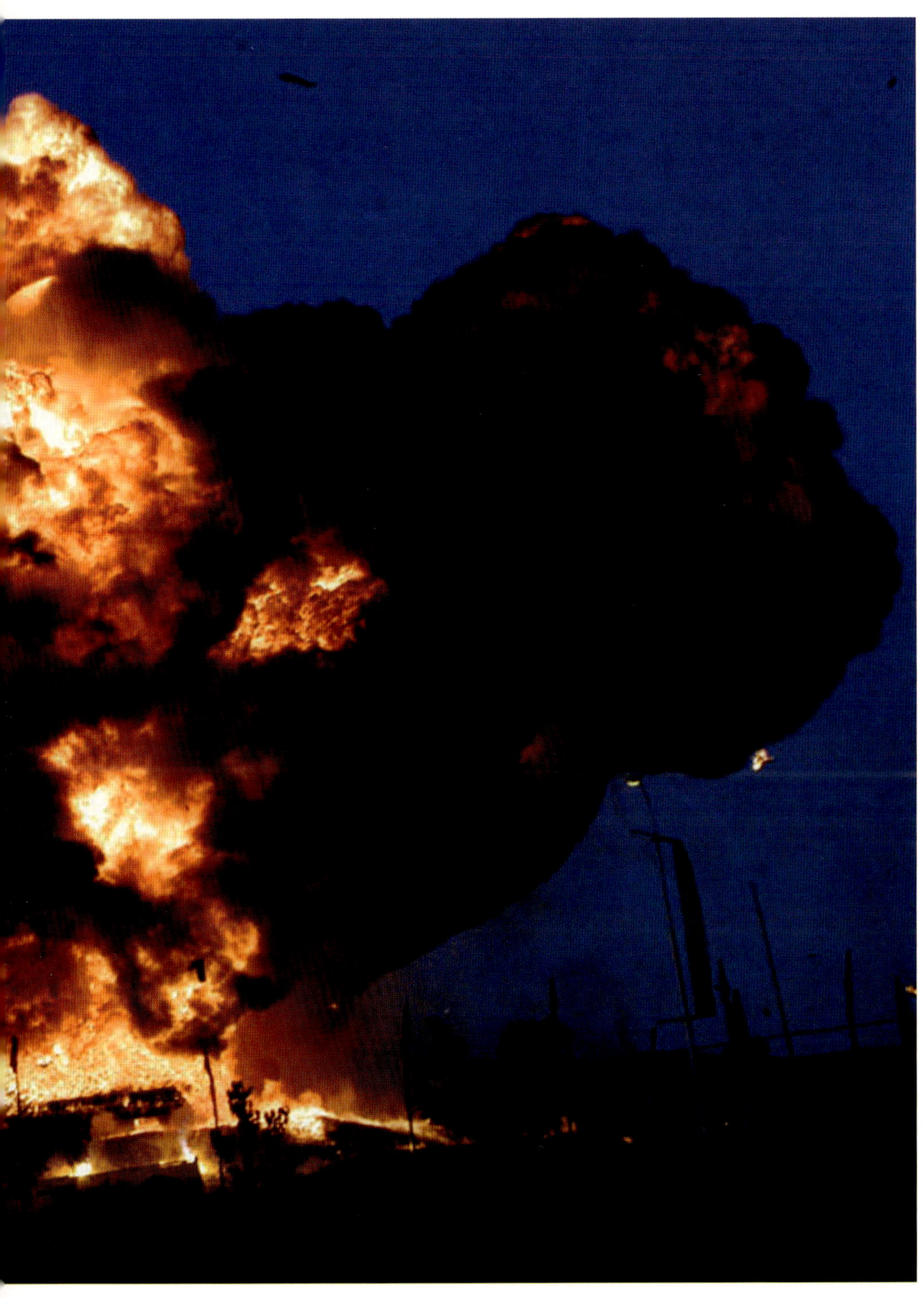

CAPTIONS

15 Hassan displaying an injury with a syringe in his arm.

16 Hassan pointing to a place where he usually buys crack.

17 Mohsen preparing the syringe again after he can't inject in his leg. His leg is bleeding.

18 *Top:* An old man "sterilizing" a needle with his saliva.
Bottom: Two addicts, high after injecting crack in a park.

19 A young boy injecting his friend with crack.

20|21 Two addicts, passed-out, after getting high a park.

22|23 An addict, lying on the ground, after getting high through injecting crack.

24 An addict smoking a cigarette with a syringe in his leg.

25 A young boy injecting his friend with crack while another man watches.

26 *Top:* Hassan mixing crack and water in a syringe.
Bottom: An old man injecting a friend with crack.

27 *Top:* A young boy pouring mixed crack into the syringe of another young boy.
Bottom: A young boy injects crack while his friend watches him.

29 Mohsen collecting plastic recyclables in a street in Tehran.

30 *Top:* Walking in a street in Tehran while a family on a motorbike passes by.
Bottom: Collecting plastic recyclables in a street in Tehran.

31 *Top:* Smoking a cigarette in a shop where he sells the plastic he collects.
Bottom: Collecting plastic recyclables in a street in Tehran.

32
33 Mohsen and Reza sitting together for a picture.

34 Fereshteh looking in a mirror in her house.

35 Fereshteh applying makeup.

36 *Top:* Smoking crack in her house.
Bottom: Her mother, and two of their friends smoking crack in their house.

37 *Top:* Looking in the mirror.
Bottom: Applying eyeliner.

38
39 Fereshteh donning a full hijab before leaving the house.

40 *Top:* Nastaran, Fereshteh's sister in law, smoking a cigarette in her house.
Bottom: Nastaran smoking crack in her house.

41 Nastaran smoking methamphetamine in her house.

43 Nastaran putting on a chador before going outside after smoking crack and meth.

44 *Top:* Shahnaz smoking crack in her house.
Bottom: Shahnaz smoking a cigarette in her house.

45 Shahnaz walking down a street in her neighborhood.

46
47 A man resting in a park after injecting crack.

49 A variety of tattoos belonging to addicts.

51 A man passed-out in a park after injecting crack.

52 A man crying while high on crack.

53 A man nodding out in a park after injecting crack.

54
55 Two men, high after using crack in a park.

56
57 One crack addict lighting the cigarette of another crack addict, in a park.

58 *Top and bottom:* A crack addict smoking a cigarette.

59 *Top:* Three crack addicts in a park. Two of them are smoking a cigarette and the other one is sleeping after getting high.
Bottom: An addict showing off his tattoo with a syringe in his wrist.

60
61 A man lying unconscious on the ground after getting high on crack. A child on a bike watches him with curiosity.

62 A man displaying his injury while high.

63 A man high on crack with the syringe still in his foot.

64 Portraits of women high on crack.

65 Portraits of men high on crack.

66 Portraits of men high on crack.

67 A man high after using crack in a park.

68 *Top:* A man sleeping in a park after injecting crack in Tehran.
Bottom: A family that lives in a park, eating bread for their lunch.

69 *Top:* A family living under a bridge in a park.
Bottom: A man sleeping in a passage.

71 A woman smoking a cigarette after smoking crack with her husband and her eldest son in their house.

72 *Top and bottom:* A man smoking a cigarette after smoking crack with his mother and his stepfather in their house. The three adult members of the family pictured are all addicts.

73 *Top:* A man, after smoking crack with his mother and mother's husband, with his younger brother standing next to him.
Bottom: A woman smoking a cigarette, after smoking crack with her husband and her eldest son, in their house with a younger son sitting next to her.

74
75 A man and his stepson smoking crack in their house.

76
77 Kids sitting in a room while their mother and stepfather get high.

78 Watching from outside the house of the family of addicts.

79 Kids washing dishes outside the house of the family of addicts.

80 *Top and bottom:* The lease on the house was up and the family of addicts could no longer afford to pay rent. Here they place their belongings on the street outside.

81 *Top:* Kids washing dishes outside the house of the family of addicts.
Bottom: A man sitting in a room in his house after smoking crack with his mother and stepfather.

83 A woman looking outside after smoking crack with her husband and her eldest son.

84
85 Shahnaz in her house in Tehran (one year later).

86 Shahnaz in her house in Tehran.

87 Shahnaz in her house in Tehran.

88 Shahnaz in her house in Tehran.

89 Shahnaz in her house in Tehran. A picture of Kim Wilde, a singer popular in the nineties, hangs on her wall.

90
91 Shahnaz in her house in Tehran.

93 Shahnaz walking home.

94
95 Fereshteh's younger brother lying on his mother's leg.

97 Picture of Fereshteh's brother on his mobile phone.

98 *Top and bottom:* Fereshteh applying makeup.

99 *Top:* Fereshteh applying makeup.
Bottom: Fereshteh in her house in Tehran.

100
101 Fereshteh and her mother smoking crack in their house.

102
103 Fereshteh and her mother smoking crack in their house, while her brother eats.

104
105 A girl outside of Shahnaz's house.

106 View of a park in a neighborhood
107 called Darvazeh Ghar (Cave's Mouth). Many addicts buy and use drugs here, especially crack.

109 *Top and bottom:* Playing in a park in southern Tehran. Many addicts come to this park to buy and use drugs.

110 Playing in a park in southern Tehran.
111 Many addicts come to this park to buy and use drugs.

112 *Top and bottom:* People in Ghar. Many drug addicts live in this neighborhood.

113 *Top and bottom:* People in Ghar.

115 Cockfighting in a park.

116 *Top and bottom:* Cockfighting in a park.

117 *Top:* A man holding a trained rooster. *Bottom:* Fighting roosters.

118 A woman waiting for methadone at a
119 DIC in southern Tehran.

120 A woman and her child waiting for
121 methadone at a DIC in southern Tehran.

122 Addicts and their families celebrating
123 the first anniversary of quitting drugs at a ceremony in Tehran held by a NGO called Congress 60.

124 *Top and bottom:* Addicts and their families celebrating the first anniversary of quitting drugs at a ceremony in Tehran held by a NGO called Congress 60.

125 *Top and bottom:* Addicts and their families celebrating the first anniversary of quitting drugs at a ceremony in Tehran held by a NGO called Congress 60.

126 A trash collector gathering used syringes
127 taken from Tehran's parks. Free needles are offered in Iran to counter the risk of HIV and other diseases.

129 A woman praying before being executed for committing drug-related crimes.

130 A guard fastens a noose around the neck of a woman before her execution for drug-related crimes.

131 A woman in a noose awaiting her execution.

133 A woman hanged for drug-related offenses.

134 Five people hanged for drug-related
135 offenses.

136 Forty thousand kilograms of drugs
137 and narcotics as they are burned by Iranian police forces as part of an annual ceremony marking Police Week in Tehran, Iran on October 8, 2003. With foreign representatives present, Iranian police burned some of the drugs they had seized from drug traffickers over the previous year, including heroin, hashish, and morphine.

Cover Image

A woman smoking a cigarette after smoking crack with her husband and her eldest son in their house.

ACKNOWLEDGEMENTS

I would like to take this opportunity to thank all the people who have helped me while taking photographs for this book.

A special thank you goes to Marcel Saba, without whose support this book would not have been published.